Current Issues in Economy and Management

T0316491

Ragıp Pehlivanlı / Nurettin Bilici (eds.)

Current Issues in Economy and Management

Multidisciplinary Perspectives

PETER LANG

**Bibliographic Information published by the
Deutsche Nationalbibliothek**
The Deutsche Nationalbibliothek lists this publication in the Deutsche
Nationalbibliografie; detailed bibliographic data is available online at
http://dnb.d-nb.de.

Library of Congress Cataloging-in-Publication Data
A CIP catalog record for this book has been applied for at the
Library of Congress.

This publication was funded by InGlobe Academy.

Cover image: www.pexels.com

Printed by CPI books GmbH, Leck

ISBN 978-3-631-80554-1 (Print)
E-ISBN 978-3-631-80832-0 (E-PDF)
E-ISBN 978-3-631-80833-7 (EPUB)
E-ISBN 978-3-631-80834-4 (MOBI)
DOI 10.3726/b16410

© Peter Lang GmbH
Internationaler Verlag der Wissenschaften
Berlin 2019
All rights reserved.

Peter Lang – Berlin · Bern · Bruxelles · New York · Oxford · Warszawa · Wien

This publication has been peer reviewed.

www.peterlang.com

Table of Contents

List of Contributors

Asst. Prof. Türkmen Taşer Akbaş,
Pamukkale University, Faculty of
Economics and Administrative
Sciences, takbas@pau.edu.tr

Asst. Prof. Pelin Ügümü Aktaş,
Antalya AKEV University, Faculty of
Art and Design,
pelin.aktas@akev.edu.tr

Lec. Bora Alkan,
Ondokuz Mayıs University, Faculty of
Economics, Administrative and Social
Sciences,
bora.alkan@omu.edu.tr

Asst. Prof. H. Işıl Alkan,
Ondokuz Mayıs University, Faculty of
Economics, Administrative and Social
Sciences,
isilalkan@omu.edu.tr

Assoc. Prof. Dr. Ali Apalı,
Mehmet Akif Ersoy University,
Vocational School,
aapali@mehmetakif.edu.tr

Asst. Prof. Bülent Arpat,
Pamukkale University, Honaz
Vocational School, barpat@pau.edu.tr

Asst. Prof. Orkun Bayram,
Antalya Bilim University, School of
Business and Social Sciences,
orkun.bayram@antalya.edu.tr

Asst. Prof. Özge Bolaman Avcı,
Adnan Menderes University, Faculty of
Economics, Department of Business
Administration, ozge.bolaman.avci@
adu.edu.tr

Lec. Mesut Bozcu,
Akdeniz University, Elmalı Vocational
School,
mesutbozcu@akdeniz.edu.tr

Elif Tuğçe Bozduman,
Uşak University, Faculty of Economics
and Administrative Sciences,
tugcebozduman@gmail.com

Assoc. Prof. Dr. Serdar Bozkurt,
Yıldız Technical University, Faculty
of Economics and Administrative
Sciences,
sbozkurt@yildiz.edu.tr

Res. Asst. Dr. Fevziye Kalıpçı Çağıran,
Ondokuz Mayıs University, Faculty
of Economics and Administrative
Sciences,
fevziye.kalipci@omu.edu.tr

Asst. Prof. Murat Çakırkaya,
Necmettin Erbakan University,
Faculty of Applied Sciences,
mcakirkaya@konya.edu.tr

Asst. Prof. Zuhal Önez Çetin,
Uşak University, Faculty of Economics
and Administrative Sciences,
zuhal.cetin@usak.edu.tr

Asst. Prof. Miraç Eren,
Ondokuz Mayıs University, Faculty of
Economics, Administrative and Social
Sciences,
mirac.eren@omu.edu.tr

Assoc. Prof. Dr. Birol Erkan,
Uşak University, Faculty of Economics
and Administrative Sciences,
birol.erkan@usak.edu.tr

Res. Asst. Dr. Alp Eren Kayasandık,
Ondokuz Mayıs University, Institute
and Graduate School of Social
Sciences

Prof. Dr. Selahattin Kaynak,
Samsun University, Faculty of
Economics, Administrative and Social
Sciences,
selahattin.kaynak@samsun.edu.tr

Assoc. Prof. Dr. Murat Koçyiğit,
Necmettin Erbakan University,
Faculty of Tourism,
mkocyigit@konya.edu.tr

Prof. Dr. Pınar Evrim Mandacı,
Dokuz Eylül University, Faculty of
Business, Department of Business
Administration,
pinar.evrim@deu.edu.tr

Dr. Mortaza Ojaghlou,
Karadeniz Technical University,
Faculty of Economics and
Administrative Sciences,
mojaghlou@hotmail.com

Asst. Prof. Sadiye Oktay,
Yıldız Technical University, Faculty
of Economics and Administrative
Sciences,
sadiye@yildiz.edu.tr

Prof. Dr. Nebiye Yamak,
Karadeniz Technical University,
Faculty of Economics and
Administrative Sciences,
nyamak@ktu.edu.tr

Asst. Prof. Hakan Yavuz,
Sakarya University,
Faculty of Political Science,
hyavuz@sakarya.edu.tr

MBA Student Kübra Yazıcı,
Yıldız Technical University,
Graduate School of Social Science
kubrayazicii21@gmail.com

Mortaza Ojaghlou and Nebiye Yamak

Tourism Sector and Dutch Disease: The Case of Turkey

1 Introduction

The term "Dutch Disease" was first used by *The Economist* in November 1977. In the related article of the journal, the possible effects of the natural gas resources in the Netherlands on the economy in 1959 were written and the macroeconomic effects of this situation were examined. According to the same paper, the Netherlands, which imported natural gas before 1959, had become a natural gas exporter with the discovery of natural gas resources, thus obtaining a high amount of foreign exchange income from natural gas exports. The rapid increase in the inflow of foreign currency to the country caused significant increases in the prices especially in the prices of non-tradable goods. It was observed that these increases caused the Netherlands to lose its competitiveness significantly in the industrial sector and therefore the economic growth rate approached to almost zero.

The advantages of natural resource exports on the economy, as well as some disadvantages such as the Dutch example, have been the subject of theoretical and empirical research from time to time. The negative effects of the natural resource wealth on the economy were first investigated by Meade and Russell (1957) for the Australian economy. According to this study, the excessive international demand for raw material has had a positive effect on the balance of payments in Australia in the first stage, but in the long run this effect has turned negative. Because, the increase in the export of raw materials raised first the export prices, then the wages and industrial costs. After a certain period, these changes created a substitution effect between export and import.

Although there were many empirical studies on the subject, the theoretical background of the Dutch disease could only develop in the 1980s. Theoretically, Dutch disease was first investigated by Corden and Neary (1982) and Corden (1984). They, in their study, proposed the Basic or Core Model of Dutch disease. They divided the economy into three different sectors. Through the rapidly developing sector, they investigated the development of non-tradable goods sector by using general equilibrium analysis. They also found that the development of the non-tradable goods sector caused a contraction in the tradable goods sector. In particular, this contraction was observed in the industrial sector. Thus, they identified the Dutch disease with the concept of deindustrialization.

The Dutch disease affects the economy through two different channels, namely the expenditure and production resources movement. The size and type of these effects differ by the economic characteristics of the countries. Thus, this diversity has negatively affected economic growth in some countries and increased inflation, current account deficit, and unemployment. It has even caused economic contraction in some countries. Even in some countries, it only changed the production characteristics and balance among sectors. The symmetric change in the volume of production and employment only decreased the industrial sector or the share of the industrial sector in GDP. In the current literature, all these effects have been examined within the scope of the Dutch disease.

In the empirical literature, after the basic Dutch disease model, the disease has been investigated mostly for the countries which are rich in natural resources. In particular, the macroeconomic impacts of oil by the OPEC countries, which have significant oil resources, were analyzed in the context of deindustrialization. However, it is clear that the Dutch disease is not only limited to natural resource exports, but it also carries a risk for all sectors and economic activities that may lead to foreign exchange inflow, except for the industrial sector according to the basic Dutch disease model. As possible risky sectors and economic activities, tourism sector, workers' money transfers, money transfers made for aid (e.g., health, education), agricultural products exports, and migration factors can be shown.

Copeland (1991) has argued that the development of the tourism sector in the long term may lead to deindustrialization and welfare loss. Copeland (1991) explored the effects of the growth in tourism sector on the welfare, output, and factor prices of host country by using general equilibrium and international trade models. In his study, Copeland (1991) claimed that the development in the tourism sector could lead the country host to tourism or to the Dutch disease by means of production factor movement and expenditure effects. Furthermore, Chao et al. (2006) expressed that the increase in the price of non-tradable goods will negatively affect the accumulation of capital in the short and medium run and reduce the welfare of the country in the long run. Some of the advantages that the tourism sector has achieved in the short term help governments temporarily solve some problems. In such a case, the income from the tourism sector is similar to the income from the export of natural resources. The rapid growth in the tourism sector or natural resources in the short term can be seen to be desirable, but this also raises the necessity of reallocation of production resource. On the other hand, in order to gain more income, workers move to the service sectors by leaving their jobs in the traditional and industrial sectors, which may lead to a decrease in the production of these sectors by affecting the redistribution of resources, industrial and agricultural sectors, and the Dutch disease or beach disease according to Holzner (2011).

The tourism sector is considered as an important source of foreign exchange inflows in Turkey. Especially in the last 20 years, very important progresses have been taken in this sector. The effects of this sector on macroeconomic indicators have been the subject of interest in the context of Dutch disease. There are almost no studies analyzing the Turkish tourism sector within the framework of the Dutch disease concept. The purpose of the present study is to econometrically determine whether the tourism sector in Turkey causes Dutch disease, whether there exists a relationship between the tourism sector and the industrial sector, and how this situation affects Turkish economy.

2 Causes of Dutch Disease

As mentioned earlier, the starting point of the Dutch disease is the availability of new natural gas resources in the Netherlands. After the theoretical framework of the Dutch disease was developed by Corden and Neary (1982), causes of the Dutch disease which were formed by the influence of other factors attracted the attention of many researchers. After Buiter and Purvis (1983), many studies have examined the Dutch disease through the petroleum sector. For this reason, more studies have been done especially for Persian Gulf and OPEC member countries. In addition, the studies of Beck et al. (2007) for the Russian economy, Egert and Leonard (2008) for Kazakhstan, for Saudi Arabia Looney (1990), for Iranian economy Karimzade et al. (2009) and Esfahani and Pesaran (2009), Peter et al. (2014) for Australian natural resources, Papyrakis and Raveh (2014) for Canada, Wei Ge and Kinnucan (2016) for the Mongolian mining sector, and Mustapha and Masih (2016) for Nigeria are among the studies examining the Dutch disease.

However, over time, this subject was not limited to natural resources and energy factors. In some countries, it has been found that other advantageous products or factors cause Dutch disease. For example, in some countries, the export of agricultural products, which is advantageous in whole economy, caused the Dutch disease. More productive production of agricultural products in agricultural countries provided an export advantage to the country. This led to a significant amount of foreign exchange inflow to the country. The high amount of revenue created an impact on the spending and resource movement by influencing the employees in the other sectors (especially the industrial sector). All these factors led to Dutch disease. For example, in Colombia, the

1910–1950 period of the bananas and the late 1970s, coffee exports have led to strong findings for the Dutch disease. Another sector that causes Dutch disease is the tourism sector, which is also the subject of this study. For the first time in literature, the concept of Dutch disease in the tourism sector has been developed by Copeland (1991). Following Copeland's research, the studies of Balaguer and Cantavella-Jorda (2000) for Spain; Nowak and Sahli (2007) and Kenell (2008) for small island economies and Thailand, respectively; Kropp and Brussels (2009) for Greece; Holzner (2010) for 134 countries; Mieiro et al. (2012) for Macau; Gylfason and Zoega (2014) for Icelandic economy; Inchausti-Sintes (2015) for Spain; and Ghalia and Fidrmuc (2015) for 133 countries are the main studies investigating Dutch disease among them.

Another factor leading to Dutch disease is foreign aid. In this factor, it has been argued that the poor countries are caught by the Dutch disease through the help of international or other aid organizations. Two important studies in this area are the World Bank's 2004 research for Ethiopia and Gupta and Yang (2005) for the African countries. In addition to the above, money transfer and direct foreign investments may cause Dutch disease. This issue has been the subject of research in more developing countries. Foreign currency inflowing to the country through money transfers creates significant effects on the country's economy, such as foreign exchange inflow through natural resources. Some of the studies investigating Dutch disease in this issue are Beja (2010) for the top 20 remittance countries, Saab and Ayoub (2010) for Egypt, Bayangos (2012) for Jordan and Syria, Bayangos (2012) for the Philippines, and Makhlouf and Mughal (2013) for Pakistan. An example of a study on foreign direct investment is the study by Botta et al. (2015) for Colombia. In addition, there are studies in the empirical literature indicating that high interest rates may cause Dutch disease. Finally, the phenomenon of international migration is one of the factors that can cause Dutch disease, by creating inter-sectoral resource movement and spending effects in the countries. The study conducted by Beine et al. (2015) for Canada is an example of this factor.

3 Tourism Sector and Dutch Disease

The tourism sector plays a major role in reducing the current account deficit by providing significant amounts of foreign exchange inflows to the economy, especially in times of economic turbulences. Moreover, this sector has a great role in the fight against possible unemployment due to the labor-intensive nature of the tourism sector (Akın et al., 2012). Although there are some problems related to the use of environmental resources, tourism sector in developing countries is seen as an indispensable locomotive sector of economic growth. Tourism sector is considered as an early sector in terms of foreign exchange gains, efficient use of scarce resources, and increase in employment and diversity (Sinclair, 1998). Tourism is an important export factor in 83% of developing countries. At the same time, the tourism sector is the main export factor in one-third of this 83%. In the less developed 49 countries, the tourism sector is an important growth factor. The added value created by the tourism sector increased by 45% in these countries in the period of 1990–2000 and by approximately 20% in developing countries (WTO, 2002). Therefore, tourism sector is an important income source for the less developed and developing countries, especially in the short term.

According to the findings of some studies, the countries' short run growth policy based on tourism has led to higher economic performance compared to other substitutable policies. However, some economists have disagreed with the results of these studies. For example, Copeland (1991) and Chao et al. (2006) argued that the growth in the tourism sector leads to a decrease in the accumulation of capital in the industry and manufacturing sector, although it reduces the consumption of non-tradable goods or improves the terms of trade. On the other hand, tourism sector is not a sector that provides or supports technological development. Solow (1956), Lucas (1988), Romer (1990), and Sachs and McArthur (2002) emphasized high technology as the most important factors that provide stable and sustainable growth in the long run. For this reason, tourism-oriented countries are more vulnerable and fragile to Dutch disease. The following four criticisms have been addressed to the growth advocates based on tourism sector, particularly in terms of sustainable development or growth (Inchausti-Sintes, 2015).

I. Will a technology-free sector, such as tourism, guarantee economic growth in the long run?
II. Will the capacity of the tourism sector be able to transform the exchange inflow into capital accumulation or guarantee its transformation?
III. Will the international competition in the tourism sector increase the efficiency of the sector?
IV. Will the return to scale of the tourism sector increase?

In addition to the above criticisms, the following question should also be answered: Will the income generated from the tourism sector generate a multiplier effect in the whole economy? In other words, how much of the tourism revenues obtained within the country can be used on national tourism capacity or how much of it will be able to develop tourism sector in terms of attracting tourists, protecting and using income?

Although the number of tourists visiting developing countries is high, the links between the tourism sector and other sectors are weak. This weakness will naturally increase the demand for imported goods. In addition, due to the capital, organization, and managerial shortcomings of national companies, foreign companies will start to operate in the tourism sector and will transfer a significant portion of their revenues abroad. Thus, a significant portion of the income from tourism will be out of the country. That is to say, tourism income and foreign exchange inflow will not be transformed into desired or expected capital accumulation due to leakage. For this reason, the tourism sector will not contribute to the development and even growth of such countries in the long term.

Holzner (2010) considers the tourism sector as one of the factors that may cause Dutch disease. The shift of employees from manufacturing to tourism and services sectors is the most important indicator of Dutch disease. According to Holzner (2010), production resources from manufacturing or industrial sector to tourism and services sectors will lead to a contraction in industrial sector. This situation will not have a positive effect on the economy in the long term. Holzner (2010) called the Dutch disease caused by tourism "Beach disease." Although the disease caused by both the tourism sector and natural resources is called Dutch disease, there are some differences between the diseases originated from tourism sector and natural resource sectors. According to Copeland (1991), the Dutch disease differs according to the sector or area of activity. The following differences can be listed in terms of tourism and natural resource sectors:

1. The rapid development of the production and export of natural resources indirectly affects the demand for non-tradable goods by changing the income of households. However, in case of rapid development of the tourism sector, non-traded goods are directly affected by international demand.
2. Tourists demand and consume non-tradable goods during their stay in the country. However, the difference between taxes on traded and non-traded goods is uncertain.
3. Tourists are demanding goods and services at national prices rather than on world prices while they are residing within the country. Therefore, national prices are affected by tariffs and quotas.
4. Since the rent obtained from natural resources is very high, it has the capacity to feed other sectors of the economy. Because resources within the country have the opportunity to move freely between sectors.

Tourists generally consume non-tradable goods, such as domestic consumers. The rapid increase in the number of tourists can lead to a loss of welfare by creating a crowding-out effect on domestic consumption. Moreover, by improving the terms of trade, it allows citizens of the country to make more consumption through imports. Excessive consumption of imported goods and the emergence of foreign currency from the country will create a resource movement and spending effect. This situation will decrease the level of welfare in the long term (Gooroochurn and Blake, 2005).

4 Econometric Method and Data

In this study, alternative variables and methods were used for determining the long-run impact of tourism sector on the economic growth in Turkey. The first method is the autoregressive distributed lag model (ARDL) developed by Pesaran and Shin (1999) and Pesaran et al. (2001). The following Models 1 and 2 were estimated under ARDL approach and then long-term coefficients were produced. The second method is structural VAR (SVAR). Variance decomposition was applied to the equations (Model 3) used in the transmission mechanism by using SVAR method. In the next step, the growth model estimated by the ARDL model was reestimated using Bayesian VAR (BVAR) method as an alternative. Thus, an opportunity to compare ARDL method findings with alternative method findings was obtained. BVAR method was applied under two important assumptions. These are rational and adaptive expectations. The estimated system under BVAR is Model 4.

Model 1: GR = f(PCI, GFC, SSE, IND, TOUR1 (TOUR2), RER, TX)

Model 2: GR = f(PCI, GFC, TOUR2, LEX, GFC^2, LEX^2, $TOUR^2$, (GFC)*(LEX), (GFC)*(TOUR2), (LEX)*(TOUR2))

Model 3: (GR, GFC, RER, TX, IND, SSE (LEX), G, TOUR1(TOUR2), TR)

Model 4: (GR, PCI, GFC, RER, TX, IND, SSE (LEX), G, TOUR1(TOUR2), TR)

The data used in the econometric analysis part of the study consist of annual data covering the period of 1975–2016. In determining the variables, studies by Ghalia and Fidrmuc (2015), Holzner (2010, 2011) and Figini and Vici (2007) were taken as reference.

The percentage of tourism income in the GNP and the percentage share of travel services in service exports were separately used as an indicator of tourism capital. The annual growth in GDP (%) represented the economic growth variable. Human capital is represented by two different variables: secondary school enrollment rate and life expectancy. The physical capital variable was used as a percentage of gross fixed capital formation in GDP. Trade variable is the share of exports, imports, and services in GDP. Industrial production value added,

Tab. 1: Definition of Data

Variable	Definition of Variable	Abbreviation of Variable	Source
Tourism I	Percentage of tourism income in GNP	TOUR1	Association of Turkish Travel Agencies
Tourism II	Percentage of travel services in service exports	TOUR2	World Bank
Growth	Annual GDP growth rate (%)	GR	World Bank
Income per capita	Income per capita (TL)	PCI	World Bank
Human capital	Secondary school enrollment rate (%gross)	SSE	World Bank
Human capital	Life expectancy at birth	LEX	World Bank
Physical capital	Ratio of gross fixed capital to GDP	GFC	World Bank
Reel effective exchange rate	Real exchange rate (based on industry consumer price index)	RER	Federal reserve Bank of St. Louis
Trade	Ratio of exports, imports, and services in GDP	TR	World Bank
Industry	Ratio of industrial production value added in GDP	IND	World Bank
Tax	Ratio of net tax revenues in GDP	TX	World Bank
Government Expenditure	Ratio of government's final consumption expenditure in GDP	G	World Bank

net tax revenues, and government final consumption expenditures were used to represent industry, tax, and public expenditure variables, respectively. All three variables are used as a percentage share in GDP. The data used in the study are summarized in Tab. 1 in detail.

5 Findings

As mentioned earlier, Models 1 and 2 were estimated by using the ARDL approach. The optimal lag length in Model 1, where economic growth is used as a dependent variable, is determined as [3,2,2,3,3,3,3,3] by using Akaike information criterion; and the calculated F-test statistics value is 11.45. Since these statistics are greater than the upper critical value of 3.9, long-run relationship exists among the variables at 1% significance level. According to the result of the LM autocorrelation test, there is no autocorrelation problem in Model 1. According to CUSUM test result, there is no stability problem at 5% significance level in the model.

According to the results of tourism-based long-term growth test, IPC has a negative effect on economic growth in the long run and this effect is also statistically significant. The coefficient of the GFC variable used for the physical capital is estimated to be statistically significant and negative at the 10% significance level. Similarly, the coefficient of SSE variable for the human capital was found to be positive and statistically significant at 1% significance level. The real exchange rate has a negative effect on economic growth at 1% significance level. However, the effect of the tourism capital on economic growth is negative and statistically significant at the 1% level. The coefficient of error correction term is between 0 and -2. This coefficient is also statistically significant.

After estimating Model 1, the long-run effects of trade, human and physical capital variables together with tourism capital on growth were investigated by using ARDL approach. Holzner (2011) and Ghalia and Fidrmuc (2015) analyzed the effects of the interactions of these variables on economic growth. Optimal lag lengths of ARDL in Model 2 were determined as [2,1,0,1,0,0,1,0,0,1,0] respectively. The calculated F-statistics for this model is 6.95. This is statistically significant at 1% level. There exists a long-term relationship among the variables at a significance level of 1%. According to the results of long-run interaction models, physical capital (GFC) and tourism (TOUR2) interaction variable in Model 2 have a statistically significant and negative effect on economic growth. In Turkey, interaction of human capital (LEX) and physical capital (GFC) affects economic growth in the long run. This effect is statistically significant at 5% level. From ARDL results, it is also seen that the interaction between tourism and physical capital has a statistically significant and negative effect on economic growth in the long run. According to this finding, hotels, airports, roads, museums, that is, physical investment in the tourism industry has made a negative impact on Turkey's economy in the long run. These results, in fact, validate the thesis that investments would be more efficient if they are in the other sectors such as industry and agriculture. On the other hand, the interaction of human capital and tourism variables positively affects economic growth. In other words, the effect of education and other human investments on the economic growth rate in the tourism sector is positive. In spite of this, it is highly probable that the labor returns will be higher if the investments are made to the industrial sector rather than to the tourism sector. Because the value added and multiplier effect of the production goods in the industrial sector is much higher than the tourism sector.

In addition to the ARDL models analyzed above, the effect of tourism on growth was also investigated with the SVAR model. Ghalia and Fidrmuc (2015) and Holzner (2011) analyzed the long-run effect of tourism on growth using the F (triangle) matrix. According to long-run SVAR impulse-response functions, the effect of one unit shock given to tourism variable (TOUR1) on other variables is as follows: The effect of shock on the first two periods on economic growth is positive. However, from the third to the tenth, this effect is negative; and from the tenth period, the impact of shock on growth is lost. The effect of the same shock on the real exchange rate, which is the most important variable in terms of the Dutch Disease hypothesis, is first decreased negatively and is positive from the fourth period. According to the hypothesis of the Dutch disease, tourism revenues will have a negative effect on the sector producing goods and services subject to trade since it raises the real exchange rate and causes spending and resource movements. In this context, the fact that the real exchange rate reacts positively to tourism revenues after the fourth period is consistent with the Dutch disease hypothesis. As a matter of fact, the real exchange rate affects the industrial variable negatively. This situation is positively increasing in the first two periods, but decreases in the following periods and approaches zero. It remains negative since the seventh period.

The effects of the shock on tourism incomes on the human capital (SSE) and tax variable are positive and also continue positively. The effect of the shock on the trade variable is negative until the ninth period and remains positive for the rest periods. The effect of the same shock on physical capital continues to be positive in the early periods and negative in the following periods. Publice expenditures respond positively to the shock of tourism revenues.Finally, the impact of the shock on tourism revenues is positive in the first period, but remains neutral since the third period. In summary, based on this analysis conducted by the SVAR method, tourism revenues cause real exchange rate appreciation. Later, this situation motivates a cross-sectoral shift of production by creating an effect of spending and resource movement. In other words, increases in tourism revenues have a negative impact on the industrial sector.

Holzner (2011), in his study, included the income per capita variable to analyze whether tourism causes Dutch disease. Following Holzner (2011), in the present study the effect of tourism capital on other variables is analyzed by BVAR method together with the per capita income variable. According to the results of BVAR with rational expectations, a positive shock to the tourism variable starts with an increasing positive effect in the first two periods on the growth variable, but it falls sharply in the third period. So, in the fifth period, the effect is negative. After this period, the effect disappears. The real exchange rate gives a negative response to tourism shock in the early periods. But this response is turning to be positive in the ninth period. In other words, a positive shock in tourism revenues causes the beginning of the effect of spending and resources movement by appreciating the real exchange rate after nine periods. Thus, it causes a contraction in the tradable sector. Therefore, the reaction of the industrial sector to the tourism sector is negative in the same period (ninth period). The economic growth rate is also affected negatively, and the effect disappears after a certain period of time when the sector is starting to be in contraction.

According to the impulse-response functions of BVAR with adaptive expectations, the effects of a unit shock given to the tourism variable (TOUR1) on other variables can be summarized as follows. The effect of shock on economic growth is positive in the early periods. However, after the fifth period, the positive effect starts to slowly decrease and turns to be negative in the tenth period and so on. The effect of the shock on the real exchange rate is negative until the fifth period, which is positive after this period. The fact that the real exchange rate reacts positively to tourism revenues after the fifth period is one of the important symptoms of the Dutch disease effect. As a matter of fact, the real exchange rate is positively affected, which in turn affects the tradable sector negatively. In this case, the impact of the shock on tourism revenues on the industrial variable is positive until the fifth period, but after that it starts to be negative.

The findings obtained from the BVAR method with rational and adaptive expectations are similar. According to the results, per capita income is positively affected by tourism revenues. However, the effect of tourism revenues on economic growth is not strong. This effect is negative in some periods. The reason for this is that the real exchange rate is firstly affected positively by the tourism revenues and that later the industry and foreign trade sectors are negatively affected by the appreciated exchange rate.

6 Conclusion

This study investigates the long-run effect of tourism sector on macroeconomic indicators in order to determine whether the tourism sector of Turkey is causing the Dutch disease. More clearly, the main purpose of the study is to determine whether there is a relationship between the tourism sector and the industrial sector; and how and in what direction if there is a relationship. In the scope of the study, the following questions are aimed to be answered: Is the Turkish economy suffering from Dutch disease because of tourism revenues? How do tourism revenues affect the other sectors of the economy? Does tourism sector affect the sectoral structure of the economy? Are the resource movement and spending effect realized?

The rapid growth in the tourism sector or natural resources in the short run can be seen to be desirable, but this also raises the need to reallocate production resources. On the other hand, in order to generate more income, the labor sector is leaving its jobs in the industrial sectors and it moves especially the non-tradable sectors. Even if the economic growth rate is positive, the growth model led by the service sector cannot achieve economic growth in the long run according to the industry-led growth model. Because, the service sector is a labor-intensive sector. Whereas the manufacturing or industrial sector is a sector that requires capital and qualified human capital, using technology and education creates a positive and multiplier effect on economic growth. In other words, it will support economic growth, knowledge and country development in the long run. In this study, using annual data for the period 1975–2016 in Turkey, Dutch disease was investigated in terms of the tourism sector. In the study, ARDL, structural, and Bayesian VAR were used as econometrics methods.

According to the results of ARDL, the effect of tourism revenues on growth in the long run is negative. The real exchange rate is positively influenced by the tourism sector. But industrial sector is later affected negatively by the appreciated exchange rate. ARDL interaction results imply that infrastructure investments which are not subject to trade in tourism sector have a negative impact on economic growth rate. In other words, it is determined that the development of the tourism sector adversely affects the sectors that are subject to trade. These results support the predictions of the Dutch disease hypothesis.

Based on Bayesian VAR analysis, any shock in tourism revenues has a positive effect on economic growth under the assumptions of rational and adaptive expectations, but this positive effect is negative in a short period of time. The same is true in the structural VAR test, where the negative effect between tourism income and growth is more pronounced. In other words, tourism revenues do not have a positive effect on growth; and moreover, sometimes the effect is negative. In addition, tourism revenues affect the industrial sector negatively by appreciating the real exchange rate. Although the effect of tourism revenues on public expenditures is negative in the early periods according to the impulse-response functions, it is positive in the long run.

In summary, there are both positive and negative effects of Turkish tourism sector on the whole economy. It is not appropriate to see and evaluate the positive aspects of tourism sector by neglecting the negative aspects. The most negative side of this sector is that in the sector the capital leakage is high and only creates a short run temporary effect. This temporary effect also spreads to the other sectors negatively. From all the findings of this study, it can be concluded that industrial sector in Turkey is still the locomotive sector of development. But, because of the Dutch disease effect of tourism sector, necessary and adequate capital of the industrial sector will be motivated to move the non-tradable sectors.

Bibliography

Akın, Aliye, Yaşar, Mustafa and Akın, Adnan (2012), "Importance of Tourism Sector in Economy (in Turkish)", **Journal of Academic Researches and Studies**. Vol. 7, N. 4, pp. 63–81.

Balaguer, Jacint and Cantavella-Jorda, Manuel (2000), "Tourism as a Long-Run Economic Growth Factor: The Spanish case", **Applied Economics**. Vol. 34, N. 7, pp. 877–884.

Bayangos, Veronica (2012), "Going with Remittances: The Case of the Philippines", https://www.researchgate.net/publication/265511106_Going_With_Remittances_The_Case_of_the_Philippines (05.11.2018).

Beck, Roland, Kamps, Annette and Mileva, Elitza (2007), "Long-Term Growth Prospects for the Russian Economy", **Occasional Paper Series**. N. 58, pp. 1–35.

Beine, Michel, Coulombe, Serge and Vermeulen, Wessel N. (2015), "Dutch Disease and the Mitigation Effect of Migration: Evidence from Canadian Provinces", **CESifo Working Paper**. N. 3813, pp. 1–51.

Beja, Edsel (2010), "Do International Remittances Cause Dutch Disease?", **MPRA Paper**. N. 39302.

Botta, Alberto, Godin, Antoine and Missaglia, Marco (2015), "Finance, Foreign (Direct) Investment and Dutch Disease: The Case of Colombia", **Springer, Econ Polit**. Vol. 33, N. 2, pp. 265–289.

Buiter, Willem and Purvis, Duoglas (1983), "Oil, Disinflation and Export Competitiveness. In Economic Interdependence and Flexible Exchange Rates", Massachusetts: MIT Press.

Chao, Chi-Chur, Hazari, Bharat R., Laffargue, Jean-Pierre, Sgro, Pasquale M. and Yu, Eden S. H. (2006), "Tourism, Dutch Disease and Welfare In An Open Dynamic Economy", **The Japanese Economic Review, Japanese Economic Association**. Vol. 57, N. 4, pp. 501–515.

Copeland, Brian R. (1991), "Tourism, Welfare and De-industrialization in a Small Open Economy", **Economica**. Vol. 58, N. 232, pp. 515–529.

Corden, Max W. and Peter, Neary J. (1982), "Booming Sector and De-Industrialisation in a Small Open Economy", **The Economic Journal**. Vol. 92, N. 368, pp. 825–848.

Corden, Max W. (1984), "Booming Sector and Dutch Disease Economics: Survey and Consolidation", **Oxford Economic Papers**. Vol. 36, N. 3, pp. 359–380.

Egert, Balazs and Leonard, Carol S. (2008), "Dutch Disease Scare in Kazakhstan: Is it real?", **Open Economies Review**. Vol. 19, N. 2, pp. 147–165.

Esfahani, Hadi S. and Pesaran, Hashem P. (2009), "The Iranian Economy in The Twentieth Century: A Global Perspective", **Iranian Studies.** Vol. 42, N. 2, pp. 177–211.

Figini, Paolo and Vici, Laura (2007), "Estimating Tourist External Effects on Residents: A Choice Modeling Application to Rimini", **FEEM Working Paper**. N. 76, pp. 1–75.

Ghalia, Thaana and Fidrmuc, Jan (2015), "The Curse of Tourism**?" Journal of Hospitality and Tourism Research**. Vol. 42, N. 6, 979–996.

Gooroochurn, Nishaal and Blake, Adam (2005), "Tourism Immiserization: Fact or Fiction**?", Fondazione Eni Enrico Mattei (FEEM) Research Paper Series**, Vol. 143, N. 05.

Gupta, Sanjeev and Yang, Yongzheng (2005), "The Macroeconomic Challenges of Scaling Up Aid to Africa", **IMF Working Paper**. Vol. 05, N. 179, pp. 1–63.

Gylfason, Thorvaldur and Zoega, Gylfi (2014), "The Dutch Disease in Reverse: Iceland's Natural Experiment", **OxCarre Working Papers**. N. 138, Oxford Centre for the Analysis of Resource Rich Economies, University of Oxford.

Holzner, Mario (2010), "Tourism and Economic Development: The Beach Disease?", Tourism Management. Vol. 32, N. 2011, pp. 922–933.

Holzner, Mario (2011), "Tourism and Economic Development: The Beach Disease?", **wiiw Working Papers**. N. 66, pp. 1–30.

Inchausti-Sintes, Federico (2015), "Tourism: Economic Growth, Employment and Dutch Disease", **Annals of Tourism Research, Elsevier**. Vol. 54, N. C, pp. 172–189.

Karimzade, Mostafa, KHadije, Nasrollahi, Saeid, Samadi, Rahim, Esfehani, Majid, Fakhar (2009), "Dutch Disease Effect on Structure of Investment", Journal of Scientific and Research on Economics. Vol. 6, N. 4, pp. 147–172.

Kenell, Lena (2008), **Dutch Disease and Tourism: The Case of Thailand** (Unpublished Master's Dissertation), Lund University, Department of Economics, Lund, Sweden.

Kropp, Manuela and Brussels, R., Kulke, R. (2009), "Greece and Its Structural Correlation with East Germany", http://www2.euromemorandum.eu/uploads/wg4_kropp_kulke_greece_and_its_scructural_correlation_with_east_germany.pdf (11.28.2018).

Looney, Robert E. (1990), "Oil revenues and Dutch Disease in Saudi
    Arabia: Differential Impacts on Sectoral Growth", **Canadian Journal of
    Development Studies**. Vol. 11, N. 1, pp. 119–133.

Lucas, Robert E. Jr. (1988), "On the Mechanics of Economic Development",
    Journal of Monetary Economics. N. 22, pp. 3–42.

Makhlouf, Farid and Mughal, Mazhar (2013), "Remittances, Dutch Disease,
    and Competitiveness: A Bayesian Analysis", **Journal of Economic
    Development**. Vol. 38, N. 2, pp. 67–97.

Meade, James E. and Russell, E. A. (1957), "The Wage and Cost of the Living
    Balance of Payments", **The Economic Record, The Economic Society of
    Australia**. Vol. 33, N. 64, pp. 23–28.

Mieiro, Susana, Nogueira, Pedro R. and Alves, José (2012), "Gaming Tourism
    Boom, Foreign Currency Inflows, and Dutch Disease Effects: An Empirical
    Model for Macau", **International Journal of Trade, Economics and
    Finance**. Vol. 3, N. 6, pp. 421–427.

Mustapha, I. Muhammad and Masih, Abul. M (2016), "Dutch Disease or
    Nigerian Disease: A Prima Facie? New Evidence from ARDL Bound Test
    Analysis", **Munich Personal RePEc Archive**. N. 69767, pp. 1–29.

Nowak, Jean-Jacques and Sahli, Mondher (2007), "Coastal Tourism and 'Dutch
    Disease' in a Small Island Economy", **Tourism Economics**. Vol. 13, N. 1,
    pp. 49–65.

Papyrakis, Elissaios and Raveh, Ohad (2014), "An Empirical Analysis of a
    Regional Dutch Disease: The Case of Canada", **Environ Resource Econ**.
    Vol. 2014, N. 58, pp. 179–198.

Pesaran, M. Hashem and Esfahani, Hadi S. (2012), "An Empirical Growth
    Model for Major Oil Exporters", **CESifo Working Paper**. N. 3780, pp. 1–27.

Pesaran, M. Hashem and Shin, Yongcheol (1999), "An Autoregressive
    Distributed Lag Modelling Approach to Cointegration Analysis", In S. Strøm
    (Ed.), **Econometrics and Economic Theory in the 20th Century: The
    Ragnar Frisch Centennial Symposium** (Econometric Society Monographs,
    pp. 371–413). Cambridge, United Kingdom: Cambridge University Press.
    doi:10.1017/CCOL521633230.011. **Econometrics and Economic Theory
    in the 20th Century: The Ragnar Frisch Centennial Symposium, Strom**,
    Cambridge University Press, Cambridge.

Pesaran, M. Hashem, Shin, Yongcheol and Smith, Richard J. (2001), "Bounds
    Testing Approaches to the Analysis of Level Relationships", Journal of
    Applied Econometrics. Hoboken, New Jersey, Vol. 16, N. 3, pp. 289–326.

Peter, Downes, Hanslow, Kevin and Tulip, Peter (2014), "The Effect of the
    Mining Boom on the Australian Economy", **Research Discussion Paper,**

Economic Research Department, Reserve Bank of Australia. N. 2014–08, pp. 1–52.

Romer, Paul M. (1990), "Endogenous Technological Change", **Journal of Political Economy**. N. 98, pp. 71–102.

Saab, Gretta and Ayoub, Maya (2010), "The Dutch Disease Syndrome in Egypt, Jordan, Lebanon, and Syria: A Comparative Study", **Competitiveness Review**. Vol. 20, N. 4, pp. 343–359.

Sachs, Jeffrey D. and McArthur, John W. (2002), **"Technological Advancement and Long-Term Economic Growth in Asia"**, Technology and the New Economy. Massachusetts, USA: MIT Press.

Sinclair, M. Thea (1998), "Tourism and Economic Development: A Survey", **The Journal of Development Studies**. Vol. 34, N. 5, pp. 1–51.

Solow, Robert (1956), "A Contribution to the Theory of Economic Growth", **Quarterly Journal of Economics**. N. 70, pp. 65–94.

The Dutch Disease. (26.11.1977), **The Economist**, pp. 82–83.

Wei, Ge and Kinnucan, Henry W. (2016), "Does Dutch Disease Hit Mongolia?", **Southern Agricultural Economics Association (SAEA)** https://ideas.repec.org/p/ags/saea16/229564.html (08.11.2018).

World Bank (2004), "Ethiopia Public Expenditure Review: The Emerging Challenge: Public Spending in the Social Sectors (English)", **Public Expenditure Review (PER)**. Washington, DC: World Bank.

World Tourism Organization (2002), "Tourism and Poverty Alleviation, WTO, Estimating Economic Impacts From, Tourism", **Annals of Tourism Research**. Vol. 24, N. 1, pp. 76–89.

Pelin Ügümü Aktaş

Analysis of Diamond Ring Commercials in the Frame of Symbolic Consumption

1 Introduction

The notion of consumption underlying the capitalist ideology has adapted to the changes in each era and transformed itself according to the tendencies; therefore, it has never lost importance or influence in social life. In the postmodern society, which is the society of the spectacle (Debord, 2012), the notion of consumption continues to be highly important and influential. In this era, the understanding of passive consumer has been erased; this shift in understanding has changed the viewpoints and perceptions about consumer behaviors. Consumption is now the determinant of culture; traditional consumption understanding, which is based on necessities, is now replaced by the understanding that consumption is a basic necessity (Baudrillard, 2013). The bearer of these newly produced meanings in this inevitable world of new consumer culture is advertisements. These visual messages are like assertions (Barthes, 1993: 157), and they have the function of directing consumption. Besides, advertisements affect socialization processes in today's world (Becan, 2016: 33). Tendencies of consumers are directly reflected in advertising copies on the basis of the dialectic relationship between advertisement and society; these reflections are in line with the dialectic relationship between advertisement and society. According to Berger (2012: 153), advertisement is the life of current culture, and capitalism cannot continue its existence without it and advertisement of modern life is surely a product of culture.

More and more modern consumers tend towards consumption in order to create identity everyday (Bocock, 2009); rather than a rational process, consumption is now an action based on psychological and social needs. The understanding about consumption at the center of postmodernism is: Consumption decisions of consumers are not only based on the features of a product, but also on the symbolic meanings of them (Elliott & Wattanasuwan, 1998: 132). In this context, the concept of symbolic consumption should be clearly understood. This modern concept is based on the understanding that consumers look for emotional and symbolic benefits besides rational benefits while choosing a product. Symbolic consumption discusses the reasons that direct individuals towards consumption. It is suggested that consumers pursue the goals of representing their identity and personality through products; they define themselves, hold a position in society on the basis of the symbolic meanings of products. It is possible to understand the social roles of products by perceiving them as symbols that function as communication methods (Grubb & Grathwohl, 1967: 24). Consumption is an action shaped according to the symbolic values, psychological and social meanings represented by a product; rational, real benefit of a product is simply another factor in this list that direct individuals towards consumption.

Symbolic values are meanings attributed to products in social processes; they are not natural, implicit meanings. Products that become meaningful on the basis of mythological elements in society tell a narrative to consumers through the meanings they develop in time (Williamson, 2001: 46). In this sense, products are no longer products; they become forms of expression. Advertisements are one of the most important instruments in this process of meaning attribution. Advertising turns products into brands by attributing specific meanings, creates attractive images and glamorizes them (Rutherford, 1996: 16); it places the glamour of a product into the center and creates a symbol on the basis of it. The basic purpose of this study is to present the methods of establishing discourses about symbolic consumption by analyzing signs used in advertising copies. The sampling of the study is commercial films about diamond jewelry – and diamond solitaire rings in private – which is one of the products with significant symbolic meaning. Semiotics, which is a method of analyzing how a meaning is created, is used in analyzing the commercial films selected by purposeful sampling.

Before opening up the findings about how symbolic consumption discourses are established in advertising copies for discussion, it is necessary to discuss the relationship between consumer society and advertisements. Understanding the concept of symbolic consumption and to present the meanings attributed to diamond products – diamond rings – in this context is highly important at this point.

2 Consumer Society and Advertisements

One of the most distinctive features of postmodern era is the effect of consumption on social life and the active role given to consumers in this context. As a natural result of this role, postmodern consumers actively reproduce and consume symbols and images at the same time (Odabaşı, 2017: 101). The basic reason behind consumption in today's world is the meanings attributed to products. While producers attribute a social meaning to a product, consumers attribute personal meanings; and at the end of this process, products become cultural items (Odabaşı, 2017: 119–120). Meanings attributed to products in this context are emotional rather than rational. Products are taken beyond being consumption materials; they get the ability to define thoughts, feelings, and relationships.

In today's world, where consumption is controller and molder, consumers tend towards emotional necessities rather than basic requirements and they consume symbols rather than the products. Consumption has become the sole objective reality of today's culture (Baudrillard, 2013), and it surrounded the social and personal life. Now, we have to live in a consumer society in the frame of this nature and determinant features of consumption. Cultural meanings are attributed to the functional values of products, and a postmodern individual communicates and interacts with these values. People are defined according to what they consume, not what they produce (Williamson, 2001: 13); thus, personalities, identities, relationships, and social environments are shaped according to these norms. According to Bauman (2010: 53), who emphasizes the thought that we now live in a global consumer society, consumption behavior patterns affect each and every part of our lives. He states that we have turned into meta-humans under the pressure of consuming more and more everyday.

Consumer society is defined as the society to whom consumption is taught; this society gets used to consumption (Baudrillard, 2013: 87). Every single individual living in this society learns to express himself through consumption in the process of socialization. Featherstone (1996: 40) mentions that consumer society has become an essentially cultural society, and he emphasizes that consistent meanings are lost at the end of overconsumption. Masses are captivated by the eternal flow of formless contiguities. Reality loses its importance; and the newly produced, unnatural realities become more important at the end of this process. Consumer society theory focuses on how consumers actively reprocess symbolic meanings coded for presenting personalities and lifestyle goals beyond specific personal and social conditions. At this point, markets present consumers a heterogeneous range of resources to make them construct personal and collective identities (Arnould & Thompson, 2005: 871). Products presented to individuals involve special attitude and behavior codes and they connect consumers with producers. Products are treated like doctrines and they are turned into lifestyles. At the end of this process, one-dimensional thought or behavior patterns are created (Marcuse, 1990: 11). Consumption patterns define these one-dimensional behavior patterns. System dictates behaviors, relationships, and lifestyles; it determines the identity of consumers who – consciously or unconsciously – contribute to the sustainability and protection of the system's power. Consumption culture states that a beautiful life can be purchased; it supports individuals as they combine products and experiences with meaningful, satisfying, and socially acceptable lifestyles (Featherstone, 2010: 200). In this way, consumption becomes a cyclical process; it is both the cause and result of social behavior patterns.

Advertisements are certainly the most efficient instruments in this dominant and determinant position of consumption. According to Williams (1993: 184), who defines advertising as a system of magic, it is the official art of capitalism. Advertisements, that affect and get affected from social processes, are one of the important determinant factors in today's consumer society. Advertisements use media and advertising instruments in order to create values, connect with consumers, and make them internalize created symbolic values (Eyice et al., 2014: 95). In consumer societies, consumers believe that they will climb the social ladder with the use of a product or service in advertisements; they think that their lives will positively change, they will belong to a certain group or become different (Odabaşı, 2009: 23). After that point, it is impossible to explain the goal of consumption only with the urge to satisfy basic needs; consumed products become determinant factors in social life and relationships. They carry these roles through the symbolic meanings they involve. Postmodern advertisements attract attention on the basis of symbolic relations they ensure instead of giving information about a product (Proctor et al., 2002: 37). In this context, while consumption plays the leading role in creating value and meaning in personal and social world, advertising is considered as the key source of symbolic meanings (Elliott & Wattanasuwan, 1998: 132). Advertisements guide people on the way to reach a life idealized by consumer society and to adapt to the behavior patterns approved by it.

The basic strategy of advertisements is addressing to necessities which can be newly created or already existing (Elden et al., 2005: 64). Advertising reconceptualizes the desire in human beings about social relationships, and it functions as a factory of fantasy that transforms this desire into something that is represented by an object. In this respect, it claims that values like love, friendship, and sexuality can be gained through objects (Jhally, 2002: 81). Therefore, meanings attributed to objects are enhanced by social relations.

According to Berger, who defines advertisement as a culture created by consumer society, society supports its self-belief through images (2012: 139); at this point, the basic anxiety used by the advertisements rises from a fear: If you have nothing, then you become nothing (2012: 143). Individuals tend towards consumption to prove their existence; they establish their personality on the basis of this framework. Advertisements create new forms of meaning in order to have a say in the world of consumption. Advertising is a complete meaning-creation process; symbols constantly change and they reproduce themselves over and over in social codes (Batı, 2012: 21–22). Advertising gives importance to emotions besides rationality in order to communicate with individuals, give them the chance to have experience, the opportunity to express themselves; it targets hearts (Odabaşı, 2017: 185). Emotional messages, thus, settle in the basis of advertisements as an important element of seduction.

Elliott and Wattanasuwan (1998) mention that there is a bilateral relationship between advertising and consumer experiences. Advertising, as a part of cultural system, has a guiding role in consumer experiences while consumer experiences shape advertisements. The researchers claim that dialectic relationship between advertisement and consumer is important. Advertising not only creates and forms cultural meanings, it also represents cultural meanings. This dialectic relationship is derived from culture and transmitted to the symbolic world of advertising. It ensures the cyclical flow of symbolic meanings used by consumers for creating personality and shaping social worlds (Elliott & Wattanasuwan, 1998: 135–136). Advertisement is an important instrument of socialization as it transforms individuals and gives them the chance to have a new identity (cit. from Kellner by Dağtaş, 2009: 23). Berger says that advertisement has an extensive power of influence in this context (2012: 153); he emphasizes that the only power acknowledged by advertisement is the power to capture; the only resource of hope, satisfaction, or pleasure are the meanings attributed to products. Williamson claims that advertisement is one of the most important cultural factors that shape and reflect human life, it is ubiquitous and unavoidable; advertising has no boundaries and covers the entire media; it establishes a superstructure which has an autonomous existence and immense power of influence (2001: 11). Advertising, thus, becomes an unavoidable part of social life, a significant resource of pleasure, and an instrument that shapes lives.

In the frame of all these, it is obvious that advertising shapes personalities and relationships, it gives form to lifestyles, and supports the way we live through consumption. It has become one of the most important instruments of socialization. It produces meanings and sustains them through symbols. Today, the face of consumption has become symbolic in the social structure which continuously consumes symbols. In this context, the nature of consumption is another discussion topic of this study.

3 Symbolic Consumption and Diamond Rings

Postmodern consumption naturally prioritizes the symbolic benefits of productions rather than their functional benefits. The methods of addressing consumers are shaped on the basis of this fact; symbols are highlighted. Individuals purchase products not only for their functions, but also for creating a valid identity, for giving meaning to life (Batı, 2012: 21); these meanings are established and conveyed through symbols. Symbol is the conventional description of a notion; it is the sign of meanings attributed to a concept by a specific society (Eyice et al., 2014: 92–95). Grubb and Grathwohl (1967: 24) define symbol as a thing that replaces or represents another thing. According to them, symbols are made of signs and meanings. The decisive role played by these meanings in consumption process refers to symbolic consumption.

In symbolic consumption, meanings conveyed, carried, or transformed by products are no less important than product functions (Odabaşı, 2017: 110). In this context, consumer goods are a part of the method used by people to represent their feelings through symbols, which are the pieces of consumer patterns (Bocock, 2009: 59). Personality and environment are framed by consuming symbols. According to Elliott (1997: 287), symbolic meanings of products have two-way functions. They construct the social world outside – social symbolism – while they construct our identity inside – self-symbolism. In this regard, meanings that consumption involves become clearer. Consumption turns into any kind of social activity used by people while revealing their features or repositioning their place in society (Chaney, 1999: 24). Consumption functions as an instrument of self-construction and self-presentation. Consumers do not consume the products at that point; they consume symbols, symbolic meanings of products. These meanings are determined in social context and product demands are shaped according to their roles in cultural practices rather than the actual functions of them in daily life (Elliott, 1997: 287). Products, thus, go beyond being consumer good; they become forms of thinking and expression.

Consumption, considered as a way of self-expression, also functions as an instrument of creating identity. Grubb and Grathwohl explain this process of consumption in seven stages: Each individual has a specific self-concept; each individual has a perception of value; each individual has behavioral tendency to improve his/her personality according to that value; personality of a human is shaped as a result of the interaction with people around him such as family and peer group; products become communication tools that function as social symbols; individuals cause interactions by conveying meanings, they are affected from these interactions and as a result of all these, the understanding of consumption is directed towards improving the sense of self through the consumption of products as symbols (1967: 25–26). As suggested by these stages, the sense of self is constructed firstly by the interaction with environment, then – and finally – by the symbolic meanings attributed to goods. Consumer rituals tell people who they are – or who they want to be. Consumer behaviors are shaped in the light of these rituals and expectations, and they establish personal and social realities that are not natural.

Every good speaks for its user in this newly formed social life. One of the most common consumer goods with symbolic meanings is diamond products, especially solitaire rings. Symbolic meanings attributed to these products, one of the most important global consumer good, is the study sampling of this research. Love, loyalty, and peace are some of the symbolic meanings represented by diamonds. In order to understand the importance of these products in advertising copies, it is crucial to analyze some researches on the issue of how these products are perceived by society.

Otnes and Lowrey (1993) carried out a research on the connection between individuals and artifacts of marriage; they had interviews about the artifacts perceived "sacred" by brides and they determined that wedding ring is one of them. According to this, when an engagement ring is presented to a woman, she becomes a part of consumer society, which is made of women with similar rings and more important than that, she can stop worrying about being cast out of that group of women. Diamond engagement rings thus function as a way of creating identity.

In another research (Schweingruber et al., 2004), American engagement proposal performances are studied. According to the findings of this study, presence of a good story and a beautiful ring during proposal is a sign of earnestness and strength of the relationship. Although verbal proposal seems to be important, a proposal without a ring is not sufficient. Proposal without a diamond ring is not a sufficient social story; it is not good enough to represent the future of a couple; such proposals can disappoint women. Viewpoint of men are also quite special; they also do not consider such proposals as reliable. They think that one is not engaged as long as he does not have a ring. In this context, size and price of the diamond ring is as important as the presence of it. Size of the diamond ring represents the sufficiency of a man. Men, therefore, feel obliged to purchase rings as big as possible. Another finding of the research shows that friends and family can involve in the process by making comments on the diamond ring of a woman.

There are studies and researches on this issue in Turkey. For instance, Eyice et al. (2014) conducted a focus group study with women. According to the findings, diamond solitaire ring means "you are unique"; it symbolizes love and marriage and ensures the approval of others in a society. Men, on the other hand, feel obliged to buy solitaire rings in order to satisfy the expectations of women rather than making personal choices.

In another study (Şabah: 2017), perception of diamonds as gifts is discussed. According to this perception, when diamond is given as a part of a ritual, it summarizes the relationship and experience; it represents the turning points. It is determined in the study that proposals without solitaire ring are not accepted as real wishes; this finding is in parallel with the findings of previous studies. Besides, according to the half of the interviewees, diamond ring is no longer a wish, it is a natural part of process, it is an obligation.

Meanings of diamond rings are presented in various studies. Diamond ring, in general, is the symbol of love; it is a symbolic consumer good, a must-have in marriage, which is the last stage of love and relationship. There is no rational benefit it delivers; it becomes meaningful and valuable through the symbolic value it carries. In this sense, it can be said that it is highly meaningful both for women and men; these products are inseparable parts of relationships and repre- sentatives of romanticism. Two important questions intersect at this point: How are these meanings created and supported, and how are they presented in advertisements?

4 Method and Sampling

Advertising combines the cultural elements created in an environment in a long time, presents meanings, and transfers them. Mutual interaction and support between visual and linguistic elements give advertisements the chance to have great impact (Becan, 2016: 37). At this point, it is important to analyze the signs created by visual and linguistic elements in order to understand the content of advertisement. We live in a world of signs, and the basic instruments in com- munication are these signs and meanings set by them. According to Barthes (1979: 41), meanings are the performances combining the signifier and the signi- fied, and sign is formed at the end of this process. Signs can be defined as words, objects, sights, or phenomena; and the domain of it is semiotics. Semiotics, also called semiology, is the scientific design studying signs and symbols as elements of communicative behavior; it researches the process of how they are created, formed, connected, and it develops a theoretical frame to demonstrate this pro- cess (Rifat, 1992: 14). Semiotics achieves integrity through interpretation studies on the basis of signs. It exhibits different meanings given to images-signs-visible objects (Şimşek, 2006: 70). Barthes approaches every advertisement as a state- ment and says that every statement is a combination of the platform of signifier or narration and the platform of signified (1993: 157). The product formed at the end of this process is the sign.

Semiotics does not perceive the act of attributing meaning as a private process. Through semiotics, people produce signs and interpret them (Alemdar & Erdoğan, 2002: 349). At this point, both creation and interpretation are significant. Visual and linguistic elements in advertisements are built to evoke audiences/consumers. According to Rifat (1996:25), copies are end products and resources of producing new meanings. Images used in forming these copies think and speak for individuals. Product replaces an image or emotion and takes credit of its meaning; this meaning transfer is possible with the cooperation of target group (Batı, 2007: 10). Taken from this perspective, audience recreates meanings over the product he/she consumes. In advertising copies, the goal is to create emotional meaning, and audience/consumer is involved in the process in line with this aim. Culture, emotional level, experiences are undoubtedly significant elements that are taken into consideration while creating and attributing meanings.

Semiotics, in the simplest terms, is interested in how meanings are created in these processes. Understanding the organization of signifier and signified in the creation process of signs is significant at this point. While making semiotic analysis of commercial films specifically chosen for this study, these elements are prioritized and analyses are carried out on this basis.

Sampling of the study is commercial films of Zen Diamond, chosen by purposeful sampling method. The common theme of two chosen commercial films broadcasted in 2017 is *It is never too late for a solitaire ring*. Discourses about symbolic consumption are established by signs in both commercial films; these discussions in the copies of the films telling two different stories on the basis of the same theme are analyzed.

5 Findings

5.1 "Zen Diamond | It is Never Too Late for a Solitaire Ring" Commercial Film Analysis

Narrative: The commercial film was firstly broadcasted in 2017. Brown tones are dominant in the film. The film starts with the image of a woman placing white flowers on a dining table by candle light. Instrumental music is heard in the background. The woman starts talking to herself, her inner voice is heard: "*Everything is okay.*" Her dress and flowers are the same color: White. She sits at the table, looks at the mirror, to her reflection and fluffs up her hair. "*I didn't exaggerate, right? It is our wedding anniversary after all.*" Excitement in her voice is replaced by an anxious tone while waiting; she checks on the clock on the wall. "*He is late.*" Her demoralization is conveyed with the look in her eyes and voice. The audience sees the white frames with family photographs. There is a happy couple with two kids in the image. There is the blurry image of wedding photos in the background. Calm rhythm continues as the woman approaches to the window and the unhappy inner voice is heard again. "*May be he forgot*

Img. 1: Frames from the Commercial Film. Zen Diamond YouTube Channel, https://www.youtube.com/watch?v=72Mdx3ajX30 (Last Accessed: 15.09.2018)

this day." At that moment, she turns around as if she hears a voice and she gets excited. The man enters the door and approaches; he starts speaking apologetically: "*I am sorry, I am late.*" The woman looks disappointed and nods her head. The man continues: "*But it is not for years, I am late only for half an hour, for one thing.*" The man shows a small black box and opens it, the woman's disappointment turns into surprise and happiness. A sound effect is heard as the man opens the box. The sound effect is magical and music becomes more dynamic as the scene continues. "*Will you continue to love me?*" The woman smiles, her eyes are full of tears. The man puts the ring on her finger. Voiceover is heard: "*It is never too late for a solitaire ring… To your only love, Zen solitaire diamond.*" The woman looks into the eyes of her husband; they hug and the diamond ring is in close-up. The advertisement ends with music and brand's slogan: "*Impossible without Zen.*" (Img. 1)

Analysis: When the discourses in commercial films are analyzed, it can be observed that the stories are established on the expectation of romantic acts. Dominance of soft brown colors and candle light that create a dim atmosphere strengthen the feeling of romanticism in the scene. Odabaşı (2017: 185) claims that romanticism, which no longer exists in real life, are experienced in advertisements and internalized. In this context, romanticism is presented as an element of attraction in advertisements. The table set for two is a sign of a private day. The scene is completed with white, the color of innocence. With their freshness, flowers are the symbols of a healthy relationship. The dress of the lady is also white, similar to bridal gown; it is another symbol of love and purity. The woman, who prepares for having a romantic dinner with her husband, checks her look in the mirror and fluffs up her hair. This act is a sign of her wish to be admired, and her excitement for celebration. She checks on the clock and continues to wait with excitement. Existence of the clock implies the value of

Tab. 1: Signifier – Signified Table

Signifier	Signified
Brown tones, pastel colors	Romanticism, peace, calmness
Candles, soft light	Romanticism
Celebration dinner/table	Special day rituals
White flowers	Romanticism, love, purity
White dress	Purity, bridal gown
Looking at herself in the mirror, fluffing up hair	The wish to be desired, excitement
Clock	The value of time, being late
Looking out of the window	Worry
Framed child-mother-father photographs	Happy family
Hugging and the diamond solitaire ring at the center of attention	Diamond as a unifying aspect, the focus of the story
Calm rhythm	Calmness
Driving rhythm	Excitement, happiness
Diamond solitaire ring	Love, loyalty, happiness, celebration, gift, being unique, the only love
The magical sound effect when the box is opened	Magical power of diamond
Advertisement slogan – *"It is never too late for a solitaire ring… To your only love, Zen solitaire diamond."*	A relationship ritual, the act of purchase that should be done sooner or later
Brand slogan – *"Impossible without Zen."*	Essentiality of diamond

time and it emphasizes that the man is late. The clock prepares for the emphasis of "being late" in the following scene. The woman completes her preparations and the audience hears her inner talk; she questions herself about whether or not she exaggerated preparations. At the end, she decides that she did not as it is a special day: The day of their wedding anniversary. There is a message to the audience underlying all these scenes: Everything should be chick and classy during such celebrations, special days are very important in relationships. The process of consumption involves specific instruments and prioritizes them in social relationships; it creates a social and cultural system with specific social behavior and interaction forms (Yanıklar, 2006: 26–27). Therefore, it can be said that celebrations in special days are the forms of interactions created by the idea of consumption. This statement is approved by the advertisement as a diamond ring is presented as a form of interaction, as a "gift in a special day."

As the time passes by, excitement of the woman is replaced by anxiety. It is seen that the probability of being forgotten makes the woman really sad. This is a reference to the discussion that special days are important in relationships, especially for women. Special days in commercial films are a significant reference point for directing audiences towards consumption and for creating a culture, a tradition of "giving presents" in those days. This discussion is especially reflected in this commercial film. The anxiety of the look in woman's eyes when she thinks that the man is "late," and the resentment in her inner voice refers to the disappointment when a special day is forgotten. Family photos that are presented to the audiences at that point represent the peace and happiness in the household, and they reinforce the dramatic structure. On the other hand, children of the couple emphasize that they are not newly married. Increase in the anxiety of woman is shown to the reader in the scene when the woman looks out of the window to see if her husband is coming. After that scene, the woman turns to the door with a hopeful look in her eyes; this scene is the breaking point of the story. The man enters the door and he looks embarrassed, he looks apologetic. Being late in a special day puts him in a difficult situation and he accepts that. The look in woman's eyes and mimics also show that the man is guilty. The woman's expression changes as soon as she sees the present: she becomes happy and emotional. The diamond solitaire ring shining in the black box makes her forget all her anxiety and disappointment; her eyes are full of tears of joy and happiness. This positive change is supported with the increase in the rhythm of music.

The man apologizes for being late: *"But it is not for years, I am late only for half an hour, for one thing."* He opens the box; the calm instrumental music is replaced by a faster rhythm. Sound effect at that point is "magical"; it refers to the feelings brought by the gift. The woman blames the man with the look in her eyes until that point, but her attitude changes magically. It is understood that the man had not bought a solitaire ring until that day. He puts his real feelings into words after opening the box: *"Will you continue to love me?"* The woman does not answer, her attention is on the ring. The man does not expect an answer, he puts the ring on her finger and they hug. The man expresses his thoughts through the ring; the most explicit answer for the woman is to accept this gift and be happy. There seems to be nothing more important or efficient than to accept the gift at that moment. As stated by Elliott (1997: 287), consumer goods are more than the objects of economic change; they are a part of thought and expression. The ring represents the feelings of the man and the thoughts of woman.

Man and woman hug, the diamond ring on woman's finger is in close-up. The focus of the story is not the relationship or feelings of the couple; it is the diamond jewelry that represents emotions. The man proves his feelings; the woman accepts the gift and forgives him. The "belatedness" in here does not refer to that night; the woman has waited for years for the diamond solitaire ring.

The man in the scene does not apologize for being late that night, he apologizes for the fact that he has not given that gift to the woman until that point. The discussion reproduced and supported in the film is that one of the emotional responsibilities of men is to buy solitaire ring. Parsons (2002: 238) states that giving gifts in newly started or older relationships is a statement of the connection between couples; the gift establishes a symbolic interaction and contributes to the development of relationship. This statement is supported by the advertisement slogan: "*It is never too late for a solitaire ring… To your only love, Zen solitaire diamond.*" Emphasizing the "uniqueness" of a woman in relationship is associated with the solitaire ring. The brand's slogan given in parallel with the jingle emphasizes the essentiality of diamond solitaire ring: "*Impossible without Zen.*" (Tab. 1)

5.2 "Zen Diamond | It is Never Too Late for a Solitaire Ring" Commercial Film Analysis

Narrative: This chosen commercial film was broadcasted in 2017. The film starts with the image of an old couple drinking coffee at home; pastel and light colors are used in general and flowers attract attention as a part of decoration. The couple startles with the excited voice of their daughter: "*Mom! Dad!*" A young woman enters the room in a happy manner: "*I've got news for you!*" She runs and sits next to the couple and says: "*Umut asked me to marry him!*" The couple smiles, the young woman continues: "*He brought huge balloons to the place where we first met and placed flowers on the ground. I was so happy I couldn't tell!*" But the mother does not listen to her any more, her attention is on her daughter's ring; she looks at it in awe and she cannot take her eyes off it. She stops her daughter: "*Your solitaire ring is very beautiful, my girl!*" She turns to her husband, implies her expectation from him with her eyes and points to the ring: "*Right, Necdet?*" The

Img. 2: Frames from the Commercial Film. Zen Diamond YouTube Channel, https://www.youtube.com/watch?v=eECLYgMxUxs (Last Accessed: 18.09.2018)

Tab. 2: Signifier – Signified Table

Signifier	Signified
Blue – White pastel colors	Silence, peace, calmness
Floral decoration	Relief, freshness, renewal
Story of marriage proposal	Ritual of relationship
Decreasing voice of young woman	Dialogue that becomes insignificant, changing focus
Diamond ring of young woman	Symbol of the wish for building a new life, new focus
Zen shop visited as a couple	Way to happiness
Different diamond ring models	Variety, the chance to make choice
Holding hands and diamond ring in focus	Diamond as a unifying aspect, the focus of story
Driving rhythm	Excitement, happiness
Calm rhythm	Romanticism, calmness
Diamond solitaire ring	Love, loyalty, happiness, celebration, gift, being unique, the only love
Advertisement slogan – *"It is never too late for a solitaire ring… To your only love, Zen solitaire diamond."*	A relationship ritual, the act of purchase that should be done sooner or later
Brand slogan – *"Impossible without Zen."*	Essentiality of diamond

man is suddenly surprised and assumes an uneasy attitude: *"I mean, a flower used to be enough, but…"* upon these words, the woman smiles with expectation and points to the ring again. The man smiles and says: *"Times have changed, right my lady?"* The woman nods and approves his words; the man puts his coffee on the table and stands up. The voiceover is heard at that point: *"It is never too late for a solitaire ring…To your only love, Zen solitaire diamond."* The couple goes to Zen Diamond shop. They choose a ring. The man holds the woman's hand; the screen goes black with the image of the ring on woman's finger. The film ends with the jingle and slogan: *"Impossible without Zen."* (Img. 2)

Analysis: Bright environment and pastel tones in the commercial film are the signs of warm home environment, trust, and happiness. Flowers and pictures of flowers are used in the decoration in order to give the impression of freshness. Fresh flowers indicate the two relationship types we see in the story; the new, fresh relationship and the old but still fresh relationship. The old couple sits, drinks coffee, and watches TV with happy expressions in their faces. They look curiously to the young woman as she enters the room. Both the couple and the woman have blue clothes; blue is also the color of the general decoration. The young woman sits between her mother and father, she is excited and happy. She starts telling how her boyfriend asked her to marry him. The first thing that she does at the beginning of her story is to show her ring: The most important object of the story. She, in a way, expects approval about this product of consumption. Odabaşı (2017: 135) states that the codes of consumption direct consumer behaviors towards the expectation of being approved by others, and he mentions that this is a kind of "social approval"; meanings of symbols are similarly interpreted and understood by different individuals. At this point, ring is used as a piece that enables parents to correctly interpret the story told by the daughter. It can be said that ring is an instrument for social approval; sufficiency and approvability of proposal is based on the ring.

The couple is interested in the story of the daughter and starts listening carefully. After a while, the mother gets distracted while the father is still interested; the voice of daughter decreases. The diamond solitaire ring on the young woman's finger distracts the mother. The young woman continues to tell the emotional details of her story while her mother looks at the ring excitedly with admiration. Finally, she cannot stop herself, interrupts her daughter and tells her how beautiful the ring is. At that point, life-changing decision of the woman loses its importance because of something "brighter." After seeing how beautiful the ring is, she looks as if she does not care about anything else; the man sees this and gets disappointed. He looks as if he did something wrong and got caught. Symbols have to represent similar meanings in groups that have interaction (Grubb & Grathwohl, 1967: 24). At this point, the ring seems to represent the same meaning for individuals from different ages and with different genders.

The story reaches the breaking point and changes direction. A significant decision about marriage seems to have lost its importance and effect both for mother and father. The mother, who does not give her daughter the opportunity to continue her story, looks at her husband with attitude and makes him accept that the ring is very beautiful. At that moment, the man gets stuck in a difficult situation; he cannot even take a sip from his coffee. He states that flowers used to be sufficient, but the time has changed; he smiles and agrees with the mother. The advertisement interprets the statements of "objects" as the statements of individuals and gives them a symbolic value (Williamson, 2001: 12). At this point, existence – or inexistence – of diamond ring is translated as an instrument of expressing feelings. The man's mistake that embarrasses him is the fact that he has not given a diamond solitaire ring; he seems ready to compensate for it. Necessity of this compensation is not a matter of discussion.

The young woman does not seem uncomfortable with the fact that she is interrupted; she looks at her father and she is curious about his reaction. She seems happy about the reaction of her mother and she does not think that there is a problem. According to Berger (2012: 134), consumer is expected to be envied as he/she reaches a certain point when he/she has a specific product. The goal of creating a consumer society is to transform individuals into objects of desire and turn them into envied beings. The young woman is not interested in completing her story, she is happy and satisfied as somebody else – her mother – envies her ring.

Jingle, an entertaining rhythm until that point, changes into an emotional tone and voiceover supports the focus of the story with the expression: "*It is never too late for a solitaire ring… To your only love, Zen solitaire diamond.*" The mother and the father enter Zen Diamond shop at that moment. They choose a ring among other models, and the ring is shown in close-up. Gifts can be used for expressing bonds that surround relationships (Parsons, 2002: 238). Here, the important point is not to have a strong marriage that continues for years, it is to give a diamond solitaire ring – although it is late – as a gift that represents the bond between the couple. Similarly, the important thing in the daughter's wedding proposal is not the content of it, it is the ring presented to her. The timing of giving that gift is not important, it can be presented during proposal or after years; the important thing is to carry out this ritual properly. It is never too late for this. The brand slogan, strengthening all the messages in the text, is heard again: "*Impossible without Zen!*" (Tab. 2)

6 Conclusion

New meanings attributed to the consumption and consumer by the postmodern era transformed the tendency and emphasis of advertising copies. Consumption is no longer a rational act of satisfying needs; it is now an action based on strong emotional decisions that form personal and social environments. This understanding of consumption, shaped by symbolic expectations beyond rational understandings, increased the importance of meanings attributed to them by individuals and society. Consumers are addicted to the search for meaning in the frame of consumption culture; they regard the symbolic meanings of products. In this context, consumption products cannot be separated from the processes of forming identities and or expressing feelings; consumption now has the function of establishing new personal and social meanings. Products are a means of expression both in daily life and in special days; they now speak for human beings.

Diamond rings are one of the most common products used for expressing feelings; they have important place in society as an essential part of rituals – like proposal; they are the most important gifts that must be given to the spouse. It is obvious that this meaning attributed to diamond ring is not created in a natural process; it is socially, artificially produced. As the cornerstone of capitalism and bearer of consumption ideology, advertisements are perceived as an important part of creating and internalizing personal and social meanings. The role of advertising copies in forming personality/identity, the responsibility of these copies in social interactions as important premises, and the part of these copies in creating and internalizing symbolic meanings and meanings formed by the signs are the basic questions of this research. The dialectic relationship between societies and symbolic meanings in advertisements are researched in the context of diamond jewelry – solitaire rings.

At the end of the research, it is seen that meanings such as love, affection, and loyalty are attributed to diamond products. Marriage – new or old – is imperfect if there is not a diamond ring in it. Solitaire ring is desired by women from all ages, so men from all ages must present their love with a ring, which has a common symbolic meaning for different individuals. Sooner or later, giving a diamond as a gift is an inseparable part of relationship rituals.

In both of the analyzed commercial films, breaking points of the stories are the appearance of diamond rings. Story until that moment ends as soon as the diamond ring is seen; all of the other elements in the story are excluded. The diamond product, which is the most important issue, is presented as the solution to conflicts and as the most exciting focus of the film. The woman who has to wait for her husband in their wedding anniversary gets very sad; she does not overcome this feeling through the words of her husband. But the diamond ring makes her happy. The most important point of the story for the mother in the second commercial film is not the proposal; it is the diamond ring of her daughter. The real storytellers in both films are not the characters, they are diamond rings.

All these symbolic meanings attributed to diamond products take over the whole story; all of the feelings and words remain in the background and the product speaks for the consumers. Diamonds are more meaningful than words; they are pictured as the symbol of the wish to build a life together. They are the representatives of strong relationships, pure love, and loyalty. In this context, diamonds are dreamt by women from all ages and social status; men are responsible for representing their love for their spouse with this specific product. Women are represented as the ones who wait for a gift; they can be sure of the love of their partner with this present. Men are obligated to buy that gift; they can prove the strength of their feelings with this present. Diamond is the unifying power in relationships with the symbolic power it holds. Therefore, both male and female consumers are included in the symbolic power; the product becomes a profoundly necessary element of relationships. The value attributed to diamond as a precious stone is associated with the value of relationships; diamond solitaire ring is equivalent of the "uniqueness," "preciousness" of the partner in relationship.

As presented by the researches, relationship between meanings attributed to diamond rings and advertisements are seen in the analyzed commercial films; the dialectic relationship between advertisement and society is sustained. These meanings attributed to products are reinforced by the stories in commercial films and by striking brand slogans; an unchangeable emotional situation is created in consumer mind. Although diamond ring is jewelry after all, it is presented as an irreplaceable object that should be used while expressing feelings. Advertisements address consumers through social meanings and symbolic values that are professionally used in them. Through the images created in minds, roles are given to individuals of all ages and genders. Discussions in these films give important data about the meaning of symbolic consumption in society. In this context, it can be said that while advertising copies present symbolic values in social practices on one the hand, they reconstruct these values and recreate meanings on the other.

Bibliography

Alemdar, K. & Erdoğan, İ. (2002). *Öteki Kuram*, Ankara: Erk Yayınevi.

Arnould, E. J. & Thompson, C. J. (2005). Consumer culture theory (CCT): Twenty years of research. Journal of Consumer Research, 31(4), pp. 868–882.

Barthes, R. (1979). *Göstergebilim İlkeleri*, (Çev.) Vardar, B. & Rifat, M., Ankara: Kültür Bakanlığı Yayınları.

Barthes, R. (1993). *Göstergebilimsel Serüven*, (Çev.) Rifat, M. & Rifat, S., İstanbul: Yapı Kredi Yayınları.

Batı, U. (2007). "Postmodern Estetiğin Bir Görünümü: Üst Gerçeklik Biçimleri Olarak Reklam Metinleri", Kültür ve İletişim Dergisi, 10, pp. 1–34.

Batı, U. (2012). *Reklamın Dili*, İstanbul: Alfa Yayınları.

Baudrillard, J. (2013). *Tüketim Toplumu*, (Çev.) Deliceçaylı, H. & Keskin, F., İstanbul: Ayrıntı Yayınları.

Bauman, Z. (2010). *Etiğin Tüketiciler Dünyasında Bir Şansı Var mı?*, (Çev.) Çoban, F. & Katırcı, İ., Ankara: De Ki Yayınları.

Becan, C. (2016). "Sembolik Tüketim Ekseninde Anti Ütopya ve Reklam", *Reklamı Anlamlandırmak*, (Ed.) Mengü, S.Ç., İstanbul: Derin Yayınları.

Berger, J. (2012). *Görme Biçimleri*, (Çev.) Salman, Y., İstanbul: Metis Yayınları.

Bocock, R. (2009). *Tüketim*, (Çev.) Kutluk, İ., Ankara: Dost Kitabevi.

Chaney, D. (1999). *Yaşam Tarzları*, (Çev.) Kutluk, İ., Ankara: Dost Kitabevi.

Dağtaş, B. (2009). *Reklam Kültür Toplum*, Ankara: Ütopya Yayınevi.

Debord, G. (2012). *Gösteri Toplumu*, (Çev.) Ekmekçi, A. & Taşkent, O., İstanbul: Ayrıntı Yayınları.

Elden, M., Ulukök, Ö. & Yeygel, S. (2005). *Şimdi Reklamlar...*, İstanbul: İletişim Yayınları.

Elliott, R. (1997). "Existential consumption and irrational desire", *European Journal of Marketing*, 34(4), pp. 285–296.

Elliott, R. & Wattanasuwan, K. (1998). "Brands as symbolic resources for the construction of identity", *International Journal of Advertising*, 17(2), pp. 131–144.

Eyice, S., İlbasmış, S. & Pirtini, S. (2014). "Sembolik Tüketim Davranışı ve Sembolik Tüketim Ürünü Olarak Tek Taş Yüzük Üzerine Bir Araştırma", *Marmara Üniversitesi Öneri Dergisi*, 11(42), pp. 83–103.

Featherstone, M. (1996). *Postmodernizm ve Tüketim Kültürü*, (Çev.) Küçük, M., İstanbul: Ayrıntı Yayınları.

Featherstone, M. (2010). "Body, image and affect in consumer culture", *Body & Society*, 16(1), pp. 193–221.

Grubb, E. L. & Grathwohl, H. L. (1967). "Consumer self-concept, symbolism and market behavior: A theoretical approach", *Journal of Marketing*, 31(4), pp. 22–27.

Herbert, M. (1990). *Tek-Boyutlu İnsan*, (Çev.) Yardımlı, A., İstanbul: İdea Yayınları.

Jhally, S. (2002). "Kıyametin Sınırında Reklamcılık", (Çev.) Aydoğan F., *Birikim Dergisi*, 159: 77–86.

Odabaşı, Y. (2009). *Tüketim Kültürü: Yetinen Toplumdan Tüketen Topluma*, İstanbul: Sistem Yayıncılık.

Odabaşı, Y. (2017). *Postmodern Pazarlama*, İstanbul: MediaCat Yayınları.

Otnes, C. & Lowrey, T. M. (1993). "Til debt do us part: The selection and meaning of artifacts in the American wedding", *Advances in Consumer Research*, 20, pp. 325–329.

Parsons, A. G. (2002). "Brand choice in gift-giving: Recipient influence", *Journal of Product & Brand Management*, 11(4), pp. 237–249.

Proctor, S., Proctor, T. & Papasolomou-Doukakis, I. (2002). "A postmodern perspective on advertisements and their analysis", *Journal of Marketing Communications*, 8(1), pp. 31–44.

Rifat, M. (1992). *Göstergebilimin ABC'si*, İstanbul: Simavi Yayınları.

Rifat, M. (1996). *Homo Semioticus*, İstanbul: Yapı Kredi Yayınları.

Rutherford, P. (1996). *Yeni İkonalar: Televizyonda Reklam Sanatı*, (Çev.) Gerçeker, M. K., İstanbul: Yapı Kredi Yayınları.

Şabah, Ş. (2017). "Pırlantam Olmadan Asla: Kadınların Bireysel Kimlik ve Pırlanta Evlilik Yüzüğü İlişkileri", *Anadolu Üniversitesi Sosyal Bilimler Dergisi*, 17(2), pp. 67–83.

Schweingruber, D., Anahita, S. & Berns, N. (2004). "Popping the question when the answer is known: The engagement proposal as performance. *Sociological Focus*, 37(2), pp. 143–161.

Şimşek, S. (2006). *Reklam ve Geleneksel İmgeler*, İstanbul: Nüve Kültür Merkezi Yayınları.

Williams, R. (1993). "Adverstising: The magic system", *Culture and Materialism*, London: Verso, pp. 170–195.

Williamson, J. (2001). *Reklamların Dili: Reklamlarda Anlam ve İdeoloji*, (Çev.) Fethi, A., Ankara: Ütopya Yayınevi.

Yanıklar, C. (2006). *Tüketimin Sosyolojisi*, İstanbul: Birey Yayıncılık.

Zen Diamond YouTube Channel, https://www.youtube.com/ watch?v=72Mdx3ajX30 (15.09.2018).

Zen Diamond YouTube Channel, https://www.youtube.com/ watch?v=eECLYgMxUxs (18.09.2018).

Hakan Yavuz

Tax Policies Concerning Lowering the Emission of Greenhouse Gas: An Assessment Specific to Turkey

1 Introduction

Environmental problems have been accepted by countries for many years as "the other country problem." However, reasons such as the population growth, industrialization, increase in the number of motor vehicles, urbanization/types of urbanization, increase in energy demand, increase in economic development and development levels, etc. have led to such an extent that the environmental problems cannot be overcome by a single country. Therefore, environmental problems are a global problem, and it is necessary to make common decisions at an international level. At a global level, it began towards the last quarter of the twentieth century with multilateral agreements, joint efforts against environmental problems, and the efforts of the United Nations.

Countries in the world faced with important environmental problems since the 1970s have become aware of the importance of acting jointly against the environmental problems that have mandatorily come to terms with the past. Environmental problems have become to expand without any limit and threaten every living and nonliving life. In the light of these developments, the Stockholm Conference was held, which was accepted as a milestone on environmental issues and provided with multilateral participation. After the conference, countries had to act together against increasing environmental problems. In this respect, the 1990s catch the attention as the years for this purpose when multilateral environmental agreements increased.

It can be said that the most important environmental problems are caused by greenhouse gas emissions. This condition has made it compulsory to put up a fight against greenhouse gas emissions at a global level. Especially developed countries want to reduce greenhouse gas emissions by increasing economic, legal, financial, and administrative measures every year. One of the most financially important measures is to implement an inclusive tax. Taxes applied to reduce greenhouse gas emissions include environmental tax, ecological tax, emission tax, eco-tax, emission tax, carbon tax, environmental cleaning tax, waste tax, vehicle tire tax, waste tax, oil waste tax, motor vehicles/means of transport tax, motor vehicles fuel taxes, alcoholic beverages additional tax, chemical waste or medication tax, agricultural inputs tax, energy taxes, air and water pollution tax, etc. There are a large number of taxes that have a field of application in different countries. No matter how effective the environmental taxes are applied to the disposal of the problem, it is not single-handed enough. Therefore, it should be supported by other tools.

Since environmental taxes are generally taken overconsumption, they are included in the indirect taxes category. However, sometimes it can be taken over capital accumulation. Pigou (1920) has a significant impact on the emergence of the idea of taxing the activities that cause environmental pollution. The main purpose of the aforementioned idea can be expressed as the protection of the environment. Pigou's analysis is more about the need to fight negative externalities. Since environmental pollution or environmental issues are types of the negative externality, Pigou's tax-based proposals have also importance in compensating for environmental problems. The main purpose of environmental taxes, which is undoubtedly irrelevant in which country it is applied, is to combat environmental pollution and to leave a cleaner environment for future generations.

Pigou (1920) states that externalities can be internalized through prices by virtue of a tax set for optimal allocation of resources. By means of this tax, because the economic activities that cause negative externality will be taxed, the difference between the private cost and the social cost resulting from the externality due to the tax is reduced to a minimum. The basis of Pigou's approach is based on state intervention. This state intervention here is ensured through accrued taxes that are subject to the legislative act (Oz and Buyrukoglu, 2012:88).

Since greenhouse gas emission is an important environmental problem, taxes are taken advantage to reduce this emission. Due to the Vienna Agreement in 1985 and the Montreal Protocol in 1987, attention was drawn to the ozone layer depletion depending upon the greenhouse gas emission and forced the world countries to take stricter measures to combat greenhouse gas emissions. Especially with the 1997 Kyoto Protocol, they accelerated their attempts to reduce greenhouse gas emission values. While developed economies achieved reduction objectives in no small measure in this regard, most of the developing countries were exempted from the reduction objective. However, in the following years, developing countries had to reduce their greenhouse gas emissions. In spite of Turkey's failure to execute a concrete reduction of greenhouse gas emissions except for some years, Turkey has not encountered any international sanctions. However, due to possible tangible sanctions in the years to come, increasing greenhouse gas emissions is a threat to be considered.

In comparison to the year 1990, Turkey's greenhouse gas emissions have increased by about 235%. Therefore, greenhouse gas emission values should be reduced by legal, economic, administrative, and financial measures. In addition to the measures to be taken, the reduction of greenhouse gas emissions through subsidy/incentive policies should be encouraged. When taking into consideration Turkey's prevention of narrowing of sectoral policies in previously applied tax incentives, generating employment, increasing tax revenues, making contributions to economic stability, the combat with the subterranean economy, and positive impacts of these areas and so on, it can be said that the said implementation may be effective in reducing the greenhouse gas emission values.

After addressing the explanations of greenhouse gases in this study (the effects of greenhouse gas emissions, global measures against greenhouse gas emissions, the development of greenhouse gas indicators from various aspects, selected OECD countries in which greenhouse gas tax practices are successful in reducing emissions), Turkey's increasing greenhouse gas emission was drawn into attention. Within this framework, the purpose of the study is the alternative tax policy that is used as an intervention tool in reducing greenhouse gas emission, which is to be evaluated specifically to Turkey.

2 Instructions Regarding Greenhouse Gas Emission

Production and consumption of fossil fuels, production and usage of various chemicals in agriculture, industrial activities, increase in waste, increase in natural resources due to the population growth, increase in the number of motor vehicles, and many other factors are directly effective in increasing greenhouse gas emissions. Regardless of the factor, all of them seem to have human actions at the source. Human beings use resources to meet their compulsory or other needs. This process affects many areas as well as the problem of increasing greenhouse gas emissions. Greenhouse gas is a gas that increases the temperature in the atmosphere due to the gases it contains. It contains carbon dioxide, nitrous oxide, methane, and various carbons (hydrofluoride, perfluoro, sulfur hexafluoride).

Greenhouse gas emissions also have a direct impact on global warming and sea level rise. Rising sea level may affect the population living in the coastal areas and production activities. In this respect, greenhouse gas emissions can cause major economic losses. In addition to economic losses, sudden seasonal movements have a negative impact on agricultural production (Latake et al., 2015:335–336). The determination of greenhouse gas emissions is very important for the standards to be used and the measures to be taken. The committed determinations directly affect the success of the applied tools. However, in some cases, the amount of emission may not be determined correctly. Even if correct detection is made, some costs may arise due to greenhouse gas emissions from other countries.

There are situations that prevent the correct determination. For example, the existence of a situation that cannot be integrated into economic life related to oil production or that is an illegal production, and therefore not reflected in economic indicators, may hinder the actual amount of emissions (Nordhaus et al., 2003:26). However factors such as setting standards correctly not making accurate measurements and personnel errors can also be effective. The competent authority for the determination of greenhouse gas emissions in Turkey is the Ministry of Environment and Urban Planning. However, TSI, TSE, Union of Chambers of Turkish Engineers and Architects, Technology Development Foundation of Turkey, private sector organizations, and NGOs are also among the relevant organizations in this topic. Responsible companies are required to report their emissions in accordance with the regulations on Greenhouse Gas Emissions and the standards specified in the communiqué on monitoring and reporting of these gases. Responsible firms are referred to as "Greenhouse Gas Confirmatory Organizations." By means of these confirmatory organizations, Turkey's annual amount of greenhouse gas emissions within the framed of obtained data is estimated. The Communique about the Verification of Greenhouse Gas Emissions and the Authorization of Confirmatory Organizations was published in the "T.C. Resmi Gazete" dated 02.04.2015 and numbered 29314. Thus, legislation on monitoring, reporting, and verifying greenhouse gas emissions has been established. This indicates that in Turkey concerned legislation has been considerably formed lately.

3 Global Measures Against Greenhouse Gas Emission

Since the problems caused by greenhouse gas emissions affect the whole world, global measures must be taken in this area. It is not possible for a country or bloc to cope with this problem. In this respect, it is very important for global organizations to develop a common language in the conflict of greenhouse gas emissions. The United Nations is one of the leading organizations in the fight against greenhouse gas emissions. However, as a form of regional organization, the EU is taking strategic decisions to combat the aforementioned problem.

The multilateral agreements carried out by the United Nations are very important in terms of creating global awareness in the fight against greenhouse gas emissions and in the way of relying on some sanctions. One of the first agreements in this context is the Vienna Agreement and the Montreal Protocol.

The main purpose of the Vienna Agreement adopted in 1985 is the protection of the ozone layer. Two years after the Agreement was signed, the Montreal Protocol was adopted in 1987. The purpose of this protocol is to ensure to bring under control the use and production of ozone-depleting substances. The aforementioned protocol is the most successful environmental agreement ever applied by the world (www.mfa.gov.tr).

In 1992, the Rio: Environment and Development Conference was held and a global roadmap was drawn on subjects like biological diversity, climate change, and combating desertification. United Nations Framework Agreement on Climate Change (UNFCCC) is the second leg of the meeting in Rio. The aim of the agreement is to reduce the negative impacts of anthropogenically emitted greenhouse gas emissions on the climate system, which reaches dangerous levels in the atmosphere. This agreement is important for being the first environmental agreement to be led by the United Nations against the threat of global warming at an international level. The countries that are party to the Agreement have set a "non-legally-binding" objective to bring their greenhouse gas emissions to the levels of 1990 towards the year 2000 (http://iklim.cob.gov.tr).

The United Nations third parties meeting was hosted by the Kyoto city of Japan. The Kyoto Agreement has influenced a wide response to the concerning reduction of greenhouse gas emissions at the global level. The fact that this protocol carries a cohesiveness element for many countries which are party to the agreement has increased the interest in the agreement. Pursuant with the third article of the Agreement, the Contracting Parties, in Appendix-I to reduce the total emissions of greenhouse gases equivalent to the carbon dioxide caused by the human activities listed in Appendix-A, to at least 5% below the 1990 level, has been obliged to comply with the digitized emission limitation and reduction commitments registered in Annex-B in 2008–2012 years of commitment period. For the entry into force of the Kyoto Protocol the Contracting Parties to Annex I shall constitute at least 55% of the total emissions, therefore the implementation of the provisions of the protocol was delayed the said ratio was reached on 18 November 2004 with the participation of Russia. The provisions of the Kyoto Protocol have been implemented in 2005 with the participation of Russia. The 55% limit prevented the entry into force of the agreement year. Thanks to this minimum limit countries which are party to the agreement have had the opportunity to put into practice their regulations on greenhouse gas emissions.

After the Kyoto Protocol, countries with mandatory reduction obligations had to take summarily legal and administrative measures in determining their economic policies by paying regard to mentioned legal and administrative measures in order to meet these obligations. After the Protocol in 1997, multilateral negotiations have continued to take place in one of the party countries each year. One of these meetings is the Copenhagen Parties Meeting.

Along with the text presented to the General Assembly of the United Nations as the Copenhagen text is not legally binding, it is more likely to have the characteristics of building a consensus and roadmap feature prospectively. Decisions in the foreground at the meeting; reduction of greenhouse gas emissions, also developing countries pursuing a low-emission development strategy, move the greenhouse gas reduction objectives reported in the Kyoto Protocol to a further stage, supporting the voluntary reduction of greenhouse gas emissions of underdeveloped countries. The conference, which is expected to take precedence over the Kyoto Protocol and has great expectations, has brought some innovations but not legally binding provisions. It is important that the two major global powers, the United States and China, take part in the conference and come to a mutual agreement with them. However, the inclusion from the process of developing countries in greenhouse gas emission is also a positive aspect of the conference (Engin, 2010:78).

After the Protocol in 2009, the Parties have continued to meet. One of them is the 2015 United Nations Climate Change Conference, which has the most impact on the global level after the Kyoto Protocol. This meeting was held with the parties who have come together 21 times. The conference, 2015 United Nations Climate Change, has had great controversy and has resulted in a two-week Paris Agreement. By 4 November 2016, the aforementioned agreement had taken effect, as the condition had been met by 5 October 2016, succeeding the requirement of entering into the agreement of at least 55 parties, which constitute 55% of global greenhouse gas emissions. This agreement is perhaps one of the most important agreements that include the issue of climate change and global warming after Kyoto and has a historical significance (Yavuz, 2017:56).

In case of the global warming, the temperature cannot be decreased, because drought, desertification, destruction of plant and animal generations, and rise of sea level are expected; and with this agreement the usage of fossil fuel is aimed to be reduced. As in many of the previous agreements, the fragile economic structures of developing countries which are party to the agreement are taken into account in this agreement (Karakaya, 2016:2–3).

The Paris Agreement aims to strengthen the global socioeconomic resilience against the threat of climate change, especially in the period after 2020. The long-term objective of the Paris Agreement is to keep the global temperature rise to as low as 2°C, compared to the pre-industrialization period. This objective can be achieved by gradually decreasing the usage of fossil fuel (oil, coal) and

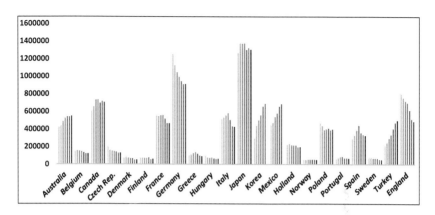

Graph 1: Greenhouse Gas Emission Indicators in Selected OECD Countries (1990–2016, tone). Source: https://stats.oecd.org

increasing the usage of renewable energy. The agreement predicts that in order to increase the adaptation and resistance capabilities of the developing countries exposed to the negative impacts of the climate change, and to increase the greenhouse gas emission reduction capacities, the developed countries have to provide financing, technology transfer, and capacity development opportunities to developing countries, least developed countries, and small island states (www.mfa.gov.tr/paris-anlasmasi).

4 Greenhouse Gas Emission Indicators

With the effect of the decisions taken in the multilateral agreements, it is more essential for countries to reduce their greenhouse gas emission indicators. More strict decisions taken every passing year have resulted in countries taking new measures for greenhouse gas emissions. The fact that the agreements made in recent years have been obligatory in many respects and that they have a cohesiveness nature and more influence in the international public opinion lead to the implementation of new policies on the greenhouse gas emissions of the party countries. In this respect, countries have to transmit accurate and reliable greenhouse gas emissions statistics to the relevant units of the United Nations in certain periods. In this section of the study, the relevant indicators related to statistics are discussed.

As can be seen from Graph 1, from 1990 to 2016, greenhouse gas emissions in many countries are in a downward trend. This decrease is particularly evident in Germany and the UK. In Turkey, there has been a steady increase over the same

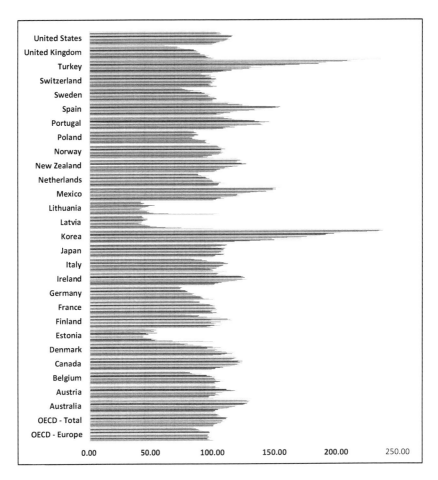

Graph 2: Greenhouse Gas Emission Indicators in Selected OECD Countries
(1990=100). Source: https://stats.oecd.org

period. Conversely, Turkey a party to international agreements concerning the
environment could cause the country to receive a financial penalty or sanction in
the upcoming years. Also, Korea and Mexico have experienced a similar upward
trend just like Turkey. In Graph 2, the development of greenhouse gas emissions
from the 1990 level in comparison with the 2016 level is discussed.

As can be seen from Tab. 1, the two countries present with the highest
greenhouse gas emissions per capita in the 1990–2016 period are the USA
and Australia. The greenhouse gas emissions per capita in both countries have

Tab. 1: Greenhouse Gas Emissions Per Capita in Selected OECD Countries

	1990	1995	2000	2005	2010	2015	2016
Australia	24.65	24.11	25.46	25.81	24.38	22.59	22.76
Belgium	14.66	15.19	14.57	13.79	12.13	10.42	10.37
Canada	21.78	22.24	23.80	22.68	20.31	19.86	19.40
Czech Republic	19.10	15.17	14.48	14.33	13.25	12.04	12.21
Denmark	13.73	14.98	13.37	12.40	11.61	8.72	9.04
Finland	14.24	14.03	13.50	13.25	14.06	10.10	10.67
France	9.64	9.36	9.31	9.10	8.20	7.21	7.19
Germany	15.82	13.83	12.82	12.16	11.65	11.10	11.10
Greece	10.06	10.12	11.34	12.06	10.34	8.50	8.19
Hungary	9.04	7.29	7.18	7.51	6.58	6.24	6.30
Italy	9.07	9.30	9.68	9.88	8.44	7.28	7.20
Japan	10.17	10.86	10.76	10.72	10.12	10.32	10.21
Korea	6.82	9.65	10.57	11.48	13.24	13.64	..
Mexico	5.21	5.01	5.27	5.33	5.60	5.43	..
Holland	14.74	14.92	13.75	13.08	12.78	11.49	11.48
Norway	12.17	11.71	12.14	11.88	11.29	10.36	10.13
Poland	12.31	11.40	10.11	10.37	10.59	10.07	10.36
Portugal	6.01	6.92	8.03	8.22	6.57	6.66	6.52
Spain	7.32	8.21	9.43	9.97	7.61	7.24	7.01
Sweden	8.35	8.32	7.73	7.38	6.86	5.51	5.38
Turkey	3.91	4.14	4.64	4.90	5.57	6.00	6.24
UK	13.99	12.99	12.16	11.56	9.72	7.82	7.39
USA	25.17	25.20	25.59	24.80	22.43	20.75	20.21
OECD Europe	11.15	10.46	10.20	10.09	9.20	8.32	8.30
OECD Total	14.08	13.98	14.15	13.96	12.95	12.15	11.97

Source: https://stats.oecd.org

declined by the year 2016 compared to the year 1990. Countries with the lowest greenhouse gas emissions per capita in 2016, respectively are, Sweden, Mexico, Turkey, and Hungary. The greenhouse gas emissions in the present period that was taken under consideration in many countries have tended to decrease per capita slightly while continuing the upward trend in Turkey. Countries with increasing greenhouse gas emissions per capita in 2016 compared to 1990 are: Japan, Korea, Mexico, Portugal, and Turkey. Turkey is one of the two countries with the lowest per capita greenhouse gas emissions in Annex-1, of the countries mentioned in the UNFCCC. Furthermore, in all years it has a value below the average of OECD Europe and its total. However, the difference is decreasing over the years.

5 Taxes Against Greenhouse Gas: Example Country Practices

Taxes are one of the most commonly used tools to reduce greenhouse gas emissions in the world. However, in empirical studies, no definitive conclusions have been found regarding the amount of taxes applied for this purpose decreases the amount of emission (Bruvoll and Larsen, 2004:493). However, as taxes affect the overall economy, greenhouse gas emission amount is also affected. For example, in the event that taxes on fuel are removed or substantially reduced, fuel consumption may increase (Nordhaus et al., 2013: 23–24). In a study, it has been determined that environmental taxes had a positive effect on environmental quality. In order to achieve this result, the impact of environmental taxes applied to environmental quality in the period of 2000–2014 over 53 countries has been examined. These countries were categorized according to their level of development. As a result of the analyses, it has been determined that environmental taxes were more effective in developed economies than developing economies (Topal and Günay, 2017:80).

i. Norway; Although empirical evidence of collecting tax on greenhouse gas emissions is very limited, environmental taxes have been widely applied in many countries. One of the Pigovian environmental taxes, carbon, is a tax used in Norway, the country where carbon taxes are applied the highest per unit ton. In early 1991, a carbon tax was introduced in Norway. Apart from the release of carbon dioxide, other emissions that cause greenhouse gas were exempt from tax (Godal and Holtsmark, 2001:653). Carbon dioxide emissions account for approximately 60% of total emissions. The carbon tax rate may vary depending on energy products and the usage of these energy products. A high tax rate is applied directly to petroleum and petroleum products, while a lower rate of the carbon tax is applied to the carbon emission resulting from the usage of mineral/mineral oil. In the following years, other emissions of gases have been added to the extent of the carbon tax.

While the national income has increased by 22% in the period of 1990–1999, the greenhouse gas emission has increased by 4% (Bruvoll and Larsen, 2004:494). The applied carbon taxes have increased the prices of fossil fuels and directly and indirectly affected greenhouse. The most energy-intensive sectors were affected by this situation (Peters and Hertwich, 2008:60). In addition to this effect, a significant amount of public revenue was obtained. The tax gathered from the emission as tax revenues on the share of total tax revenues was 1.7% (Metcalf, 2009:11).

Direct effects include; energy efficiency and the spread of replacement products while indirect impacts include total cost transfer industry competition and labor market regulations. With the impact of the taxes on the price level, there has been a process in which energy efficiency has increased in both residential and industrial production facilities in the long term. With the introduction of a more technological production process, regular storage, and carbon taxes, a greenhouse gas emission reduction has been achieved. However, there was no significant change in greenhouse gas emissions in the sectors with high crude oil and energy intensity. When all applications were evaluated as a whole, the highest impact was experienced when the carbon tax application increased the price level. In the same study, the carbon tax of $ 21 per ton unit was found to reduce the greenhouse gas emissions by approximately 14% (Bruvoll and Larsen, 2004:494–495). Environmental taxes applied in Norway include: taxes collected from oil extraction activities, mineral products tax, sulfur tax, basic taxes on fuel oil, car fuel tax, coal and coke tax, electricity production and consumption tax, tax on non-refillable beverage bottles, tax on alcoholic and carbonated beverage bottles, final waste tax, artificial fertilizer tax, motor vehicle tax, annual weight tax on vehicles, motor vehicle registration tax, insecticide tax, battery tax, environmental and health damaging chemical waste tax, agricultural pesticides tax collected from plastic-glass and metal products, etc.

ii. England; One of the countries that have succeeded in reducing greenhouse gas emissions is the UK. There is no direct carbon tax in the UK. However, there are two climate-related applied taxes. These are climate change tax (2001) and the variable annual inflation and fuel taxes used in the highways (1993). Climate change tax is collected from fossil fuels (natural gas, lignite, coal, coke, gaseous hydrocarbons) and electricity. Due to political concerns, climate change tax could not be applied according to the carbon content/quantity of fossil fuels. For example, taxes were collected from coal 16 pounds per ton, 30 pounds from gas, and 31 pounds from electricity. The tax collected from coal and electricity is lower than it should be. However, due to the increasing protests in the following years, the automatic increase of this tax was abandoned. This situation prevented the implementation of the tax according to the carbon emission amount (Pearce, 2003:378–379).

The aim of the climate change tax is to reduce greenhouse gas emissions by encouraging enterprises to use more efficient energy. This applies to tax, industry, trade, agriculture, public administration, and other service areas (Sumner et al., 2011:932). However, it is not taken from consumer goods, gasoline, diesel, heating, and some wastes which are taxed by domestic consumers. The rates of this tax have been increasing since 2007 (except for 2010) according to the possible inflation rate every April. The sectors where energy is used intensively can benefit from the reduced rate. However, a significant amount of public revenue is obtained. In the 2001/2002 fiscal year of implementation, 714 million pounds of revenue was generated. In 2016/2017 fiscal year, this income has increased to 1 billion 925 million pounds. About half of this income is derived from gasoline consumption (www.uktradeinfo.com).

Fuel tax, which varies according to annual inflation and used in highways, is applied to tackle climate change by reducing greenhouse gas emissions from the road transport. This tax also has objectives such as solving the traffic congestion problem and regulating the flow of traffic, improving air quality, providing more efficient resource utilization, and internalizing externalities resulting from transportation. The rate of this tax, which was introduced as 3%, was increased to 5% in 1995. This tax led to a significant increase in fuel prices. In this way, the drivers have been aimed to save fuel. The tax has had three types of effects on drivers. These are: the purchase of more fuel-efficient technological vehicles, the adoption of more economical driving styles, and less vehicle use. On the other hand, vehicle manufacturers are also expected to pay more attention to the investment of alternative fuel-efficient vehicles and engine technologies (www.env.go.jp/earth).

Since 1 April 2013, a carbon pricing tax has been implemented in fossil fuels to reduce carbon emissions in addition to the two taxes. It is aimed to promote the transition to a low-carbon economy through taxation. After this implementation, significant reductions were made in the amount of electricity produced from coal, one of the energy sources causing most carbon emissions. However, there are also critics of this tax. Because of this tax, domestic companies have a significant cost. In return, a small number of emission decreases. Nevertheless, some environmental groups and large-scale domestic companies have argued that this practice should continue as it encourages low-carbon investments (Hirst, 2018:3).

iii. Sweden; Among the Scandinavian countries, the country with the highest economic size is Sweden. Sweden is one of the countries that is an example to the countries of the world among environmentalist countries like Norway. Since 1991, one of the most important instruments that have guided climate policy in the country where the carbon tax is applied is the taxation of greenhouse gas emissions inflicted by transportation, housing, industry, and agriculture. Having said that, Sweden is also one of the oldest, most efficient and maker of highest carbon pricing countries in the world. In 1991, sulfur was started to be collected over value-added tax and on nitrogen oxide and energy; the same tax was collected in 1992. These tax rates increased from 25 to

120 euros per ton in the period from 1991 to 2017. Thanks to the extra taxes applied, the opportunity to reduce the tax burden on the labor force has been achieved (Raab, 2017:4).

However, low carbon tax is applied to prevent loss of production in sectors where energy is concentrated. With the implementation of carbon taxation, imported fuels based on carbon emission and thus external dependence on energy may be reduced (Ackva and Hoppe, 2018: 1, 16). However, in order to achieve this objective, the prices of low-carbon alternative energy sources should be at reasonable levels (Martinez and Silveira, 2013:117).

One of the first countries to approve the Kyoto Protocol, Sweden is the country that stands out with the lowest GDP emissions per unit in the world. One of the objectives of 2020 is the objective of increasing the share of renewable energy to approximately 50% in energy production. Having reached the afore-mentioned objective by the year 2013, Sweden has also increased hydroelectric power production significantly in recent years. The share of nuclear power plants in electricity production is approximately 40%. It was stated that the tendency to decrease greenhouse gas emissions will increasingly continue in the medium- and long-term country plans. All carbon emissions originating from energy in the European Union Emission Trading Scheme are within the context of the carbon tax applied in this country. In this respect, it is shown as an example to the EU. In spite of the low greenhouse gas emission in the country, it is noteworthy that the 2020 objective has been determined to be 17% below the 2005 level. According to the estimates of the Swedish Environmental Protection Agency, the objective, which is 17%, is expected to come true as 30% (Ackva and Hoppe, 2018:2).

iv. Germany; Germany has been one of the countries that significantly reduced greenhouse gas emissions from 1990 onwards. To achieve this reduction, increase in energy efficiency and increased share of renewable energy sources in energy consumption are highly effective. Wind and solar energy production have been increased dramatically within the scope of renewable energy sources (Sterner and Köhlin, 2015:260). On the other hand, Germany is one of the few member states in the 1990–2011 period in which the greenhouse gas emissions from transportation within the EU did not increase. In this period, transportation-related greenhouse gas emissions have been reduced by approximately 6%. Increasing fuel prices, road tolls, eco-taxes, and increasing usage of biofuels have been effective in achieving this reduction. In the same period, the emission caused by industry has been reduced by 23%, and the emission caused by agriculture has been reduced by 18%. The declining trend in the emission continued until the end of 2012 with the effect of the Kyoto Protocol. As for

Germany, 2020 greenhouse gas emission objective is 14% lower than the 2005 level (Bozsoki, 2013:6).

A comprehensive environmental tax reform, called eco-tax in Germany, has been carried out in 1999. With this reform, a significant increase has been made in the fuels of motor vehicles. In addition, taxes on natural gas, heating fuels, heavy fuels (petroleum), and electricity consumption in housing have been also increased. In order to reduce the impact of this increase on the employee and the employer, social insurance contributions have been reduced. The purpose of this aforementioned tax reduction is to eliminate the negative impact of environmental taxes on production (Heine et al., 2012:19, Andersen, 2010:6). By this means, both the amount of greenhouse gas emissions can be reduced and the employment problem will be contributed. However, due to the possible decrease in the amount of consumption (decreasing domestic demand), the markets may be adversely affected, as the price of final consumption will increase due to the aforementioned taxes (Böhringer et al., 2003: 50).

The environmental taxes applied in Germany are not taken directly according to the carbon content of energy products, such as those countries in Scandinavia (Sweden, Norway, the Netherlands, Denmark, and Finland). In this respect, the direct carbon tax is not applied in Germany. However, coal, which is subject to various taxes in many countries due to the carbon emission it contains, is an energy product supported by incentives on the contrary in Germany (Ekins and Speck, 1999:374). Among Germany's medium- and long-term objectives for greenhouse gas emissions in comparison to 1990 are among the reduction targets; There are 40% in 2020. 55% in 2030 and 95% in 2050. This reduction objective in 2050 was committed in the Paris Agreement. The increase of the share of renewable energy sources objective falls within the reduction objective.

v. Finland; Cold climate and long distances reveal a high energy need in Finland as well as in many Scandinavian countries (Smith et al., 2014:1). The first country in the world to implement the carbon tax and one of the countries that have taken measures related to greenhouse gas emissions at the global level that have raised awareness is Finland. However, as Finland is a party to the UNFCCC, the Kyoto Protocol, the Montreal Protocol, and the Paris Agreement, the country has a significant commitment to reducing greenhouse gas emissions. Finland's greenhouse gas emissions, which have largely met its commitment in these agreements, are approximately 18% below the 1990 level as of 2017 (www. stat.fi/static).

The carbon tax has been increased in certain periods from 1990 until today. However, the industrial sector and households have been largely exempted from this increase. Today, the country that has the highest carbon tax after Sweden is Finland. In 2011, a significant change in taxes was made in order to further reduce greenhouse gas emissions. Accordingly, it has been decided to give more importance to the amount of carbon dioxide contained in the fuel type, especially when determining the price formation in the taxes collected from fuel consumption. This has resulted in a high increase in fuel prices (including motor vehicles, boats, yachts, and aircraft fuel). Nevertheless, despite the intense debate, the introduction of a new tax (windfall tax) for nuclear and wind power plants was introduced in 2012 and 2013. The purpose of this tax is to increase energy prices. Because the carbon content of these energy sources is very low and tax revenues from these areas cannot be achieved at the desired level (Smith et al., 2014:13–17).

On the other hand, since the transportation sector is considered to be one of the key sectors in achieving the objective of the reduction of emissions in international agreements, the tax collected from gasoline and diesel is above the EU average. Much the same in Turkey, because less tax is collected from diesel compared to gasoline in recent years, it has been a significant increase in the demand for diesel vehicles. When the passenger cars are purchased for the first time, a one-time "car tax" is charged. This application can be likened to the SCT received in the purchase of new vehicles in Turkey. This tax varies between 3.8% and 50%. Moreover, the vehicle tax paid annually varies according to the carbon emission of each vehicle. The aforementioned tax varies between 106 and 654 euros. The second part of the annual tax is based on the type of fuel used by the cars. While gasoline-powered cars are not charged, diesel vehicles are charged (www.stat.fi/static).

In 2013, the action plan was adopted in order to increase energy efficiency and further reduce greenhouse gas emissions; the concepts of intelligent and efficient energy usage, intelligent housing production, and sustainable food production and transportation are highlighted (www.stat.fi/static). Some taxes applied in addition to the carbon tax include: waste tax, beverage and alcoholic beverages tax, beverage packaging tax, petroleum waste tax, nuclear power tax, hydroelectric tax, carbon dioxide–based taxes collected from fuel consumption, liquid fuel tax, electricity fuel tax, coal and natural resource tax, oil transportation and import tax, etc.

6 Measures Taken Against Greenhouse Gas Emission in Turkey

Global warming-based climate change has directly affected the geography where our country is also located. Seasonal fluctuations depending on global warming resulting in an addition of sudden, incorrect urbanization/types of urbanization have emerged as a high cost in terms of economy for Turkey. Economic and political instabilities experienced for many years has prevented the implementation of an effective environmental policy in Turkey. Economic stability due to the political stability in the 2000s brought about important developments in the context of environmental policy. Today, environmental policy is among Turkey's policy prioritization. Particular attention was drawn to this area with the new laws and regulations introduced in the context of harmonization efforts in the field of environment depending upon especially the relations with the EU. However, according to the developed countries, environmental policy has areas to be developed.

One of the strategic objectives of "Climate Change Action Plan: 2011–2023" of the Ministry of Environment and Urbanization concerning the greenhouse gas emissions is the statement of "contribution to limiting the rate of increase of greenhouse gas emission by not disrupting the development program harmonized with sustainable development principles developed for the purpose of reducing the greenhouse gas emissions through global policies and it's own means." Turkey has been decided to be exempted from the binding provision in the stated agreements for having the lowest value of greenhouse gas emission, taking place in the category of middle-income country, the country's geopolitical position, and the fact of the economic condition among the countries of the UNFCCC Annex-I list. But many of the new linking provisions set forth in the following years may be valid with regards to Turkey. For this purpose, within the scope of conducting a transformation or reform work in the related sectors, certain goals and objectives have been set for the medium and long term. In the stated plan, the goals and objectives signified that stand out to reduce greenhouse gas emissions in areas such as energy, buildings, transportation, industry, waste, agriculture, land use, and forestry are as follows:

✓ The topic regarding *energy* and among its goals; there are objectives of reducing the energy density, increasing the share of usage and production of clean energy, and reducing the emissions of the greenhouse gas caused by the coal usage of clean coal technologies.

✓ The topic regarding *buildings* and among its goals; there are objectives of increasing energy efficiency and the usage of renewable energy in buildings, limiting the greenhouse gas emissions caused by the habitations. In order to achieve these goals, objectives such as "In 2023, at least 1 million housings and commercial buildings with up to a plot of 10,000m2 and systems established for heat insulation that is providing standards and energy efficiency in public buildings," "In public institutions buildings and facilities, reduction of yearly energy consumption to 10% until 2015 and 20% until 2023," and "As of 2017, at least 20% of the annual energy need of new buildings are provided from renewable energy sources" have been determined.

✓ The topic regarding *transportation* and among its goals; there are main objectives such as ensuring the dissemination of the usage of alternative fuel and clean vehicle technologies and the efficiency of energy consumption in the transportation sector. In order to achieve these stated goals, objectives such as: as of 2023, the objectives of the railroads to increase the share of freight (5% in 2009) to 15% and the share of passenger transport (which is 2% in 2009) to 10% have been determined. In addition, objectives of "as of 2023, the share of highways in passenger transportation (which was 80.63% in terms of tonne-kg) to below 60% and the share in passenger transport (which is 89.59% in passenger-km in 2009) to be reduced to 72%" are also included.

Under the same heading, sub-objectives like "Limiting the rate of increase in the emission arising from the usage of individual vehicles in urban transportation," "Making legislative regulations in order to increase the usage of alternative fuel and clean car until 2023 and improving the capacity," "Taking incentive local measures for the usage of alternative fuel and clean car in the urban transportation until 2023," and "Limiting energy consumption used in transportation until 2023" have been determined. As can be seen, very important goals in order to reduce greenhouse gas emissions from transportation and objectives in order to achieve these goals have been determined.

✓ The topic regarding *industry* and among its goals; there are main objectives such as ensuring more efficient energy usage in the industrial sector and reducing the carbon dioxide density per GDP that have been determined. In order to achieve these goals, there are sub-objectives such as: "Making legislative regulations devoted to limiting the greenhouse gas emissions and energy efficiency," "Limiting greenhouse gas emissions from energy usage (including electricity share) in industrial sector," "Development of financial and technical infrastructure devoted to limiting greenhouse gas emissions," and "The development and usage of new technologies to limit greenhouse gas emissions in the industrial sector by the 2023 year" that have been determined.

✓ The topic regarding *agriculture* and among its goals; in order to reduce greenhouse gas emission in the agriculture sector, "Determining and increasing the amount of carbon stock kept in the soil" and "Determining the limiting opportunity of greenhouse gas emission inflicted from the agriculture sector" have been determined as sub-objectives.

As is seen, in order to reduce greenhouse gas emissions in areas such as energy, industry, transportation, agriculture, and housing; various objectives and important sub-objectives have been determined to achieve these goals. On the other hand, in order to achieve these goals, it has been decided to make regulations regarding the legislation by different institutions, to ensure coordination among the legislation, to limit greenhouse gas emissions, and to make new legal arrangements for energy efficiency. However, the action of providing training and consultancy support to limit the greenhouse gas emissions to KOBIs (SMEs) has been included.

In the 2023 action plan, "Forming a taxation and pricing system based on limiting greenhouse gas emissions in motor vehicles" has been also mentioned. Another conspicuous aspect of the plan is providing low-cost crossing opportunity to vehicles in highway and bridge tolls which have low greenhouse gas emissions. The plan also includes encouraging the production of land, air, and sea vehicles with high energy efficiency and by the selection of pilot cities, the preparation and implementation actions of high-efficiency and climate-sensitive urban transport strategy.

As the stated goals and objectives show in the plan, the steps taken towards the reduction of greenhouse gas emissions in Turkey for a while now will continue in the medium and long term. However, the transformation of these steps into the economic life and adoption by the actors that cause greenhouse gas emissions should be put into practice of a transition period en masse. Within this scope, it is also necessary to increase the audit activities, generalize the training and information meetings to be given on this point, and to provide the necessary financial support and information sharing to ensure the technological transformation that will reduce the greenhouse gas emissions.

7 Turkey's Taxes as a Tool of Alternative Intervention for Increasing Greenhouse Gas Emission

Turkey, which is a party to the international agreement for the reduction of greenhouse gas emissions, due to the increase in emissions from 1990 until today seems to be the harbinger of possible future sanctions. Therefore, concrete steps should be taken in many sectors to reduce related greenhouse gas emissions. It has been expressed in different studies that taxes can be used as a financial intervention tool in achieving the goals and sub-objectives stated in the Climate Change Action Plan.

Prepared in 2011 "Greenhouse Gas Reduction Potential Emissions: Marginal Reduce Cost Curve for investment" in the project named. 2010–2030 period examining the greenhouse gas emissions reduction resources in Turkey in various sectors of the economy were estimated cost of this decline. This study was prepared from the perspective of the private sector investor, and the estimates of the related cost and benefits of different investment opportunities were made. According to the macroeconomic results of the present policy scenarios discussed in the study, the cost of additional investments to reduce carbon accounts for 3% of the total cost with 5 billion euros per year. The savings generated from the operation of these investments account for 3% of the total consumption and save 19 billion euros per year. It has also been expressed that Turkey can receive payment for the international carbon markets or emission reduction with bilateral agreements. This income can be accrued to the government or distributed between firms that reduce emissions. However, even when emission reductions are achieved, the value of irreducible emissions is quite high. Therefore, it is stated that a carbon tax to be introduced at the default prices will be a highly loaded source of income for the state.

According to OECD data, as of 2016, it is the seventh country that has the highest share of environmental tax revenues in national income. It is the sixth country in the share of environmental tax revenues in total tax revenues. Considering Eurostat data, the share of environmental tax revenues (when social security premiums are included in total tax revenue) is the highest among European countries in the share of total tax revenues. (www.oecd. org/environment, http://appsso.eurostat.ec.europa.eu). The aforementioned indicators suggest that a high amount of environmental taxes are collected in Turkey. Approximately 65% of the environmental tax revenues are composed of energy taxes. In a study in 2011, the implied tax rate on energy was calculated and the effects of tax practices on energy efficiency and environmental pollution have been examined. On the contrary to the EU countries in the study and despite Turkey's high implied tax rate, these taxes have been determined to not have a positive impact on environmental pollution. In order to reduce the high implied tax rate on energy, it is stated that renewable resource utilization should be encouraged and thus environmental pollution may decrease (Aytaç, 2011).

In the other study in 2013, Turkey's carbon tax implementation in comparison with the emission trade would be more cost-effective. Also, the adverse effect on national income was estimated to be more under favors of the General Equilibrium Model. Based on this aforementioned determination, it is stated that the emission trading system on a national scale and the carbon stock exchange to be established will be effective at reducing the greenhouse gas emissions by bearing a small cost (Mercan and Karakaya, 2013).

In a study conducted in 2015, the subject of "Low-carbon development ways and priorities for Turkey" are examined through the help of the general equilibrium model. According to the model, the collection of the carbon tax and the transfer of collected taxes to renewable energy sources through renewable investment fund may be effective in reducing greenhouse gas emissions. However, the cost of reducing 1 kg of carbon dioxide varies between 7 and 23 cents (US $). With a tax burden corresponding to 1.2% of the total GDP, carbon dioxide emissions can be reduced by up to close to 25%. It can be said that the resulting cost is at a reasonable level to accelerate the transition from fossil fuels to renewable energy usage. In the case of an implementation of a carbon tax in the same study, some of the collection of revenues to be used to reduce the fragility towards the climate change at the local level could be effective in reducing the greenhouse gas emissions. Finally, the transfer of some sources of electricity to the wind turbines is about 44%.

Although there are some studies in the literature on the positive effect of taxes on reducing greenhouse gas emissions, there are some studies that have no effect. In this respect, in addition to taxes on reducing greenhouse gas emissions, spending/incentive/subsidies and penal policies should also be implemented. Tax incentives and penalties may change the greenhouse gas emission values that the companies have released. The lower and upper limit of incentive amounts can be determined according to the sectors.

Companies that do not exceed these limits may be given incentives. However, companies that exceed the specified limits may be subject to the tax penalty. By this means, it will be possible to determine which tax incentive amounts can encourage more conservationist production models after which level, current production techniques that are the reason of cause of greenhouse gas emissions, policies towards environmental sensitivity of companies, and whether these companies have the awareness of greenhouse gas emission values they release.

Through incentives; reducing greenhouse gas emissions, encouraging new and clean technologies, R&D activities and sustainability making more efficent use of available resources and improving environmental awareness can be ensured. In addition the adoption of a growth model based on green growth can reduce Turkey's greenhouse gas emissions. However, the European Union's relations with Turkey may also affect positively. On the other hand, progress can be made in the fight against greenhouse gas emissions, especially through the usage of some changes in high taxes on fuel oil. Thus, the amount of OTV (SCT) and KDV (VAT) may be reduced by a certain amount. A new tax called carbon dioxide tax may apply. In this way, awareness can be created on energy-intensive industries and in the areas where the fuel oil is used.

Thanks to the additional tax/taxes, prestige in international meetings can be increased.

8 Conclusion

The increasing emissions of greenhouse gas are one of the most conspicuous and important issues in the field of environment especially with the effect of international meetings. The process, which started with the Vienna Agreement on a global level in the fight against greenhouse gas emissions, continued with the Montreal Protocol in 1987. The 1997 Kyoto Protocol has been one of the most internationally world-shaking agreement on emissions. The fact that the protocol contains binding provisions on the reduction of greenhouse gas emissions for the developed countries has further increased the effect. After this year, struggles with greenhouse gas emissions have accelerated and reached a peak point with the 2015 Paris Agreement.

Turkey is a country that has signed the Paris Agreement but has not passed it through the parliament. One of the most important reasons why the agreement has not been passed through the parliament is that the commitments would affect the industrial sector negatively. Especially in the 2000s due to population and economic growth in Turkey, industrial production has increased over the years. Initially, in spite of the efforts of the Ministry of Environment and Urbanization and various public and private institutions, the emission rates could have not been reduced in these years. After 1990, the years that amount of emissions have decreased are 1994, 1999, 2001, and 2008. The common feature of these years is that these are the years of recession or stagnation. The decrease in emission has caused a significant economic cost to our country.

The most important aim of our country is to reduce the amount of emission without loss of production. It is expressed in empirical and practical studies that taxes will be an effective tool in achieving this goal. In order to reduce greenhouse gas emissions, incentives or subsidy policies can be influential as well as taxes. In the following years, greenhouse gas emissions are emphasized in some plans and programs in which the rate of increase will be limited. For this, significant mitigation objectives for the future are determined: initially energy, then building, transportation, industry, and agriculture sectors. In order to reach these objectives, it is important to expand renewable energy resources. However, it can be said that the incentive policies should be brought into action quickly and that the taxes on energy should be altered to be more environmentally oriented.

Until now, due to the level of emission Turkey has not faced any sanction but may so in the future. Although the amount of emissions per person in Turkey

is below the OECD and European countries' average, the difference is declining
by years. Turkey's previous excuses in the last years may not be accepted in the
next years by the international public opinion. However, since 2020, considering the one hundred billion dollars fund that will be transferred to the developing countries by the United Nation's green climate fund, it can be said that
considering all the risks, Turkey has to be a party to the Paris Agreement. In
order to reduce greenhouse gas emissions, a new taxation and incentive mechanism should be applied.

Bibliography

Ackva, Johannes ve Hoppe, Janna (2018), "The carbon tax in Sweden", federal
    ministry for the environment, **Nature Conservation and Nuclear Safety**,
    Vol. 1, N. 31, September.

Andersen, Mikeal Skou (2010), "Europe's experience with carbon-energy
    taxation", **Sapiens**, Vol. 3, N. 2, pp. 1–11.

Aytaç, Deniz (2011), "Türkiye'de Enerji Etkinliğini Sağlama ve Çevresel
    Kirlenmeyi Engellemede Enerji Üzerindeki Zımni Vergi Oranlarının Etkisi",
    Maliye Dergisi, Vol. 160, January–June, pp. 392–410.

Bozsoki, Ingrid (2013), "Assessment of climate change policies in the context
    of the European Semester", Country Report: Germany, Ecologic Institute,
    Vol. 1, N. 34, January.

Böhringer, Christoph, Conrad, Klaus and Löschel, Andreas (2003), "Carbon
    taxes and joint implementation", **Environmental and Resource Economics**,
    Vol. 24, pp. 49–76.

Bruvoll, Annegrete and Larsen, Bodil Merethe (2004), "Greenhouse gas
    emissions in Norway: do carbon taxes work?", **Energy Policy**, Vol. 32,
    pp. 493–505.

Ekins, Paul and Speck, Stefan (1999), "Competitiveness and exemptions from
    environmental taxes in Europe", **Environmental and Resource Economics**,
    Vol. 13, pp. 369–399.

Engin, Billur (2010), "İklim Değişikliği İle Mücadelede Uluslararası İşbirliğinin
    Önemi", **Sosyal Bilimler Dergisi**, Vol. 2, pp. 71–82.

Godal, Odd and ve Holtsmark, Bjart (2001), "Greenhouse gas taxation and
    the distribution of costs and benefits: the case of Norway", **Energy Policy**,
    Vol. 29, pp. 653–662.

Heine, Dirk, Norregaard, John and ve Parry, Ian W. H. (2012), "Environmental
    tax reform: principles from theory and practice to date", **IMF Working
    Paper**, Vol. 1, N. 38, July, WP/12/180.

Hirst, David (2018), "Carbon Price Floor (CPF) and the price support mechanism", **Briefing Paper, Vol. 05927**, January.

Karakaya, Etem (2016), "Paris İklim Anlaşması: İçeriği ve Türkiye Üzerine Bir Değerlendirme", **Adnan Menderes Üniversitesi Sosyal Bilimler Enstitüsü Dergisi**, Vol. 3, N. 1, pp. 1–12.

Latake, Pooje, Pawar, Pooje and Ranveer, Anil C. (2015), "The greenhouse effect and its impacts on environment", **International Journal of Innovative Research and Creative Technology**, Vol. 1, N. 3, pp. 333–337.

Martinez, Clara Inés Pardo and Silveira, Semida (2013), "Energy efficiency and CO2 emissions in Swedish manufacturing industries", **Energy Efficiency**, Vol. 6, N. 1, pp. 117–133.

Mercan, Mehmet and Karakaya, Etem (2013), "Sera Gazı Salımının Azaltımında Alternatif Politikaların Ekonomik Maliyetlerinin İncelenmesi: Türkiye İçin Genel Denge Analizi", **Erciyes Üniversitesi İktisadi ve İdari Bilimler Fakültesi Dergisi**, Vol. 42, July–December, pp. 123–159.

Metcalf, Gilbert E. (2009), "Market-based policy options to control U.S. greenhouse gas emissions", **Journal of Economic Perspectives**, Vol. 23, N. 2, Spring, pp. 5–27.

NERA (2011), "Sera Gazı Emisyonlarını Azaltma Potansiyeli: Yatırımlar İçin Marjinal Azaltma Maliyet Eğrisi", **NERA Economic Consulting**, England.

Nordhaus, William Dawbney,, Merrill, Stephen A. and Beaton, Paul T. (2003), **Effects of U.S. Tax Policy on Greenhouse Gas Emissions**, The National Academies Press, Washington.

Öz, Ersan and Buyrukoglu, Selçuk (2012), "Negatif Dışsallıkların Önlenmesinde Çevresel Vergiler: Türkiye ve OECD Ülkeleri Karşılaştırılma sı", **TİSK Akademi**, Vol. 2012, N. II, pp. 85–107.

Pearce, David (2003), "The social cost of carbon and its policy implications", **Oxford Review of Economic Policy**, Vol. 19, N. 3, pp. 362–384.

Peters, Glen. P. and Hertwich, Edgar G. (2008), "Post-Kyoto greenhouse gas inventories: production versus consumption", **Climatic Change**, Vol. 86, pp. 51–66.

Pigou, Arthur C. (1920), **The Economics of Welfare**, Macmillan and Co., Limited, UK.

Raab, Ulrika (2017), "Carbon tax – determining the tax rate. Swedish Experiences", Presentation at the PMR Technical Workshop on Carbon Tax: Design and Implementation in Practice, Swedish Energy Agency, March, Sweden.

Smith, Lucy Olivia, Velten, Eike Karola, Donat, Lena and Duwe, Matthias (2014), "Assessment of climate change policies in the context of the

European Semester, Country Report: Finland", **Ecologic Institute**, Vol. 1, N. 26, January.

Sterner, Thomas and Köhlin, Gunnar (2015), **Pricing Carbon: The Challenges, Towards a Workable and Effective Climate Regime**, Chapter 18, https://voxeu.org/sites/default/files/file/sterner%20and%20kohlin.pdf, (26.10.2018).

Sumner, Jenny, Bird, Lori and Smith, Hillary (2011), "Carbon taxes: a review of experience and policy design considerations", **Climate Policy**, Vol. 11, pp. 922–943.

Topal, Mehmet Hanefi and Günay, Hamdi Furkan (2017), "Çevre Vergilerinin Çevre Kalitesi Üzerindeki Etkisi: Gelişmekte Olan ve Gelişmiş Ekonomilerden Ampirik Bir Kanıt", **Maliye Araştırmaları Dergisi**, Vol. 3, N. 1, pp. 63–83.

Yavuz, Hakan (2017), **Çevre Sorunları ve Maliye Politikası**, Savaş Yayınevi, Ankara.

Yeldan, Erinç and Voyvoda, Ebru (2015), **Türkiye İçin Düşük Karbonlu Kalkınma Yolları ve Öncelikleri**, İstanbul Politikalar Merkezi, Bion Matbaacılık, İstanbul.

https://stats.oecd.org/Index.aspx?DataSetCode=AIR_GHG, 20.10.2018.

www.mfa.gov.tr/viyana-sozlesmesi-ve-montreal-protokolu.tr.mfa, 23.10.2018.

www.uktradeinfo.com/Statistics/Pages/TaxAndDutybulletins.aspx, 26.10.2018.

https://www.env.go.jp/earth/g8_2000/forum/g8bp/detail/uk/uk07.html, 26.10.2018.

https://www.stat.fi/static/media/uploads/tup/khkinv/fi_nir_un_2016_20180415.pdf, 28.10.2018.

http://iklim.cob.gov.tr/iklim/AnaSayfa/BMIDCS.aspx?sflang=tr, 29.10.2018.

http://www.mfa.gov.tr/paris-anlasmasi.tr.mfa, 29.10.2018.

https://webdosya.csb.gov.tr/db/iklim/editordosya/file/eylem%20planlari/Iklim%20Degisikligi%20Eylem%20Plani_TR.pdf, 30.10.2018.

http://www.oecd.org/environment/tools-evaluation/environmentaltaxation.htm, 30.10.2018.

http://appsso.eurostat.ec.europa.eu/nui/submitViewTableAction.do, 30.10.2018.

Ali Apalı and Mesut Bozcu

Interaction Between Accounting Information Systems and Other Information Systems Created in Terms of Functionality

Introduction

Today, it is observed that the concept of knowledge is regarded as one of the concrete values of the business – like human, material, machine, and money. This is because the value of businesses is shaped by the value of the knowledge, they obtain and use. For businesses to be successful and managers to make accurate and strategic decisions, it is necessary that they need to have knowledge first and then use it effectively and efficiently. Furthermore, it is of great importance that businesses obtain and use knowledge as soon as possible.

In order for businesses to be successful, decisions must be made and implemented at all levels of the business unit, and organizations must work in a healthy manner. In other words, businesses can achieve their goals only by making successful decisions. We encounter knowledge at this point as "indispensable source" in order to make the necessary decisions. (Gökçen, 2007: 3).

Today, when knowledge is regarded as power for both people and businesses, clarifying the concepts of knowledge and information systems will contribute to the integrity of the subject.

1 Conceptual Discussion

1.1 Concepts of Data, Knowledge, and Information

Nowadays, the key element that enhances the strategic superiority of businesses against their competitors and their success in the market is the power of the knowledge they possess. With the transition to the information society in an industrial society, businesses have knowledge beyond current and fixed assets. However, having knowledge alone is not enough. In fact, everything begins with data that is considered the source of knowledge. The concept of data can be briefly defined as the raw material of information or raw material. Data are the expressions formed by a combination of signs, symbols, and numbers.

Data is the form of observations objectified as text, numbers, or live presentation. As such, data is regarded as the input of information. As it is known, the first stage of information generation since the early ages is observation. Historical events, economic events, or social events were all observed and recorded after observations. The purpose here is to ensure that the relations obtained as a result of observations facilitate the human life (Tonus, 2009: 4). In fact, data is the stored form of an operation and is kept easily available by being stored. For example, the procurement manager may record the quantity, the purchase price, the date, and the amount of a product to be delivered or shipped. All of these examples are data that can be derived in certain forms (Yuva, 2002: 43). In terms of accounting, data is any kind of accounting that is recorded without any system. For example, only 100 cash accounts or 255 inventory accounts are data on their own. However, associating this data with the process from the systematic classification of this data till the preparation and interpretation of financial statements expresses information.

Determining the recording time and recording format of the data needed by the information users, determining which subject data is related to, when or under what circumstances it will be collected means creating data. Knowledge is, on the other hand, meaningful symbols and figures used in the decision-making process (Altuğ, 2014: 72). Knowledge is designed and systematized data. Therefore, knowledge is the data, which is found randomly in the market, made meaningful. Another concept closely related to knowledge is the concept of information. Information is the organized set of data. The common point of data and information concepts is that both are internalized and recorded forms from outside the brain. The information is taken from outside by receivers and processed in the brain with old information and converted into new information, thus taking its place in memory. In this way, the brain continuously functionalizes information in the process of transformation of information (Akgül and Keskin, 2003: 176).

1.2 Classification of Knowledge

Knowledge is categorized in almost every area according to various purposes during various periods. While classifications are made in different branches of science for their own purpose, it is possible to list some of them as follows: business knowledge, accounting knowledge, sociological knowledge, philosophical knowledge, technical knowledge, and scientific knowledge. Barutçugil (2002: 60–67) studied knowledge in three main classifications: It is possible to list them as knowledge classifications according to the type of use and arrangement of knowledge, the source of knowledge, and quality of knowledge.

1.2.1 Types of Knowledge by the Ways They Are Organized and Used

The types of knowledge are separated as idealistic, systematic, pragmatic, and automatic knowledge according to the way they are organized and used

(Barutçugil, 2002: 61–62). **Idealist knowledge** is what an individual needs in order to make the necessary decisions to create a vision, set goals, and build values and beliefs. Such knowledge is seen in managers, who have idealistic knowledge in benchmarking and in-house knowledge production. In terms of accounting, financial advisors' improving standards by using accounting knowledge and creating new accounting applications take place within the borders of idealistic knowledge. **Systematic knowledge** is the attempt to solve problems encountered with past experience and educational knowledge. Such knowledge will be used to identify errors in financial crises or accounting failures occurring in businesses. While systematic knowledge is used, various models and regulations can be applied. The source of **pragmatic knowledge** is the rules, procedures, and instructions. Application of accounting knowledge within the enterprise with certain rules is the result of pragmatic knowledge. Uniform accounting plan is the most important source of pragmatic knowledge in the accounting information system. **Automatic knowledge** type is the automated knowledge that is routinely applied. As an example of this knowledge in the accounting information system, cash collection will be debited to 100 cash accounts. This is the type of knowledge that everyone who has some relation with accounting knows. On the other hand, the fact that rational increase in sales suggests that profitability will rise in the accounting information system is another example of automated knowledge.

1.2.2 Types of Knowledge by Source

Knowledge is divided into explicit and tacit knowledge according to its source. **Explicit knowledge** is the knowledge that can be expressed formally and systematically (Bayram, 2010: 297). Explicit knowledge is the knowledge that anyone can access. The secrets that people do not have are the knowledge that is used and that is made available when necessary. The period-end financial statements in the accounting information system are the most used examples of explicit knowledge. Period-end financial statements are presented in a raw form for the use of stakeholders in stock markets, company pages, national newspapers, and magazines. **Tacit knowledge** is, on the other hand, a kind of knowledge that is personal, contextual, and hard to structure-express and transfer (Bayram, 2010: 297). Tacit knowledge consists of personal knowledge. People often do not realize that they are using this knowledge. The fact that financial advisors make accounting knowledge explicit knowledge by using it from different angles or the difference between the financial advisors who reach a different output of knowledge with the same data or accounting output result from tacit knowledge.

To give another example, even if the accountant who performs the computer-based accounting records is distracted during certain periods, his/her making the accounting records correctly and not remembering it later is the result of using tacit knowledge.

1.2.3 Types of Knowledge by Quality

It is possible to divide knowledge by quality into three as the knowledge found in persons, the knowledge found in clients, and knowledge on systems and processes as customers and structural capital (Barutçugil, 2002: 64–65). The knowledge found in persons, which is the first one of this knowledge, is the knowledge of the values that everything about the accounting profession contributes to the one doing the profession. In addition, the number of employees in the accounting department of the business, for how many years they have been working there, and the number of subunits are the elements of this knowledge type within a business. The number of customers interested in business, their qualifications, and frequency of shopping can be shown as examples to the customer knowledge; and patents and trademarks developed within the business can also be shown as an example of structural capital knowledge.

2 System, Information System, and Classification of Information Systems

2.1 Concepts of System and Information System

It is possible to define the system as a combination of two or more elements to reach a purpose. Systems that are in constant relation with the environment are called "open systems," and systems that do not interact with the environment are called "closed systems." Each business is a system. The units, departments, and fields of activity within businesses are each subsystems. The elements that the systems should carry are listed as follows (Ağca, 2013: 9):

- Systems must have common objectives.
- Systems must consist of at least two elements.
- Systems must have input, process, and output mechanisms.
- Each element in the system must have a function.
- Each element in the system can have a separate purpose. However, the purpose of the system should be superior than the purpose of each of these elements.
- Each piece in the system can gain a different function when they come together. The combination of these elements should result in the top function of the system.

- The components of the system must interact with at least one other component.
- Each component in the system must be dependent on another component.
- There are subsystems within a system. All of these subsystems must form a superior system.

The concept of the system needs to be dealt with the concept of the information system. The information system is a whole aimed at providing information and information services to set up and control subsystems (Munteanu et al., 2011: 56). Information systems are a set of rules that contain processes such as obtaining, shaping and interpreting the data and recording, transforming, retrieving, and transmitting it to the sources when requested. At the same time, an information system is a group that contains planning, controlling and analyzing where elements that collect, preserve, and disseminate information come together. Information systems make it possible to transform raw data into a useful format, and access that information when needed (Meral, 2016: 84). It is possible to classify information systems in different ways.

2.2 Classification of Information Systems

Laudon and Laudon (2002, 40–45) examined information systems in each organization under six headings: (Electronic) data processing system, office automation systems, management information systems, decision support systems, manager support systems, and information processing systems (Laudon and Laudon, 2002: 40–45).

2.2.1 Electronic Data Processing Systems

One of the units that use electronic data processing systems in most business is the accounting unit. In order to obtain accounting information, the data processing system which expresses the recording of raw data on a daily basis needs to be computer based.

Electronic data processing systems, also known as registration processing systems, operation processing systems, information processing systems, atomic business processing systems, and data processing systems (Canbaz, 2016: 53), are realized through journal entries in accounting information systems. Transfer of the journal to the general ledger in the second stage is also a part of electronic data processing systems. In addition, processing of stock cards, request slips, sales operations, invoice preparation, preparation of collection vouchers, and recording salary and payroll transactions in accounting programs are other examples of electronic data processing systems that are subsystems of accounting information generation within a business. The features of electronic data processing systems in accounting applications can be listed as follows:

- Electronic data processing systems in accounting applications should be document-based.
- These systems are for storing recorded data/information.
- They can be presented to business stakeholders at any time.
- They are used for accounting output at certain intervals.

2.2.2 Office Automation Systems

Office automation systems are used in decisions made for technical processes in businesses. The use of technological tools within the business is achieved through office automation systems. This results in less labor and lower costs (Ersöz and Ersöz, 2015: 102). Office automation systems are used quite effectively in the implementation of accounting information systems. Automation systems are utilized in many stages of accounting systems from the documentation process to the registration, reporting, analysis, or interpretation stages. Thanks to automation, the accounting information system output is prepared very quickly for users both inside and outside the enterprise. This reduces the information costs of the accountant and therefore the information costs of the enterprise.

There are elements of computer technology in office automation systems. The internalization of the external elements of computer technology and the formation of accounting information are based on package programs and software. When computer technology is used in information technology and accounting information creation, the benefit that it creates is high.

2.2.3 Management Information Systems

With this system, top managers can get the information they want from within the enterprise or outside the enterprise. The purpose of this system is not to present all the information within the business to the top management. On the contrary, unnecessary information is filtered at lower levels and only analyzed, and useful information is delivered to the top managers. There are some questions in the top management information system for which answers are sought. These questions are listed as follows (Canbaz, 2016: 74):

- What job should be carried out?
- What is the situation of the competitors?
- What should be done against market fluctuations?
- Which units should be brought to the fore in order to increase income?

When answers are started to be sought to these questions, it appears that all the answers pass directly or indirectly through the accounting information system. If the current business is not profitable, then the necessary cost research will be obtained from accounting information. Not only costs but also the determination of the position of competitors in the current product market is conducted by examining the accounting information systems of the competitors. If there is a price and sales volatility in the market, these are again analyzed by accounting data. Accounting information is also used to increase the profitability or to reduce the loss. In short, information to be obtained from within or outside the enterprise and presented to the managers within the top management system can be obtained either from a business' own accounting information system or from accounting information systems of competitors.

2.2.4 Decision Support Systems

The concept of decision support systems was first used by Peter G. Keen in 1972 (Şahin, 2009: 209). Decision support systems are systems that were established to assist managers in making decisions. The main purpose of these systems is to support the managers when they make decisions. The information available is analyzed with various methods and models, and these help managers to make decisions (Ersöz and Ersöz, 2015: 109). In this system, managers can get the desired information by giving the commands they want to the computer. They do not need a separate computer user or programmer. Decision support systems are mostly used by mid-level and high-level managers. Managers may or may not use the information they get through the computer (Sevim, 2006: 28–29). Ersöz and Ersöz (2015, 111) list the characteristics of decision support systems as follows:

- These systems should be particularly helpful in making decisions that are semistructured and unstructured.
- They should help the managers at all levels while making decisions.
- They should provide support in all stages of the decision-making process.
- They should support independent decisions as well as interdependent decisions.
- Decision support systems should be easy to use.
- They should be for planning the future.
- They should have access to data and model bases.
- They should be able to use analytical models to analyze data and produce solutions.

- They must be user-interactive.
- They should be able to produce alternative decisions and possible costs at strategic, tactical, and technical level.
- They should be able to provide support for decisions in many areas.
- They should provide individual or group-based decision support.
- They should be flexible to adapt to changing conditions.
- They should be able to be used at irregular time intervals.
- They should be web-based.

Accounting information system which is effective in business management is in constant interaction with decision support systems. In fact, the accounting information system is a decision support system in itself.

2.2.5 Artificial Intelligence and Expert Systems

One of the information systems needed for the effective management of businesses is artificial intelligence and expert systems. Artificial intelligence was introduced in 1956 with a study carried out at Dartmouth College in New Hampshire (Ersöz and Ersöz, 2015: 113). The basis of artificial intelligence is the ability of technological machines to do things that human intelligence can do. Thus, it is expected that machines will respond differently to different situations like people.

Artificial intelligence is an artificial communication system that is expected to exhibit cognitive action or independent behaviors such as learning, perception, interpretation, decision-making, and communicating, which are specific to human intelligence. The other system component, which is usually mentioned together with artificial intelligence, is the concept of expert systems. Expert systems are basically computer programs based on knowledge of an expert in solving problems. That is, they are defined as systems which are used to solve complex problems with the computer technology based on human knowledge (Canbaz, 2016: 77–78). It is possible to list the advantages of expert systems as follows (Koza, 2008: 79):

- Businesses will not have to pay high fees to experts.
- Experts' efficiency will increase.
- The expertise will be preserved and reapplied, and the accuracy level will increase.
- In areas where they are used, the consistency and accuracy of decisions will increase.
- Expert systems provide documentation that is more qualified in terms of rationality when compared to experts with special knowledge.

- They provide predictions for decisions.
- They guide inexperienced employees.

In today's accounting information systems, expert systems are utilized more than artificial information systems. The data/information obtained only using computer technology will not work for users of accounting information. When accounting information is combined with the power of computer technology by experts, the true information will be meaningful to users. For example, if certain models are not made after the presentation of the main financial statements, it means that it is raw information. Financial statements have to be analyzed via computer technology and the rates have to be determined.

2.2.6 Top Management Support Systems

It is the main aim in top management support systems to obtain, combine, and present available information without using any tools. Although this system is similar to decision support systems, it differs at some points. Accordingly, while analytical modeling is used more in decision support systems, top management support system offers less analytical methods. According to this system, although the personalities and experiences of top managers are different from each other, they all demand information in a radical way. Therefore, it is necessary to construct flexible structures that will be shaped according to the managers while designing this system (Ersöz and Ersöz, 2015: 125). Top managers' using computers not only reduces information processing costs and duration but also results in the effective use of available resources and directing the surplus of resources to more productive areas. Furthermore, another advantage of the system is that activity results and developments are assessed to shed light on long-term planning (Sevim, 2006: 27).

3 Knowledge for Businesses

3.1 The Importance of Quality Knowledge for Businesses

It is not sufficient for a business to only have information. Each business has some knowledge. Sometimes the surplus of knowledge can also be a factor that increases operating costs. In that case, the quality of knowledge is ahead of the existence of knowledge. According to the first element of qualified knowledge, knowledge is considered as of high quality as long as it is relevant to the subject. The second factor that determines the quality of information is that it should be obtained at the desired time. There is no point in using the information later that is not available when it should be used. It is better to have no information rather than have incorrect information. Therefore, the other factor that affects the quality of information is the correctness of information. The quality of information is actually directly related to cost. The cost of the information should be at a lower level than the value of the advantage that it provides. The use of costly information will have no effect on a business other than operating costs.

In order for information to be converted into quality information, it must be supported and accepted by managers. The information should even be accepted by all system members, not just business managers. For example, the problematic and unacceptable inputs of packaged software that are not adopted by accounting personnel in the accounting department will cause problematic output in the same way. In addition, information should be in harmony with technological developments in order to produce healthy results. It will be difficult for businesses to use the information that does not use technological information and will cause time losses.

3.2 Information Management and the Continuity of Information in Businesses

In today's world of information, businesses need endless information. However, the fact that the information that the business possesses is not well managed is a barrier to the meaning of information. In fact, information management is a discipline that updates the ever-increasing information capacity in the corporate environment, makes the information available by identifying the required actions, and enables this information to be shared with the employees in a business (Bayram, 2010: 87). Information management is the result of the developments in the last 50 years based on organizational learning movements, also referred to as Taylorist management philosophy, total quality management, and business renaissance. However, because information is related to the processes of human intelligence and is often tacit, information management in a business mostly emerges on the basis of information management (Akgül and Keskin, 177).

Acquiring knowledge in businesses is possible either from internal sources or from external sources. In the event that the information obtained from internal sources is not sufficient, it is inevitable that the external sources will bring about some negative factors. Since the information obtained from external sources always leads to dependence on external sources and the source of information is never available, it is necessary to develop different strategies for the continuity of the business (Çukacı, 2005: 13). The ability of businesses to capture continuity is also dependent on their constant dynamism and ability to change. Change is all about managing knowledge efficiently. The protection of business assets and being able to sustain relations with the environment and in-house communication depend on the efficient use of available information. While the capital of the businesses constitutes their continuity in the traditional sense, today, businesses obtain the continuity through the institutional and internal knowledge they have. However, businesses need to filter the information they have and leave out the unnecessary information. This is because unnecessary information not only increases the burden of businesses but also increases the transaction costs (Yılmaz, 2015: 1016).

4 Relationship Between Information Systems and Accounting Information System

Today, businesses need accounting knowledge as well as traditional knowledge. Traditional accounting systems are inadequate for the collection, storage, and presentation of data to relevant parties. Those who ask for information demand more than these. This led businesses to new quests and brought accounting information system to the foreground (Ertaş, 2016: 67). Rowney and Steinbart (2000) list the contribution of the accounting information system to a business as follows (Ertaş, 2016: 79):

- Increasing quality and reducing product service costs: Accounting information system warns business managers when quality limits are ignored within the system. This helps to preserve the quality of the products, reduce wastes, ultimately resulting in lower costs.
- Increasing productivity: Designing an accounting information system effectively will result in timely and accurate information being produced at the desired time and will increase productivity. For example, businesses that implement a just-in-time production approach will provide inventory control and prevent all production inputs from running with empty or incomplete capacity.
- Effective decision-making: By using the accounting information system correctly and on a timely basis, business managers will be able to make business decisions in a timely and effective manner.
- Sharing of information: Designing accounting information system well provides the sharing of the experience that emerges as the result of the information accumulated. Correct use of shared information will provide a competitive advantage to businesses.

General tasks of accounting units in businesses are to follow-up receivables – debts, bank accounts, current term and adjusting process transactions, and determination of resource needs or surplus in any unit. However, fulfilling all these will not make sense for the functioning of the accounting. The information obtained should be converted to knowledge in a form that can be used through the accounting information system. This process, which can be interpreted as the transition from the accounting function to the accounting information system, will end when it reaches the final knowledge users.

Businesses need to be established, sustainable, achieve success, and be able to survive intense competition within a globalized world structure. In an environment where internal and external threats pose a risk and the rate of technological change is high, businesses must be able to survive. The ability of businesses to hold onto the market and achieve success is directly proportional to the way top management views the business within the framework of system understanding. It is clear that in the decisions taken and in the works performed, it is an obligation to view equally and in a coordinated manner to all the functions of the business. No matter whether businesses produce goods or services; the activities of businesses come to the forefront among four main functions such as production, management, marketing, and finance (Ersöz and Ersöz, 2015: 4).

4.1 Management Function and Accounting Information Systems

While the management understanding puts forth the structure that determines the objectives of the business, accounting information system provides a tool that ensures the most accurate and speedy delivery of the necessary information in order to make healthy decisions in reaching the objectives of businesses and also provides the basic data source for management mechanisms in the evaluation of the performance results of applications (Güney, 2013: 279). An effective management understanding will arise by management's taking information about cash, receivables, assets, fixed assets, investments, etc., from the accounting information system and sources of these assets (Acar and Dalgar, 2005: 30). However, in order to carry out successfully the management concept, it is necessary to attach importance to the accounting information system and to have a significant positive relationship between the management understanding and the accounting information system. The principle of transparency of management is based on ensuring that all information regarding the operation of the management is properly transmitted to the public to regularly and continuously monitor company activities. Periodical activity reports, financial statements, and footnotes are prepared by the accounting information system in the businesses within the framework of existing legislative provisions and international financial reporting standards and presented to the public by a declaration of conformity by the managers. Investors can better understand the key issues affecting the business and make sure that their investment decisions are appropriate. Accounting information systems and management practice mechanisms have some responsibilities in making the information to be disclosed to the public in a timely, accurate, complete, understandable, interpretable, low-cost, easily accessible, and simultaneous manner to help the people and organizations that will benefit from the disclosure of information make decisions. In accordance with the principle of transparency, financial and nonfinancial information of the company's activities is presented to the users of accounting information, the business which performs this behavior assumes the democratic enterprise mission of accountability and transparency (Çelik, (2007) 41). Furthermore, such businesses will contribute to the corporate management understanding if they fulfill the requirements of transparency, accountability, responsibility and justness principles.

4.2 Production Function and Accounting Information Systems

The production function in businesses is in constant communication with accounting information systems. Information flows are provided for the control of the stocks used in production and for the timely introduction of all inputs such as raw materials and materials to be used in production. For businesses that cannot fully implement the just-in-time production system, accounting information system is important in terms of access to instant production input. On the other hand, the production function also provides the necessary information for the determination of the capacity utilization rates of the machines, devices, or installations used during production and the calculation of the labor required for production.

In order to make productions in businesses, sales must be at the desired level. The output of accounting information systems should be used to make production plans in the direction of the indicators that emerge as a result of sales. The cost per unit and the total cost information within the cost information that is assessed in the production planning can also be obtained from the accounting information system. Productivity and waste quantities during production are also other information obtained from the accounting information system.

Accounting information system takes data from the production unit in the production process. The data obtained are processed in the classical accounting process and presented as output for the use of the production unit. However, all of the information required for production cannot be obtained from within the enterprise. Sometimes the raw materials and other materials or factors derived from external sources such as electricity, water, and natural gas are included in the information processing process together with production unit inputs and presented to the information users.

4.3 Marketing Information System and Accounting Information Systems

Marketing information system produces the information required for the planning, execution, coordination, and control of all kinds of marketing activities that the marketing department managers are interested in. While the marketing information system in the businesses takes important decisions such as sales forecasting and planning, market research, advertising, and promotion and pricing; it uses the information produced by the accounting information system.

The marketing information system transforms the business into a structure different from its competitors by the marketing mix and strategies developed for the business, its environment, and customers. Marketing information system with a broader definition is making a necessary analysis about marketing provision and arrangement of necessary information and provision of correct flow of information. This information system contains computer hardware and software like other information systems (Timur, 2013: 103–104). According to another definition, the marketing concept of the businesses has turned into a marketing information system over time. Marketing information systems are a structure designed to obtain, process, and present the information marketing managers need (Kılıç and Dündar, 1994: 50). The relationship between marketing information systems emerging in the direction of marketing function of business and accounting information systems is circular, and marketing information system uses the information of accounting information systems as input.

Accounting information system output is used during the sale of the product produced by the business. The internal part of the information that the marketing unit needs from the determination of the price of the goods to the market selection is obtained from the accounting information systems. Information such as annual sales forecasts, advertising, and marketing and promotion expenditures prepared using the enterprise's budgets are internal information and are accessible through accounting information systems. In addition, after-sales service plans are prepared using the outputs of accounting information systems.

4.4 Financing Function and Accounting Information Systems

The financing information system can be defined as an information system that fulfills the managerial responsibilities of the management of an enterprise and plans the actions of the enterprise regarding its present and future assets and meets the information requirements that occur in the direction of that plan (Ertaş, (2016) 63). It is highly difficult to distinguish financial information systems from accounting information systems. Although finance and accounting are separate information systems, the functional link between them is strong.

The financial information system means that the necessary funds are obtained and maximum benefits are obtained from these funds in order to realize the objectives of the enterprise. In other words, it is the most efficient use of the money of the enterprise. The objective of the financial information system intersects with that of the accounting information system at this point, and it is regarded as an information system that provides information to users (Önce, 2013: 184). On the other hand, the strategic importance of the accounting information system, which provides financial information to the enterprise, increases. Accounting information system determines the financial targets of the enterprise, compares the realized and targeted financial results, and keeps the results for later transactions (Yılmaz, 2015: 1015).

Accounting information systems and financial information systems in businesses are the two systems that interact with each other the most. Finance departments obtain all the information from the accounting information system regarding whether to make or postpone investments, in which areas investments should be made, and how the investments will be financed. Much information is obtained from the accounting information system outputs such as possible long- and short-term business profitability, cash flows, programmed budget information of the units in the enterprise, cost data, and product profitability. In accordance with this information, the financing information system makes the most appropriate decisions with management information system.

Conclusion

Increasing information needs of accounting information users and their desire to use this information in decision-making processes have made information today's most precious asset. Information systems affect decisions made by all managers who have decision-making authority together with management processes in businesses. Developments in information and information systems also bring forward the concepts of data, knowledge, and information in businesses. Innovations in information technologies, especially electronic data processing systems, office automation systems, management information systems, decision support systems, artificial intelligence and top management support systems, have enabled significant steps to be taken to restructure information systems. Due to increasing competition among businesses, expectations from information systems have also increased in relative terms; and these systems have played a part in establishing management policies of businesses and taking important strategic decisions. Instead of any kind of information, the concepts of quality information and continuity of knowledge have become more important for businesses. Since accounting information systems are located at the center of management, production, marketing, and financial information systems created functionally in businesses; it is inevitable that these information systems interact. Therefore, the accounting information system has facilitated the decision support systems that are being established in the businesses. This is because if the business decides to make a production decision or if it creates a marketing mix, all information will be provided from the accounting information system. Since management and finance information systems will also obtain all kinds of information from the accounting information system, the accounting information system will inevitably interact with other information systems created functionally in the businesses.

Bibliography

Acar, D., Hüseyin D. (2005), Entelektüel Sermayenin Ölçülmesinde Muhasebe Bilgi Sisteminin Katkısı, Muhasebe ve Denetime Bakış, 1, 23–40.

Ağca, A., (2013), Muhasebede Bilgi Yönetimi, Açıköğretim Yayınları, ed. Necdet Sağlam ve Arman Aziz Karagöl, Açıköğretim Yayınları, Eskişehir.

Akgül, A. E., Keskin, H., (2003), Sosyal Bir Etkileşim Süreci Olarak Bilgi Yönetimi ve Bilgi Yönetimi Süreci, Gazi Üniversitesi İ.İ.B.F. Dergisi, 5(1), 175–188.

Altuğ, M., (2014), Muhasebe Bilgi Sistemleri, Sosyal Bilimler Araştırma Dergisi, 23, 57–85.

Barutçugil, İ., (2002), Bilgi Yönetimi, Kariyer Yayıncılık, İstanbul.

Bayram, H., (2010), Bilgi Toplumu ve Bilgi Yönetimi, Etap Yayınevi, İstanbul.

Canbaz, S., (2016), Yönetim Bilgi Sistemleri, Paradigma Akademi, Ankara.

Çelik, O, (2007), Accounting Information and Business Democracy in Businesses, Siyasal Bookstore, Ankara.

Çukacı, Y. C., (2005), Ekonomik Değer Olarak Bilginin Muhasebe, İşletmeler ve Genel Ekonomi Açısından Değerlendirilmesi, Doğu Anadolu Bölgesi Araştırmaları, 3(3), 11–19.

Ersöz, O., Ö., S., Ersöz, (2015), İşletmelerde Bilgi Sistemleri, Nobel Yayınevi, Ankara.

Ertaş, F. C., (2016), Muhasebe Bilgi Sistemi ve Organizasyonu, Seçkin Yayınevi, 4. Baskı, Ankara.

Gökçen, H., (2007), Management Information Systems, Palme Publishing, Ankara.

Güney, A., (2013), Yönetim Anlayışında Muhasebe Bilgi Sisteminin Yeri, Eğitim ve Öğretim Araştırmaları Dergisi, 2(3), 276–280.

Kaderli, Y., Köroğlu, Ç. (2014), İşletmelerde Muhasebe Bilgi Sistemi ile Kurumsal Yönetim Anlayışı Arasındaki İlişki, Muhasebe ve Finansman Dergisi, 2014, 21–38.

Kılıç, Ö., Dündar, S., (1994), Pazarlama Bilgi Sistemlerinin Gelişimi ve Önemi, Yönetim, 5(17), 47–53.

Koza, M., (2008), Bilgi Yönetimi, Kum Saati Yayınları, İstanbul.

Laudon, K. C., Laudon, J. P. (2002), Management Information Systems, Prentice-Hall, New Jersey.

Meral, E., (2016), Türkiye'de Bilgi Sistemleri Denetimi ve Kamu Gözetimi Kurumu'nun Bilgi Sistemleri Denetiminde Üstlendiği Misyon, Muhasebe ve Denetim Dünyası, 1(1), 83–99.

Munteanu, V., Zuca, M., Tinta, A., (2011), "The Financial Accounting Information System Central Base in The Managerial Activity of an Organization", Journal of Information Systems & Operations Management, 5(1), 63–74.

Önce, S., (2013), İşletme Bilgi Sistemleri, ed. Hasan Durucasu, Anadolu Üniversitesi Yayınları, Eskişehir.

Rowney, M., Steinbart, P. J., (2000), Accounting Information Systems, New Jersey.

Sevim, Ş., (2006), Muhasebe Bilgi Sistemi, Dumlupınar Üniversitesi Yayınları No.13, Kütahya.

Şahin, M., (2009), Yönetim Bilgi Sistemleri, Anadolu Üniversitesi Yayınları, Eskişehir.

Timur, N., (2013), İşletme Bilgi Sistemleri, ed. Hasan Durucasu, Anadolu Üniversitesi Yayınları, Eskişehir.

Tonus, H. Z., (2009), Yönetim Bilgi Sistemi, ed. Mehmet Şahin, Anadolu Üniversitesi Yayınları, Eskişehir.

Yılmaz, F. Ö., (2015), Kurumsal Yönetim ve Muhasebenin Sosyal Sorumluluğu Açısından Muhasebe Bilgi Sisteminin İşletmelerdeki Rolü, Uluslararası Sosyal Araştırmalar Dergisi, 8(39), 1011–1018.

Yuva, J., (2002), Knowledge Management: The Supply Chain Nevre Center, Inside Supply Management, 34–43. www.semanticscholar.org, erişim: 16.02.2018.

Orkun Bayram

Evaluation of Participation Banking in Turkey from the Perspective of Performance and Positioning and Suggestions for Growth

1 Introduction

As stated in the Holy Qur'an, in the Bakara, Ali Imran, Nisa and Rum suras, the interest (ribâ), which is a type of gain that is not obtained by working and producing, is defined as haram. However, the payment of interest at a certain rate to the collected deposits has become an ossified practice in the classical banking sector, which has been tasked with forming the basis of contemporary economic systems. In the countries where only classical or traditional banking institutions and organizations exist, depositors with the abovementioned sensitivities do not want to transfer their savings to the banking system; instead, they intend to use their savings in types of investments such as gold, foreign exchange, and real estate, which are not directly utilized in production. As a result, these funds cannot contribute directly to the economy of the country. Islamic banking practices have emerged to prevent this situation. The first Islamic bank in the world was established in Egypt in 1963 (Kara, 2006: 11), and in the following years, the Islamic banking sector has spread rapidly in Gulf countries such as Saudi Arabia, Bahrain, Iran; Malaysia, Tunisia, and other countries with the majority of the population being Muslim, and in countries such as the United Kingdom (Yanıkkaya and Pabuçcu, 2017: 48). Since its emergence, the Islamic banking sector has made significant progress worldwide in terms of market share and industry size. The vast majority of the population in Turkey is also Muslim, and the need for Islamic banking practices in this country has led to the industrialization of this sector in Turkey.

The first application of Islamic banking in Turkey, established in 1975, is the State Industrial and Labor Investment Bank (DESİYAB). This bank started to work on the basis of the profit/loss partnership principle instead of interest, but in 1978 this decision was abandoned to return to the interest system (Polat, 2009: 87). Therefore, this bank did not constitute a successful example of Islamic banking; the new legislation created in the later years provided the opportunity for a permanent initiation of Islamic banking activities in Turkey. It was first made possible by the decree published in 1983 that private financial institutions, which could work on Islamic Banking procedures, could become operational

(Battal, 1999: 22); and in 1984, the first private financial institution started to provide services. With the participation banking law issued in 2005, private financial institutions which were previously governed by decrees from the Council of Ministers started to be governed by laws issued by the Parliament, and became a more reliable business type for their prospective customers.

Assigned with the task of bringing Islamic banking applications to the banking sector in Turkey with the law filed in 2005, following this development, participation banks in Turkey had launched different products based on the Islamic banking market procedures in an accelerating manner. During the establishment phase of the participation banking system, these banks started to serve their customers in the form of participation accounts which are focused on private current accounts and participation in profit or loss to collect funds. In order to make use of the fund, the services they provided were partnership (Mudaraba and Mushareke), which is also focused on profit or loss, production support based on the principle of profit share (Murabaha), rental (İcare), and provision and sale of goods. Other services such as electronic fund transfer and bill payments are also offered to the customers by participation banks. Then, in 2009, the first participation insurance (Tekâfül) company started its activities. In 2010, the first interest-free bond (lease certificate or Sukuk) was issued. These developments were followed by the first Participation Index product in 2011, the start of the first participation retirement company's services in the same year, and similarly, followed by other innovations that increase the product range (Aslan and Özdemir, 2015: 30). Thus, the participation banking sector in Turkey, with the legal support provided by the government, has submitted various Islamic banking products to the appreciation of its potential customers since its inception. In light of these efforts and due to the Islamic faith of the vast majority of the population in Turkey, the participation banking in Turkey can be expected to have a market share at least on par with the traditional banks.

When the market shares of the participation banks in the sector are analyzed by the end of 2017, it is seen that despite the supportive structure of the religious beliefs of the Turkish public and the legal regulations, they cannot reach the expected levels. The fact that participation banks have a market share of 6.1% in the funds collected and a 5% market share in the funds allocated indicates inferiority in performance in terms of competition compared to traditional banks. Again, based on total assets, equity, net profit, and other key performance indicators; participation banking sector is observed to be unable to exceed market share even as low as 5% (Participation Banks Association of Turkey (TKBB), n.d.).

On discussing the fact that the market share of the participation banks in the entire banking sector is insufficient, besides the religious beliefs of the public and the regulations at the country under consideration, there exist many environmental factors to reveal this result. The general environmental conditions affecting participation banking, the impact of economic, technological, sociocultural, and legal environmental conditions can be considered to be undeniable. For example, the global economic crises, as in 2008, affect all countries. If the credit rating of the country in which a participation bank operates is decreasing due to an economic crisis in the global scale, the participation bank issuing Sukuk may experience difficulties in the international arena. In the current situation, three of the five participation banks in Turkey are owned by foreign participation banks, the other two are owned by the state, and another one is currently being established by the state as well. Foreign-owned and state-based participation banks may be affected differently from global economic crises, and sector managers should take this into consideration.

Another group of environmental factors affecting participation banking is technological innovations. Now, technological innovations have enabled us to withdraw money without a card in ATM devices, to ensure that the approvals of individual loans are only done at the headquarters in a centralized manner; and through block chains, international money transfer can be made much more quickly without the approval of a central authority. Participation banks need to bring these innovations to their systems. Bank customers in Turkey, due to the intensive use of social media, could make informed comparisons between different options for banking services; thus, participation banks need to keep up with their competitors in terms of the use of technology.

To investigate the problems affecting the participation banking in Turkey and presenting an obstacle for them in obtaining the expected market share and for the development of relevant solutions, the abovementioned conditions must be considered. If accurate solutions can be developed, it will be possible to reach the real potential of participation banking. For example, in the current situation, all countries around the world increase gold reserves to protect their economies against exchange rate fluctuations (Anadolu Agency, 2018). Turkey is estimated to have around 2500–5000 tons of gold in squirrelled away funds (Para Analiz, 2018); and participation banks, compared to traditional banks, can collect these funds more effectively to save the country's economy. While the value of squirrelled away gold is estimated to be more than 110 billion dollars (Para Analiz, 2018), the total value of funds collected in the participation banking sector as of February 2019 is 146,317 million Turkish liras (TKBB, n.d.).

Through this comparison, the size of the potential of participation banking not yet implemented is better understandable.

It would be useful to compare the ratio of total amount of assets owned by participation banks in Turkey to the total amount owned by the whole banking sector in the country with the other countries to estimate the potential of participation banking in Turkey. According to the 2017 data, participation banks in Turkey, in terms of share in the entire banking sector's asset size, rank 19th in the world, which is behind many of the share in Yemen, Qatar, Malaysia, Bangladesh, and many other countries (Atar, 2017: 1042). To reveal the existing potential and to reach a better place in terms of Islamic banking worldwide, it is paramount to identify the problems encountered in participation banking in Turkey and develop solutions. The purpose of this chapter is to analyze these problems through the use of expert opinion from the participation banking sector in Turkey and to develop solutions. It also aims to identify the shortcomings of participation banking applications from the perspective of potential banking customers in Turkey. In this respect, it aims to contribute to the participation banking sector via enriching the solution proposals by evaluation of the problems experienced with the customers' view.

In the following sections of the study, firstly literature review will be provided; then, the methods used will be explained in the next section, followed by findings and comment sections. The study will conclude with the section on the results and future research.

2 Literature Review

Academic activities related to participation banking in Turkey especially gained momentum after support through relevant legislations have been provided. In this literature review, the emphasis has been on the articles which have contributed to the research questions constituting this study: evaluation of participation banks in terms of performance and positioning in Turkey and suggestions for solution. In this context, the resource books about Islamic finance and banking, publications containing the definition of the participation banking conducted in Turkey, the reasoning of the developments in participation banking in Turkey, and the description of the banking products offered to the customers in Turkey are included. One of the arguments highlighted in the studies is the advantages participation banking activities provide for financial stability during times of economic crisis in Turkey. Afterwards, articles focusing on the state of participation banking worldwide have been mentioned, and current research conducted in connection with the participation banking problems in Turkey are indicated. In particular, the proposed solutions in recent studies were compiled, and recent developments in Turkey to realize these solutions are included. In the last part of the literature review, the contribution of our study to the literature is emphasized.

In Islamic understanding, in the conduct of economic and other activities, the main theme is interest-free banking (ez-Zerqa, en-Neccar, 2009: 26; Nyazee, 2016: 73), which should be well understood by all stakeholders of the Islamic banking sector. The Islamic economy is in continuous development to create an alternative to the interest-oriented system in the conventional banking and finance sector (Dikkaya and Kutval, 2015: 77; Kuforiji, 2019: 71; Abdul-Rahman, 2010: 13), but it also has the potential to pose as a holistic alternative to existing economic systems (Hazıroğlu, 2018: 119;). In addition, Islamic banks have shown more stable performance in times of global economic crises than traditional banks (Rasid, Nizam and İsmail, 2014: 59). Because of this success, the interest in Islamic banking in the global sense has increased.

Among the present studies, the articles and theses focusing on the definition of Islamic banking, its global development, organization stages and legal structures of participation banks in Turkey, and the methods they use for fund-raising and collecting have been on the rise. One of the main ideas highlighted in these studies is that participation banks are more resistant to economic crises than traditional banks. Therefore, the advantages offered by participation banking to provide financial stability (Tenekeci, 2017: 70), and their principle of work for production-based economic activities on the use of funds and profit or loss partnership (Aysan, Dolgun and Turhan, 2013: 100) allows participation banks to contribute to the economy of their country in times of crisis. One of the methods used in the studies making this judgment is the comparison of the values of various financial ratios, especially in times of crisis, for traditional banks and participation banks. The reason for the use of this method is the idea that participation banks in Turkey should compete with conventional banks rather than their own counterparts to increase their market share, which depends on the fact that participation banking sector is far from reaching its true potential in Turkey yet.

The ratios of profitability and asset management are among the values used to compare the performance of participation banks and traditional banks in times of crisis (Erol, Baklacı, Aydoğan and Tunç, 2014: 115). In addition to these ratios, risk levels and convertibility ratios are used. Besides direct benchmarking, the financial ratios such as capital adequacy ratios are also determined by methods such as stress test (Akkuş, 2017: 210). In times of economic downturn, it was observed that participation banking had more stable values compared to the traditional banking sector in terms of said financial ratios, which is among the advantages of participation banking. Regarding the reasons for this advantage, studies emphasizing step by step the problems in markets functioning with traditional interest principle having chain reaction not only in national but in global scale, and also indicating the supporting role of participation banking for noninterest bearing activities that contribute to the economy (Yazıcı, 2016: 79) are observed in Turkey's participation banking literature.

Considering the studies on the current situation of Islamic banking practices around the world and the current situation of Islamic banking in global terms, it can be seen that one of the important dynamics supporting the sector is the preference of Islamic banking applications for the investment of the funds obtained from the oil sales of the Gulf countries (Atar, 2017: 1039). Islamic banking practices around the world have shown a tendency to develop differently in different countries, which can be said to be due to the impact on Islamic banking of the environmental conditions mentioned in the previous section and the changes in these conditions. According to 2017 data, the first three countries in which Islamic banking has the highest value in terms of market share in the whole banking sector are Iran (100%), Sudan (100%), and Brunei (57%) (Atar, 2017: 1041). For the total volume of assets belonging to the Islamic banking sector, Iran still ranks first and Turkey ranks 7th according to the 2016 data (Atar, 2017: 1053). Thus, Turkey, which was among the first 20 countries given the global performance of the participation banking sector in terms of market share, is among the top 10 countries in terms of asset volume. This shows the potential of participation banking in Turkey which was indicated by various figures in the previous section.

Regarding the developmental stages of Islamic banking practices in different countries, it can be said that the support of the state and legal regulations has a positive effect on this development (Yanıkkaya and Pabuçcu, 2017: 47). One of the contributions of legal regulations to the banking system is the regulation of the usage and dissemination of banking products. As one of the dimensions of development for the Islamic banking system, the diversity of Islamic banking products used can be counted. According to 2015 data, Murabaha product has more than 50% usage rate in many countries except Malaysia and United Arab Emirates (TKBB, 2015: 15). An Islamic banking approach based on the Murabaha banking product to this level leads to criticism worldwide. The reason for this criticism is that Islamic banking's principle of realizing economic activities against profit or loss in return for partnership is the reason that products of Mudaraba and Mushareke should be brought to the forefront in terms of Islamic philosophy compared to other products which are focusing on buying and selling and debt (Azmat, Skully and Brown, 2015: 269). Over the years, Turkey expanded its participation banking product range. Alongside products such as Sukuk and Tekâful, via a legal arrangement made in 2008, interest-free private pension system was also offered to participation banking customers (Altuncuoğlu 2017: 57). However, it can be said that the expansion of the product range on the basis of profit or loss partnerships will be more beneficial to reflect the philosophy of participation banking on the economy and share the risks arising from economic activities.

In order to evaluate the overall performance and the current status of participation banking in Turkey different methods were used in the literature. Multi-criteria decision methods such as TOPSIS and usage of data from the balance sheet and income statements of participation banks in Turkey to determine financial performance scores (Esmer and Bağcı, 2016: 28), as well as values of financial data on specific years being compared via statistical methods such as t-test or comparison of financial data based on Basel III criteria (Bildirici-Çalık and Aygün, 2017: 59) are some of the methods used to measure the performance of participation banks in Turkey.

To delineate the current status of the participation banking in Turkey, methods such as comparison of Islamic banking legal regulations and products, and examining the banking strategies implemented in Turkey (Yanıkkaya and Pabuçcu, 2017: 58) are used. In some sectors, overall analysis of strengths, weaknesses, opportunities, and threats; arranging surveys with participation banking employees (Aslan and Özdemir, 2015: 40); and conducting interviews with industry experts (Egresi and Belge, 2017: 36) were used to illustrate the current status of the participation banking sector in Turkey. When we compile the conclusions of previous research on our topic, recommendations for development of the participation banking sector in Turkey can be summarized as follows:

- Standardization of board decisions on confirmation of participation banking practices in Turkey being compatible with Islamic lifestyle and philosophy (formerly each bank had a separate advisory board, in 2018 Union of Participation Banks in Turkey established a committee for overseeing standardization efforts),
- Increasing the diversity of participation banking products (in particular through an increase in profit/loss-sharing-oriented products and thus, the lowering transaction volume focused on Murabaha),
- Create awareness for the destruction of the perception that participation banking as applied in Turkey does not really represent Islamic philosophy and interest-free banking,

- Increasing the efficiency of participation banks and ensuring that they benefit more from economies of scale,
- Increasing undergraduate and graduate education programs, publications, and other academic studies on participation banking.

When studies analyzing specific topics or issues on participation banking in Turkey are considered, various research topics can be encountered. One of these topics aims to assess whether participation banking in Turkey has acquired sufficient level of human capital having the required competencies and sensitivities on Islamic banking and to provide helpful recommendation on this subject. Besides the industry-specific subjects such as the dynamics of interest-free finance system, participation banking employees should possess sufficient level of knowledge and skills on topics such as macroeconomics, foreign exchange, foreign trade, and financial mathematics (Kara, 2006: 108). For measuring efficiency of participation banks in Turkey in comparison with their counterparts, other participation banks overseas, and with conventional banks in Turkey; optimization methods such as Data Envelopment Analysis (DEA) were applied (Eyceyurt-Batır, 2016: 157; Öztürk, Canbaz ve Gür, 2017: 5; Yıldırım, 2015: 295; Şekeroğlu ve Kayhan, 2018: 333).

It is another participation banking research area to identify shortcomings in existing practices through surveys applied to participation banking customers. A wide variety of studies have been carried out on this subject and new ones continue to be made. The results from such studies confirmed that, as noted above, there may be false or incomplete perception of participation banking, while other results have been revealed. A survey conducted in the city of Kastamonu showed that participation banking customers were satisfied with the quality, speed, and effectiveness of the services; but they did not have enough knowledge about participation banking products, they mostly owned not participation but current accounts, and they were also working with traditional banks due to the lack of internet services and branch network provided by participation banks. In addition, it was stated that participation banks should increase their customer base with the type of customers who were young, working, and with a high educational level (Dilek and Küçük, 2017: 25). Following this suggestion, participation banks should enhance their product diversification to attract these type of customers (Anaç and Kaya, 2017: 179). In another study conducted in Uşak province, the result of satisfaction, knowledge level, preference, and interest-free banking perception related to participation banking was found to be low (Özen, Şenyıldız and Akarbulut, 2016: 13). A study conducted in the province of Istanbul found that customers had a lack of confidence that the participation banks applied interest-free banking and also the deposits in the participation banks were under state guarantee; shortcomings of customers were detected for awareness and education level in terms of Islamic finance (Egresi and Belge, 2017: 48).

An important topic included in survey-based research on participation banking customers is to measure the service quality with SERVQUAL scale (Parasuraman, Valarie and Leonard, 1985: 42). While there was no significant difference between the participation and traditional bank customers in Gaziantep province in terms of demographic characteristics, the satisfaction of the customers of participation banking was higher whereas there was no difference between the two types of bank customers in terms of loyalty (Tan, İğde, Çelik and Buğan, 2016: 56). In the survey study conducted on a participation bank belonging to the state, which used the same model, it was concluded that the customers in İstanbul who participated in the survey were satisfied with the services of the bank.

In the studies carried out to measure various values such as satisfaction and perception with participation banking customers, as stated above, while different results are obtained for different samples in some respects, it is seen that the problems mentioned in the studies and the related recommendations are similar and also resembles the abovementioned items. For example, inadequacy in branch network and banking products and high commissions and fees (Bülbül, 2017: 57); employees' level of insufficient financial consultancy provided to the customers and also the bank's internet services (Artar, Okumuş and Güneren-Genç, 2016: 267; Güneren, Okumuş and Artar, 2016: 240); these are mentioned as issues that need to be improved by participation banks.

Through the research done on the participation banking in Turkey and in the light of developments in this area, innovative business models are now being developed for participation banking. These studies have intensified the efforts to create a vision and strategies. In this context, for participation banking to use venture capital funds via partnership with appropriate monitoring and auditing provided to transition participation banking from Murabaha-oriented transaction intensity. In a study, the likelihood of such a business model was assessed in consultation with different stakeholders of the business model through an in-depth interview (Demir, 2018: 256).

Turkey's strategic goals on participation banking for 2025 were announced (TKBB, 2015: 7). Strategies and stakeholders were identified as increased sector-wide coordination, product diversity, formation of advisory boards, and enhancement of training for human resources, corporate communication, and reputation. The duty to researchers at this point, with Turkey having such a high potential in the participation banking sector, is to present the current trends in participation banking, and to improve, identify, and propose solutions to problems. A further task is to determine the deficiencies by making measurements related to the values such as participation banking positioning, perception and awareness, and also to strive to develop solutions. This study contributes to the participation banking in Turkey and to the literature to answer this need.

3 Methodology

Firstly, interviews were made with senior executives in the participation banking sector, and the current situation of the sector was tried to be illustrated. Human resource and positioning-oriented evaluation was demanded from the interviewees, and the innovations that could be made and practices that could be adapted from other countries were also inquired.

In the study, the participants were selected to have at least 15 years of experience in participation banking and are working in different institutions operating in the sector.

In the interview study, semistructured open-ended questions were asked to the participants. In order to ensure that the participants feel comfortable during the interview and respond to the questions in detail, before the start of the interview, the personal information of the participants and the institutions they work with, as well as their titles, were guaranteed to be kept private. The questions asked during the interview were as follows:

1. Do you believe the total market share of the participation banking over the entire banking sector is sufficient?
2. According to the data on the overall banking sector, participation banking cannot raise its total market share to a value higher than 5% since its establishment. Regarding this fact, please indicate the five most important problems the sector is having in Turkey.
3. Please indicate your suggestions for solution to the abovementioned problems.
4. Do you think that the personnel working in the participation banks are have sufficient skills and competency on both the banking technique and sensitivities regarding the participation banking system?
5. Do you find strategies applied for penetration of participation banking in Turkey adequate and accurate?
6. What kind of innovations is needed for the development of participation banking in Turkey?
7. What are the participation banking applications that are applied overseas but not yet implemented in Turkey and can be helpful to the development of the sector?

Tab. 1: Participation Banks' Asset Volume and Market Share in the Sector (Million Turkish Liras, 2013–2017)

Years	Total Assets	Change (%)	Market Share %
2013	96.022	36,7	5,5
2014	104.073	8,4	5,2
2015	120.252	15,27	5,1
2016	132.874	10,5	4,9
2017	160.136	20,5	4,9

Source: TKBB, BDDK

The purpose of the first question is to assess the impact on participation banks' managers of the average 5% total market share the sector has. According to the data of TKBB and Banking Regulation and Supervision Agency (BRSA), in 2013–2017, it is seen that the share of participation banking in the banking sector stayed between 4.9% and 5.5%. In 1983 the Cabinet allowed to establish Private Finance Institutions, and in 1985 Albaraka Turkish Private Finance Corporation and Faisal Finance Institution started their activities (TKBB, n.d.); thus, the sector is active for 34 years, and it is stuck on such a low level of market share (Tab. 1).

A survey conducted in 2014 by the Ministry of Religious Affairs named Religious Life Survey in Turkey showed that 99.2% of the population of Turkey is seen as belonging to the Islamic religion. In this survey conducted on 21632 people across the country, it was stated that 50.9% of the respondents were women and all of the participants were 18 years of age or older. In the study, the percentage of those who stated that all of what is told in the Qur'an is true and applies at all times was 96.5% and the percentage of those who did not attend was 1% (TRT Haber, 2014). In light of this survey it is quite surprising that participation banking sector in Turkey is active for 34 years and still unable to extend the only 5% total market share. The purpose of the second question is to find reasons and explanations for this result.

On the other hand, in the holy books that are sent to humanity there are verses referring to interest being harmful and should not be consumed. For instance, Qur'an, surah Al-Baqara verse 275 clearly forbids interest, and also in Torah it is written to give back a percent of interest. At this point, the survey conducted by the Ministry of Religious Affairs of Turkey raises a great contradiction between the market share of the participation banks and the religious beliefs of the public. If Turkey assumes Islam with 99.2% of the population and interest is certainly forbidden by Qur'an, then Turkey is expected to favor the participation banks; however, market share of participation banks operating in Turkey could surpass 5%. Therefore, it would be an appropriate attitude for participation banks not to link the problems they face to the lack of "conservative customer" profile. In the current situation, it is seen that participation banks did not reach their potential customers properly. The reason to ask the interviewees to list the major problems of participation banking is to address this surprising phenomenon from their perspectives.

The aim of the 3rd question addressed to the participants is to raise the awareness of the participants about how to solve the problems identified in the participation banking sector.

The aim of the 4th question addressed to the participants is to determine their views on whether the reason the participation banks do not have sufficient market share is they employ personnel who do not carry the sensitive approach for Islamic banking principles and technical banking knowledge.

For example, if a marketing portfolio manager working in a participation bank does not know the specifics of discount post finance or discountable letters of credit when visiting a potential corporate customer representative, it will lead to the loss of the potential customer or marketing a product that does not comply with the Islamic Banking sensitivity.

The purpose of the fifth question posed to participants is whether they know their market well and whether they can develop strategies that are Turkey-specific and will contribute to the development of Turkey's economy.

The aim of the sixth question addressed to the participants was to determine whether the senior executives working in the participation banks are aware of the problems they have identified and the innovations, new business models, and creative products that need to be produced in order for the participation banking to reach the targeted sector share.

The purpose of the seventh question is to determine whether senior managers of participation banks in Turkey have awareness for their products are services on the global scale (In particular, foreign capital-oriented participation banks in Turkey are expected to have the capability to transfer know-how from their main conglomerate.).

As a second data collection method, surveys were conducted on employees of various institutions and organizations as well as households. The questionnaire, which was prepared online, was distributed through social media and was answered by 111 people. The survey was designed to comprehend the awareness and perception of the effectiveness of participation banking in Turkey in the minds of the participants and has a total of 47 questions in the survey. In the first seven questions, the participants' level of awareness and experience related to participation banking was tried to be determined by an open-ended question plus six Yes/No types of questions.

In the following sections of the questionnaire, the participants form the scale of semantic difference (Kurtuluş, 2010: 104) with 20 different dimensions (e.g., level of success, confidence level) to reveal two profiles of Participation Banks and Traditional Banks in their minds. Evaluation of each dimension was made in 5-point Likert type.

4 Findings

In this section, the data collected by the above methods will be presented and interpreted. First of all, the answers to the interview questions directed to the senior executives working in the participation banking sector will be compiled.

4.1 Interview Results

1) *The adequacy of the market share of participation banking:* All of the interviewed senior executives declared that they are not satisfied of the market share. As can be seen from Tab. 1, participation banking sector in Turkey has tended to decline in the last five years and its market share declined in 2017 to lower than 5%. Some of the participants stated that despite the high percentage of government support and the religious beliefs of the public, market share developments have been quite slow, while some stated that this was due to the challenges faced by the participation banking sector with the focus on political and economic conjuncture.

2) *The most important issues causing participation banks not being able to raise the total market share over 5% in Turkey:*
   - The community being not sufficiently aware that interest and dividends are different from each other of the main activity of participation banks,
   - The technological infrastructure being inadequate and their systems being too slow to keep up with technological developments,
   - The lack of product diversity, the difficulty in introducing new products, due to the constraints created by the fatwa and regulations similarity of new products to traditional banking products,
   - Having inadequate human resources in terms of education, knowledge and experience, inadequate investment in personnel, inadequate or incompetent human resources focused on participation banking,

- Hiring personnel from traditional banks instead of educating new graduates based on their own principles, and this leading to adaptation problems during communication with the customer,
- The exchange of participation bank employees, in the course of time, with traditional bank professionals due to not having any increase in the scale of this sector, and therefore under senior management mentality; the high level managers' tendency to serve the needs of the bank partners and short-term plans to be negatively affecting the customer image,
- Inadequate Customer Relationship Management activities, especially in the social media, the posts lacking Islamic banking-oriented sensitivity and creating discomfort,
- Inadequate promotion activities,
- Distribution of loans being concentrated in certain sectors,
- Lack of equity,
- The ownership of the capital being almost entirely foreign, and the foreign shareholders' tendency to obtain high profit in short-term, rather than focusing on long-term plans and this tendency having a negative effect on the personnel,
- The recruitment of new public participation banks from within the sector causes marketing efforts to concentrate on the same customer portfolio; this leads to a decline in the sector's profitability due to the intense competitive environment, thus enabling participation banks to work with even more competitive approaches.

3) *Solution proposals for problems of participation banking:*
- Intensively providing financial literacy trainings, and acquire instructors with Islamic banking thinking and product knowledge to illuminate current and potential customers,
- Intensive training of the personnel working in the participation banking sector on the philosophy of Islamic banking, its mission and vision,
- Keeping up-to-date with technology developments and fintech-oriented innovations,
- Examining the worldwide Islamic banking product range of banks especially as HSBC and Citibank to offer new products to the Turkish market,
- Having state or government institutions to be able to provide new legislation so that the participation banks can launch new product to the market faster,
- Sending personnel to their personal development trainings and also to technical trainings such as foreign trade,

- Encouraging staff to receive training in graduate programs in Islamic banking and finance,
- Abandoning the tendency to satisfy the staffing needs via transferring staff from other participation banks or from traditional banks, and so to abandon the competition-oriented approach and to train their own human resources, through proper training of new graduates with a career plan it is possible to obtain human capital with proper know-how, good knowledge of banking and technical skills, appropriate sensitivity towards interest-free Islamic banking philosophy,
- BRSA or other regulatory agencies taking effect to transform participation banks' perspective from short-term return-oriented approach to long-term strategic planning, so the pressure on the personnel and hence the turn-over will be reduced,
- Employment of people with an Islamic banking sensitivity in the executive positions of participation banks (otherwise the credibility of the institution may be harmed, especially if managers post social media photos that do not correspond with Islamic banking principles, which could lead to serious image loss from the perspective of the client),
- Having Participation Banks Association of Turkey provide more active support on creating new products and other subjects,
- To have a stronger asset quality via addition of capital or bank mergers to work more effectively for products and profitability,
- Increasing the frequency of promotion and advertising activities.

4) *The adequacy of the personnel working in the participation banks in terms of the banking technology and the sensitivity towards the participation banking system:* All of the interviewed senior managers indicated that they find the staff working in participation banks in Turkey to be insufficient with technical competence and also lacking the necessary sensitive approach to Islamic banking. Especially in recent years, it has been noted that there has been a significant decrease in the sensitivity required by the personnel to be demonstrated to the customers. The reasons for this situation are the transfer of nonqualified personnel from traditional banks and the distancing of the personnel of the participation banks from the mission and vision that they should have. Personnel who do not have the appropriate competencies and sensitivities perceive such philosophies in the form of principles and rules, and this perception causes difficulties in persuading the customer. As another reason, it is stated that the personnel are guided by sales models that are not in line with the participation banking objectives.

5) *The adequacy of the strategies implemented in assuring the penetration of participation banking in Turkey:* All of the interviewed executives stated that the participation banking in Turkey lacks proper strategies for penetration. The reasons for this are the fact that the number of branches and personnel of participation banks is insufficient, and the areas where they affect the economy are limited proportionally to the lack of versatility of their products. The shareholders' risk and profit perception may also cause fluctuations on penetration and positioning status depending on conjunctures.

6) *Required innovation for the development of the participation banking in Turkey:*

   • Getting more support from regulatory agencies on legislation and fatwa,
   • Arrangement of the laws and regulations of participation banking as much as possible and separately from the legislation for traditional banking,
   • Participation Banking audit and consultancy mechanisms should be independent and centralized,
   • Determining the competition conditions among the participation banks within the framework of legislation,
   • Having foreign capital–oriented participation banks being subject to the same positive discrimination as the public participation banks,
   • Correction of falsely aimed competition areas,
   • Renewal of wage and price policies,
   • To work with relevant departments of universities to increase product diversity,
   • Accelerating the digitization process and thus reducing costs.

7) *Potentially beneficial industry applications that are made in the world, but not yet implemented in Turkey:*

Some participants stated that participation banking in Turkey should exert significant research and development efforts to increase its product range with original products so, rather than world examples, they should produce their own unique solutions. By increasing the variety of products, new customers can be added to the sector and the market share of the sector in the whole banking sector can be increased. In addition to the use of existing products, Murabaha applications could be minimized with the support of TKBB. Another proposal from the participants is that the participation banks should contribute to the economy by providing detailed and intensive support for the establishment of joint companies with the entrepreneurs as profit sharing models and the training and development of these entrepreneurs.

Tab. 2: The Level of Recognition and Awareness for Participation Banks in Turkey

n=111	Yes		No		No Answer
Questions	**# responses**	**%**	**# responses**	**%**	**# responses**
Awareness on two categories of banks; conventional vs. participation banks	84	76.36	26	23.64	1
Knowledge on the differences between conventional and participation banking principles	61	55.96	48	44.04	2
Being exposed to promotions by participation banks	77	71.30	31	28.70	3
Ever visited any branch of participation banks	49	45.79	59	55.14	4
Ever worked as a corporate or retail customer with a participation bank	35	32.11	74	67.89	2
Ever worked as a corporate or retail customer with a conventional bank	83	76.15	26	23.85	2

Tab. 3: The Rememberability of Participation Banks in Turkey

Most well-known participation banks in Turkey n=111	# responses	%
Kuveyt Türk	27	24.32
Ziraat Participation Bank	17	15.32
Albaraka Türk	12	10.81
Türkiye Finans	14	12.62
Vakıf Participation Bank	8	7.2
Total	78	70.27

4.2 Survey Results

The responses of the participants to the questions indicating their awareness and experience regarding the participation banks were compiled as follows (Tabs. 2, 3, and 4).

In order to reveal two different profiles for Participation Banks and Traditional Banks, the distributions regarding the semantic differential profile (Kurtuluş, 2010: 104) having 20 different dimensions (e.g., level of success, level of reliability) are shown in the following tables (Tabs. 5 and 6).

Tab. 4: The Rememberability of Conventional (Working on Interest-Based) Banks in Turkey

Most well-known conventional banks in Turkey (n=111)	# responses	%
İş Bank	27	24.32
Garanti Bank	19	17.12
Ziraat Bank	13	11.71
Yapı Kredi	10	9
Akbank	9	8.1
Halkbank	2	1.8
Finansbank	1	0.9
Şekerbank	1	0.9
Total	82	73.87

Tab. 5: Semantic Differential Profile for Participation Banks

1: Strongly disagree 2: Disagree 3: Undecided 4: Agree 5: Strongly agree (n=111)	Avg.	Frequencies for answers (in percentage)				
		1-%	2-%	3-%	4-%	5-%
Participation banks in Turkey are modern.	3.11	7.27	16.36	41.82	27.27	7.27
Existence of participation banks in Turkey is meaningful.	3.25	9.09	16.36	26.36	37.27	10.91
Participation banks in Turkey operate in an aggressive manner.	2.55	9.09	38.18	42.73	8.18	1.82
Participation banks in Turkey operate in a friendly atmosphere.	3.26	5.45	7.27	47.27	35.45	4.55
Participation banks in Turkey have well-established systems.	3	5.45	20.91	47.27	20.91	5.45
Participation banks in Turkey have attractive exterior.	3.11	4.59	18.35	40.37	34.86	1.83
Participation banks in Turkey are reliable.	3.2	5.56	12.96	40.74	37.04	3.7
Participation banks in Turkey appeal to small companies.	3.06	6.42	11.93	54.13	23.85	3.67
Participation banks in Turkey are active in community life.	3.03	5.5	20.18	44.95	24.77	4.59
Participation banks in Turkey make you feel at home.	2.72	11.93	24.77	45.87	14.68	2.75
Participation banks in Turkey have a strong image.	2.99	6.54	20.56	42.99	27.1	2.8

Tab. 5: (continued)

1: Strongly disagree 2: Disagree 3: Undecided 4: Agree 5: Strongly agree (n=111)	Avg.	Frequencies for answers (in percentage)				
Participation banks in Turkey provide helpful services.	3.11	7.34	15.6	38.53	35.78	2.75
Participation banks in Turkey are nice to deal with.	2.95	10.09	18.35	43.12	22.94	5.5
Participation banks in Turkey are inviting.	3.29	4.59	5.5	49.54	36.7	3.67
Participation banks in Turkey have no parking or transportation problems in their branches.	2.62	8.26	28.44	56.88	5.5	0.92
Employees of participation banks in Turkey are my kind of people.	2.92	9.26	20.37	45.37	19.44	5.56
Participation banks in Turkey are successful.	2.98	11.11	14.81	40.74	31.48	1.85
Participation banks in Turkey have ads that attract a lot of attention.	2.95	7.41	27.78	32.41	26.85	5.56
Participation banks in Turkey have interesting ads.	2.77	6.48	34.26	37.96	18.52	2.78
Participation banks in Turkey have influential ads.	2.52	14.81	37.96	30.56	13.89	2.78

Tab. 6: Semantic Differential Profile for Conventional Banks

1: Strongly disagree 2: Disagree 3: Undecided 4: Agree 5: Strongly agree (n=111)	Avg.	Frequencies for answers (in percentage)				
		1-%	2-%	3-%	4-%	5-%
Conventional banks in Turkey are modern.	3.75	4.59	5.5	14.68	60.55	14.68
Existence of conventional banks in Turkey is meaningful.	3.92	2.78	3.7	8.33	69.44	15.74
Conventional banks in Turkey operate in an aggressive manner.	3.51	3.7	22.22	16.67	34.26	23.15
Conventional banks in Turkey operate in a friendly atmosphere.	2.97	5.56	27.78	34.26	28.7	3.7
Conventional banks in Turkey have well-established systems.	3.81	2.8	8.41	12.15	57.94	18.69
Conventional banks in Turkey have attractive exterior.	3.75	2.8	7.48	14.95	61.68	13.08

(continued on next page)

Tab. 6: (continued)

1: Strongly disagree 2: Disagree 3: Undecided 4: Agree 5: Strongly agree (n=111)	Avg.	Frequencies for answers (in percentage)				
		1-%	2-%	3-%	4-%	5-%
Conventional banks in Turkey are reliable.	3.42	8.33	10.19	21.3	51.85	8.33
Conventional banks in Turkey appeal to small companies.	3.2	3.7	14.81	42.59	35.19	3.7
Conventional banks in Turkey are active in community life.	3.46	4.63	12.04	24.07	50.93	8.33
Conventional banks in Turkey make you feel at home.	2.59	12.96	33.33	36.11	16.67	0.93
Conventional banks in Turkey have a strong image.	3.72	2.78	5.56	23.15	53.7	14.81
Conventional banks in Turkey provide helpful services.	3.69	2.78	6.48	15.74	68.52	6.48
Conventional banks in Turkey are nice to deal with.	3.09	6.54	18.69	36.45	35.51	2.8
Conventional banks in Turkey are inviting.	3.07	7.41	18.52	37.04	33.33	3.7
Conventional banks in Turkey have no parking or transportation problems in their branches.	2.59	10.28	40.19	33.64	12.15	3.74
Employees of conventional banks in Turkey are my kind of people.	2.84	5.56	27.78	45.37	19.44	1.85
Conventional banks in Turkey are successful.	3.69	2.78	3.7	26.85	55.56	11.11
Conventional banks in Turkey have ads that attract a lot of attention.	3.94	2.78	3.7	9.26	65.74	18.52
Conventional banks in Turkey have interesting ads.	3.79	2.78	2.78	23.15	55.56	15.74
Conventional banks in Turkey have influential ads.	3.09	4.63	25	33.33	30.56	6.48

In order to reveal two different profiles belonging to Participation Banks and Traditional Banks, the evaluations that constitute the semantic differential profile (Kurtuluş, 2010: 104) having 20 different dimensions (e.g., level of success, reliability level) were compiled as a snake diagram (Tab. 7). With this presentation, it was aimed to present the associations in the minds of the participants about the activities of Participation Banks and Traditional Banks. It is possible

Tab. 7: Snake Diagram Based on Semantic Differential Profile of Participation Banks and Conventional Banks

Participation banks	1	2	3	4	5	Conventional banks
Old-fashioned						Modern
Meaningless						Meaningful
Defensive						Aggressive
Unfriendly						Friendly
Not well-established						Well-established
Unattractive exterior						Attractive exterior
Unreliable						Reliable
Appeal to big companies						Appeal to small companies
Inactive						Active in community life
Make you feel uneasy						Make you feel at home
Weak						Strong
Indifferent to customers						Helpful services
Hard to deal with						Nice to deal with
Cold						Inviting
Parking or transportation problems						No parking or transportation problems
Not my kind of people						My kind of people
Unsuccessful						Successful
Haven't noticed ads						Ads attract a lot of attention
Uninteresting ads						Interesting ads
Not influential						Influential ads

to make comparisons because the survey questions contain the same kind of evaluations for Participation Banks and Traditional Banks. As mentioned in the previous sections, participation banks should not only gain access to the squirrel away funds but also aim for the traditional banks rather than other participation banks as competitors. The following assessment may be useful in this respect.

The values marked for each dimension are the average values of the responses to the survey questions as presented in the tables above.

According to the survey results, while the existence of participation banks in Turkey is known, the number of participants who does not know the difference between traditional banks and participation banks are too high to be denied. At this point, participation banks need to express themselves better in society. On the other hand, it is seen that the penetration strategy used by the participation banks contributes to a level of awareness in the society, but this strategy does not lead the corporate or individual customers to work with participation banks. In another respect, we observe that 76% of the survey participants work with a traditional bank. When we look at the positioning of participation banks between each other, 24% of the respondents mention Kuveyt Türk as the first that comes to mind among participation banks in Turkey. Kuveyt Türk was followed by Ziraat Participation Bank in the second place through being listed by 15% of the respondents as the first participation bank name they would mention. Again, the indecisiveness of the participants on the activities of the participation banks, branch positioning, and personnel quality shows that the participation banks are unable to fully introduce their founding philosophy and convince their potential customers to work with them.

5 Conclusion

In this study, the main objectives are to contribute to the participation banking in Turkey and in this direction to develop solutions and suggestions for development. In this context, following the literature review, a survey was conducted to determine the awareness and perception of the participation banking sector; and interviews with senior executives were conducted to assess the effectiveness of participation banking. In the light of the survey and interview data obtained, the deficiencies of participation banking applications in Turkey in terms of reputation and perception were emphasized. The following recommendations were compiled to develop participation banking in Turkey to reach its potential:

• The development of participation banking in our country and also in the world is quite new compared to traditional banking. For this reason, participation banking business model is a much more open business model. Brainstorming of leading industry leaders and advisory boards, not only for a specific participation bank, but also from a macro perspective, can be a major contributor to the sector. It is recommended to emphasize the difference from traditional banking and to form a business model that can create a sense of belonging.

- The creation of much more intensive support and training programs for entrepreneurs for the loan process will reinforce the sense of belonging in customers and the difference with traditional banking will be revealed in a much healthier way. For this to happen, there is a need to abandon the short-term profitability-oriented perspectives as mentioned above.
- When using the Murabaha method, it is only possible to carry out transactions via invoices without seeing the goods purchased. Therefore, it may be useful to check the purchased product. In addition, the use of Bank Payment Obligation instead of letter of credit in the import of goods by Murabaha method will result in more revenue from foreign trade transactions and registration of informal transactions.

For the purposes of the study, more than one data source and an intensive literature review were executed on the basis of assessing the potential, performance, and positioning. Following the study, it can be considered that as future research that collecting data on the imposition of weights on items of the perception and awareness scale, an index or a similar measurement would be obtained; and more interviews could be made with the employees of public institutions regulating the participation banking to obtain information about the feasibility of the development proposals.

Bibliography

Abdul-Rahman, Yahia, (2010), **The art of Islamic banking and finance: tools and techniques for community based banking.** New York, USA: Wiley & Sons.

Akkuş, H. Tunahan, (2017), **Türk bankacılık sektöründeki katılım bankalarının finansal istikrarının stres testi yöntemi ile analizi** (Doctoral Dissertation, Balıkesir University), Retrieved from http://www.tkbb.org.tr/Documents/Yonetmelikler/201312548001-Tez-(%C4%B0mzal%C4%B1).pdf (06.03.2019).

Altuncuoğlu, Mehmet, (2017), **Faizsiz bireysel emeklilik sisteminin. İşleyişi: 2008 sonrası Türkiye örneği** (Master's Dissertation, Bahçeşehir University) Retrieved from http://www.tkbb.org.tr/Documents/Yonetmelikler/Mehmet_Altuncuoglu_Faizsiz_Bireysel_Emeklilik_Sisteminin_Isleyisi_2008_Sonrasi_Turkiye_Ornegi.pdf (06.03.2019).

Anaç, Turhan and Kaya, Ferudun, (2017), "Bireysel Müşterilerin Katılım Bankacılığını Tercih Etmesini Etkileyen Faktörler", **Bartın Üniversitesi İktisadi ve İdari Bilimler Fakültesi Dergisi**, Vol. 8, N. 15, pp. 145–182.

Anadolu Agency, (2018). "Merkez bankaları altın topluyor" https://www.ntv.com.tr/ekonomi/

merkez-bankalari-altin-topluyor,imRJ7JZ-kkydbCszV190Dg?_ref=infinite (04.03.2019).

Artar, Okşan, Okumuş, Şaduman, Güneren Genç, Elif, (2016), "Assessing Customer Awareness and Selection Criteria Of Islamic And Conventional Banks In Turkey", Doğuş Üniversitesi Dergisi, Vol. 17, N. 2, pp. 255–271.

Aslan, Hakan and Özdemir, Mücahit, (2015), "Development of the Islamıc finance in Turkey: a questionnaire study", **Proceeding – Kuala Lumpur International Business, Economics and Law Conference 7**, 15-16 August 2015, Zes Rokman Resources **(publisher), ISBN** 978-967-11350-6-8, Kuala Lumpur, Malaysia.

Atar, Abdulkadir, (2017), "Başlangıcından Günümüze Dünyada ve Türkiye'de İslâmi Bankacılığın Genel Durumu", **Journal of History Culture and Art Research**, Vol. 6, N. 4, pp. 1029–1062.

Aysan, Ahmet Faruk, Dolgun, Muhammed Habib, and Turhan, M. Ibrahim, (2013), "Assessment of the participation banks and their role in financial inclusion in Turkey", **Emerging Markets Finance and Trade**, Vol. 49, N. 5, pp. 99–111.

Azmat, Saad, Skully, Michael and Brown, Kym, (2015), "Can Islamic banking ever become Islamic?", **Pacific-Basin Finance Journal**, Vol. 34, pp. 253–272.

Battal, Ahmet, (1999), **Bankalarla karşılaştırmalı olarak hukuki yönden: Özel finans kurumları**. Ankara, Turkey: Research Institute for Banking and Trade Law.

BDDK, Banking Regulation and Supervisory Agency Turkey, (2019), https://www.bddk.org.tr/ (04.03.2019).

Bildirici-Çalık, Esra, and Aygün, Mehmet, (2017), "Comparing the financial performance of conventional and participation banks with basel III criteria", **Journal of Researches on Business and Economics**, Vol. 7, N. 2, pp. 47–64.

Bülbül, Sadık, (2017), **Türk bankacılık sektöründe müşteri memnuniyetinin katılım ve mevduat bankalarında karşılaştırılmalı olarak değerlendirilmesi**, (Doctoral Dissertation, Gebze Technical University), Retrieved from http://www.tkbb.org.tr/Documents/Yonetmelikler/201312548001-Tez-(%C4%B0mzal%C4%B1).pdf. http://www.tkbb.org.tr/Documents/Yonetmelikler/Turk-Bankacilik-Sektorunde-Musteri-Memnuniyetinin-Katilim-ve-Mevduat_Bankalarinda-Karsilastirmali-Olarak-Degerlendirilmesi.pdf (06.03.2019).

Demir, Zafer, (2018), **Küçük ve orta büyüklükteki işletmelerin (kobi) finansal problemlerinin çözümünde girişim sermayesi fon'larının önemi ve rolü: katılım bankacılığına yeni bir model önerisi**. (Doctoral Dissertation,

İstanbul Sabahattin Zaim University), Retrieved from http://www.tkbb.org. tr/Documents/Yonetmelikler/doktoratezibaski.pdf (06.03.2019).

Dikkaya, Mehmet, and Kutval, Yunus, (2015), **Katılım Bankacılığı Türkiye Örneği**. Ankara, Turkey: Savaş Publishing.

Dilek, Serkan, and Küçük, Orhan, (2017), "Customer satisfaction in participation banks", **International Journal of Research in Business and Social Science**, Vol. 6, N. 4, pp. 22–33.

Egresi, Istvan, and Belge, Rauf, (2017), "Islamic banking in Turkey: population perception and development challenges", **Romanian Review on Political Geography/Revista Româna Geografie Politica**, Vol. 19, N. 1, pp. 30–55.

Erol, Cengiz, Baklaci, Hasan F., Aydoğan, Berna and Tunç, Gökçe, (2014), "Performance comparison of Islamic (participation) banks and commercial banks in Turkish banking sector", **EuroMed Journal of Business**, Vol. 9, N. 2, pp. 114–128.

Esmer, Yusuf, and Bağcı, Haşim, (2016), "Katılım Bankalarında Finansal Performans Analizi: Türkiye Örneği-Financial Performance Analysis of Participation Banks: The Case Of Turkey", **Mehmet Akif Ersoy Üniversitesi Sosyal Bilimler Enstitüsü Dergisi**, Vol. 8, N. 15, pp. 17–30.

Eyceyurt-Batır, Tuğba, (2016), *Türkiye'de katılım bankaları ve konvansiyonel bankaların kârlılık belirleyicileri ve etkinlik yönünden karşılaştırılmaları*, (Doctoral Dissertation, Atatürk University), Retrieved from http://www. tkbb.org.tr/Documents/Yonetmelikler/tugba-ececyurt-doktora-tezi.pdf (06.03.2019).

ez-Zerqa, M. Ahmet., en-Neccâr, Abdülaziz, A. Muhammed (2009), **İslâm düşüncesinde ekonomi, banka ve sigorta**, (H. Karaman, Trans.), İstanbul: İz Publishing.

Güneren, Elif, Okumuş, Şaduman, and Artar, Oksan. K., (2016), "Household and corporate customers of participation banks in turkey: customers' satisfaction and bank patronage factors", **Maliye ve Finans Yazıları**, Vol. 106, pp. 213–241.

Hazıroğlu, Temel, (2018), **Katılım Ekonomisi Yeni Zihin, Yeni İktisat**. İstanbul: İz Publishing.

Kara, Mustafa, (2006), **Katılım Bankalarında Personel Eğitimi**, (Master's Dissertation, Gazi University), Retrieved from http://www. tkbb.org.tr/Documents/Yonetmelikler/Kat%C4%B1l%C4%B1m%20 bankalar%C4%B1nda%20personel%20e%C4%9Fitimi.pdf (06.03.2019).

Kibritçi Artar, Okşan, Okumuş, Şaduman, and Güneren Genç, Elif, (2016), "Assessing customer awareness and selection criteria of Islamic and conventional banks in Turkey", **Doğuş Üniversitesi Dergisi**, Vol. 17, N. 2, pp. 255–271.

Kuforiji, John Oluseyi, (2019), **The Essentials of Islamic Banking, Finance, and Capital Markets**, Lanham, Maryland: Lexington Books.

Kurtuluş, Kemal, (2010), **Araştırma yöntemleri**, İstanbul: Türkmen Publishing.

Nyazee, Imran Khan, (2016), **Concept of Riba and Islamic Banking**, Malaysia: Islamic Book Trust.

Özen, Ercan, Şenyıldız, Leyla, ve Akarbulut, Kenan, (2016), "Faizsiz Bankacilik Algisi: Usak Ili Örnegi/Islamic banking perception: the case of Usak City", **Journal of Accounting, Finance and Auditing Studies**, Vol. 2, N. 4, pp. 1–19.

Öztürk, Doğan, Canbaz, Muhammed Fatih, ve Gür, Murat, (2017), "Katılım bankaları ile mevduat bankalarının 2009–20016 yılları etkinliklerinin VZA ile karşılaştırılması", http://www.tkbb.org.tr/Documents/Yonetmelikler/ Katilim-Bankalari-ile-Mevduat-Bankalarinin-VZ-ile-2009-2016- Etkinliklerinin-Karsilastirilmasi.pdf (06.03.2019).

Para Analiz. (2018). "Yastık altındaki servete inanamayacaksınız!" http://www.paraanaliz.com/2018/guncel/yastik-altindaki-servete- inanamayacaksiniz-21855/ (06.03.2019).

Parasuraman, A. Parsu, Zeithaml, Valarie. A., and Berry, Leonard. L., (1985), "A conceptual model of service quality and its implications for future research", **Journal of Marketing**, Vol. 49, N. 4, pp. 41–50.

Polat, Ali, (2009), "Katılım Bankacılığı: Dünya Uygulamalarına İlişkin Sorunlar-Fırsatlar; Türkiye İçin Projeksiyonlar", (Aydın Yabanlı, Ed.) *Finansal Yenilik ve Açılımları ile Katılım Bankacılığı*, İstanbul: TKBB, pp. 77–120.

Rasid, S. Zaleha A., Nizam, Mohamad A. and İsmail, W. Khairuzzaman W, (2014), **Weathering the Global Crisis: Can the Traits of Islamic Banking System make a Difference?**, Singapore: Partridge.

Şekeroğlu, Sinan and Kayhan, Furkan, (2018), "Türkiye'deki katılım bankalarının etkinliğinin veri zarflama analizi ile karşılaştırılması", (Sezer Bozkuş Kahyaoğlu, Zülfi Umut Özkara, Eds.), *Katılım Finans Teorik ve Ampirik Çalışmalar*, Ankara: Gazi Publishing, pp. 316–338.

Tan, Ahmet, İğde, Medet, Çelik, Tarık Ziyad, and Buğan, Mehmet Fatih, (2016), "Algılanan Hizmet Kalitesinin Katılım ve Mevduat Bankalarında Müşteri Memnuniyeti ve Müşteri Sadakati Üzerine Etkisi", **International Journal of Academic Values Studies**, Vol. 5, pp. 45–59.

Tenekeci, Mehmet, (2017), **Katılım Bankacılığının Finansal İstikrara Etkisi: Türkiye Örneği**, (Doctoral Dissertation, Karatay University),

Retrieved from http://www.tkbb.org.tr/Documents/Yonetmelikler/Mehmet_Tenekeci.pdf (06.03.2019).

TKBB, Participation Banks Association of Turkey, (n. d.), http://www.tkbb.org.tr/Documents/Yonetmelikler/TKBB_2017_TR-Final.pdf (06.03.2019).

TKBB, Participation Banks Association of Turkey, (2015), "Participation Banking Strategy Document 2015–2025, Participation Banks Association of Turkey", www.tkbb.org.tr/Documents/Yonetmelikler/TKBB-Strateji-Belgesi.pdf (06.03.2019).

TRT Haber, (2014), "Türkiye nüfusunun %99.2'si Müslüman", https://www.trthaber.com/haber/yasam/turkiye-nufusunun-yuzde-992si-musluman-136243.html (06.03.2019).

Yanıkkaya, Halit, and Pabuçcu, Yaşar Uğur, (2017), "Causes and solutions for the stagnation of Islamic banking in Turkey", **ISRA International Journal of Islamic Finance**, Vol. 9, N. 1, pp. 43–61.

Yazıcı, Resül, (2016), "Finansal Krizlerin Önlenmesinde Katılım Bankacılığı Sisteminin Rolü Üzerine Bir Değerlendirme", **Sakarya Üniversitesi İktisat Dergisi**, Vol. 1, N. 1, pp. 59–82.

Yıldırım, Ismail, (2015), "Financial efficiency analysis in Islamic banks: Turkey and Malaysia models", **Journal of Economics Finance and Accounting**, Vol. 2, N. 3, pp. 289–300.

Selahattin Kaynak and Miraç Eren

Forecasting Turkish Manufacturing Industry's Sales Income and Export by Genetic Algorithm–Based Grey Model-GAGM (1, 1)

1 Introduction

In the economies of developed countries, manufacturing industry is the most important element of growth, productivity, exports, and technology transfer. In Turkey, the weight of the manufacturing sector in the economy has increased with the adoption of free market economy and has become a driving force of the Turkish economy.

Companies operating in the Turkish manufacturing industry show their presence in the status of public, private, and foreign capital in terms of capital ownership. However, state-owned firms have been constantly criticized for being behind the private sector in terms of efficiency and competition, and have mostly operated in areas such as energy, transportation, telecommunication, and infrastructure. It has always been argued that foreign-owned firms need to increase their weight in the economy because they accelerate economic growth; create production, employment, and competitive environment in developing country economies; and also provide the technology transfer and the opportunity to open up to foreign markets. The weight of domestic private firms in the Turkish economy has increased because of the adoption of the open market economy concept, the globalization of the economy, and privatization policies.

Knowing which firms in the Turkish manufacturing industry are or will be predominant in their sales income in terms of the ownership of the factors of production (especially capital ownership) is important for researchers, firm owners, and those who have the authority to make decisions. It is possible to predict and forecast of the total sales revenue shares of public-, foreign-, and private-owned firms through several models such as regression analysis, time series analysis, artificial neural network, semi-parametric, parametric, and non-parametric methods. However, in order to forecast the future sales of the firms operating in the Turkish manufacturing industry, since the use of the techniques mentioned in the literature requires a large number of observations, assumptions, and complex input factors; the grey prediction model which provides estimation with limited data set instead of traditional prediction models has been used in this study. Thus, the future sales revenues of different types of capital have been revealed.

In the Data Sets section, information about the data of each capital ownership type according to the total sales income of public-, private-, and foreign-owned firms in the Turkish manufacturing industry in terms of capital ownership between 1993 and 2014 is provided. In the Methodology section, titles describing the grey prediction procedure are included. In the Finding and Results section, estimates of the share of sales income of each capital ownership in the Turkish manufacturing industry have been obtained. In addition, future forecasts of total sales revenues were found. Under Conclusions, a number of proposals have been made for researchers, firm owners, and political decision-makers on behalf of which capital ownership type sales income is/will be weighted.

2 Data Sets

In the study, data set consists of the sales and export revenues of the largest 500 foreign-, private-, and public-owned firms operating in the Turkish manufacturing industry between 1993 and 2014. The obtained data are given in Tab. 1.

Along with the adoption of open foreign economic policies, in Turkish manufacturing industry, both the numbers and sale revenues of private- and foreign-owned firms have increased. In addition, along with the adoption of the liberal policy approach in the economy and the acceleration of privatization after 2004, the public sector has left its place to the private sector in many areas.

3 Methodology

3.1 Grey Prediction Model GM (1, N)

Assume that $X_1^{(0)} = \left\{ x_1^{(0)}(1), x_1^{(0)}(2), ..., x_1^{(0)}(n) \right\}$ is a sequence of data of a system's characteristics, $X_i^{(0)} = \left\{ x_i^{(0)}(1), x_i^{(0)}(2), ..., x_i^{(0)}(n) \right\}$ $i = 1, 2, ..., N$ sequences of relevant factors, $X_i^{(1)}$ the 1-AGO sequence of $X_i^{(0)}$, $i = 1, 2, ..., N$.

$$\frac{dX_1^{(1)}(t)}{dt} + a_1 X_1^{(1)}(t) = b_2 X_2^{(1)}(t) + b_3 X_3^{(1)}(t) + ... + b_N X_N^{(1)}(t)   \quad t = 1, 2, ..., n \tag{1}$$

is called as a whitenization equation of a GM (1, N) grey differential equation. The derivative $\frac{dX_1^{(1)}(t)}{dt}$ for the dependent variable is represented as

Tab. 1: Total Income Sales and Export of Capital Ownership Types

	Public		Private		Foreign	
	Revenue Sales (Million TL)	Export (Thousand Dolar)	Revenue Sales (Million TL)	Export (Thousand Dolar)	Revenue Sales (Million TL)	Export (Thousand Dolar)
1993	174.885.406	948.594	68.764.663	3.947.888	330.696.016	623.574
1994	349.758.343	978.822	116.713.513	5.894.643	618.901.998	821.081
1995	534.899.910	570.114	260.785.599	4.577.690	856.687.840	1.059.327
1996	1.012.772.980	774.836	504.354.894	7.046.169	2.452.916.381	1.480.535
1997	2.310.377.930	977.735	1.155.639.311	7.905.400	4.790.810.733	1.535.845
1998	3.536.645.104	853.999	2.057.576.416	7.978.637	7.904.649.954	1.961.806
1999	3.195.791.613	676.344	3.010.522.791	7.678.360	11.983.530.550	2.613.802
2000	6.588.356.573	880.103	4.998.346.414	8.008.901	19.023.606.264	2.768.782
2001	10.882.089.460	1.193.333	8.569.627.591	9.380.592	30.051.579.096	3.485.348
2002	12.450.598.962	784.930	13.614.457.880	11.166.224	45.609.237.026	4.406.495
2003	14.447.461.892	1.053.235	18.999.727.589	15.407.221	61.600.240.859	6.201.428
2004	16.757.765.786	1.205.735	25.949.950.581	21.724.079	83.697.267.855	9.019.668
2005	5.786.082.091	290.230	27.203.108.009	25.271.737	105.153.854.880	10.163.505
2006	6.306.512.702	456.391	36.359.309.192	29.288.519	126.983.688.220	12.662.840
2007	7.355.017.908	466.743	39.553.221.077	35.670.636	139.851.822.678	16.162.515
2008	5.375.583.979	48.153	40.218.878.909	48.487.660	173.917.520.636	15.678.211
2009	5.254.524.454	42.021	38.879.481.106	30.391.519	142.052.171.848	12.619.747
2010	5.881.512.079	48.134	42.586.017.800	35.270.067	178.003.585.511	14.012.531
2011	7.086.169.244	83.216	53.067.814.940	44.291.330	232.228.063.066	14.408.207
2012	7.387.937.383	883.951	55.323.051.965	44.463.528	258.592.759.742	14.158.170
2013	7.927.823.123	902.601	57.841.813.557	43.961.116	281.370.138.368	12.528.879
2014	8.475.577.962	948.170	71.410.318.978	37.324.287	305.796.052.232	13.041.420

$$\frac{dX_1^{(1)}(t)}{dt} = \lim_{h \to 0} \frac{X_1^{(1)}(t+h) - X_1^{(1)}(t)}{h}, \quad \forall t \geq 1 \tag{2}$$

Since the collected data is a time-series data, the sampling time interval between period t and $t+1$ is assumed to be one unit. Then, the derivative $\frac{dX_1^{(1)}(t)}{dt}$ can be approximated to an inverse accumulated generating operation (IAGO) variable $X_1^{(0)}(t)$ of the original dependent time series data as

$$\frac{dX_1^{(1)}(t)}{dt} \approx \frac{X_1^{(1)}(t+1) - X_1^{(1)}(t)}{1} = X_1^{(0)}(t), \quad \forall t \geq 1 \tag{3}$$

After the solution of grey differential equation, the obtained parameter values are placed into the whitening equation of the solution. Thus, the solution of the grey differential equation is given by

$$\hat{X}_1^{(1)}(t+1) = \left[x_1^{(1)}(0) - \frac{1}{\hat{a}_1} \sum_{k=2}^{N} \hat{b}_k X_i^{(1)}(t+1) \right] e^{-\hat{a}t} + \frac{1}{\hat{a}_1} \sum_{k=2}^{N} \hat{b}_k X_i^{(1)}(t+1), \quad where \quad x_1^{(1)}(0) = x_1^{(0)}(1)$$

$$(4)$$

When $N = 1$, then the solution of GM $(1, 1)$ is rewritten as

$$\hat{X}_1^{(1)}(t+1) = \left[x_1^{(1)}(0) - \frac{\hat{b}}{\hat{a}} \right] e^{-\hat{a}t} + \frac{\hat{b}}{\hat{a}}, \quad where \quad x_1^{(1)}(0) = x_1^{(0)}(1). \quad (5)$$

Thus, GM $(1, 1)$ is essentially a kind of exponential prediction model.

After the obtained parameter values are placed into the whitening equation of the solution, the predicted result $\hat{X}_1^{(0)}(t)$ from inverse accumulated generating operation by $\hat{X}_1^{(0)}(t+1) = \hat{X}_1^{(1)}(t+1) - \hat{X}_1^{(1)}(t)$ is obtained; and $\hat{X}_1^{(0)}(t)$ is the prediction result for the next observation.

The original grey model uses the least square method to estimate the coefficients. Furthermore, the use of this method requires a large number of data and good behavior of distribution data in order to estimate the parameters. However, when a grey forecasting model uses a limited sampled data (about four sample data), such estimates would result in a significant error. Particularly, for data with obvious fluctuation, the least square method used to estimate the coefficients will have a considerable error [1]. Therefore, both to improve mentioned shortcomings and to provide a better performance prediction, an improved multivariable grey forecasting models GAGM(1, N) solved by genetic algorithm approach with the global search and rapid convergence is more suitable to estimate the grey differential equation coefficients for both improving the relevant shortcomings and providing a better performance prediction.

3.2 Grey Model Estimation Procedure-Genetic Algorithm Grey Prediction Model, GAGM (1, N)

In order to solve the development coefficient "a_1" and grey input coefficients "$b_1, b_2, ..., b_N$", Genetic Algorithm (GA) is adopted to the GM $(1, N)$ model. GA uses crossover, reproduction, and mutation and evaluates the advantage of the model on each generation to produce a better target optimal solution [1]. The performance of solution of the problem is evaluated by a fitness function, which corresponds to the objective function of the optimization problem. The fitness

Tab. 2: Parameter Values of Model Solution

	Parameter values	
	b1	b2
GAGM(1,1)(log(Sales revenue))	-0.005	25.488
GAGM(1,1)(log(Export))	-0.005	17.116

function in this study is Mean Absolute Percentage Error (MAPE), which is defined as the minimum of in sample-average error, which is

$$min \quad MAPE = \frac{1}{N-1} \sum_{t=2}^{N} \left| \frac{X_1^{(0)}(t) - \hat{X}_1^{(0)}(t)}{X_1^{(0)}(t)} \right| \times 100 \tag{6}$$

subject to

$$\hat{X}_1^{(1)}(t+1) = \left[x_1^{(0)}(1) - \frac{1}{\hat{a}_1} \sum_{k=2}^{N} \hat{b}_k X_i^{(1)}(t+1) \right] e^{-\hat{a}_1 t} + \frac{1}{\hat{a}_1} \sum_{k=2}^{N} \hat{b}_k X_i^{(1)}(t+1), \quad \forall t = 1, 2, ..., N-1$$

$$\hat{X}_1^{(0)}(t+1) = \hat{X}_1^{(1)}(t+1) - \hat{X}_1^{(1)}(t) \quad \forall t = 1, 2, ..., N-1$$

4 Finding and Results

4.1 The Forecasting of the Total Sales and Export Revenues of Capital Ownership Types by GAGM (1,1) Procedure

Following the calculation of the proportional estimate of the sector transition structure via the QP-Markov model according to Turkey's total sales revenue and export, it benefited from the Genetic Algorithm Grey Prediction Model-GAGM(1,1) procedure for simulation and forecasting total amounts of Turkey's sales revenue and export. According to the procedure of GAGM (1, 1) model defined in Section 3.2 "Grey Model Estimation Procedure-Genetic Algorithm Grey Prediction Model," the parameters' values of the sequences data created for the total amount of Turkey's sales revenue and export are shown in Tab. 2.

The simulation and forecasting results according to the parameters' values results are provided in Tabs. 3 and 4.

Tab. 3: Simulation and Forecasting of Sales Revenue

	Years	Real Value of Sales Revenue	Simulative and Forecasting Values	Absolute Percentage Error (%)
Simulation	2005	138.143.044.980	142.128.867.414	2.885
	2006	169.649.510.114	161.650.106.508	4.715
	2007	186.760.061.663	183.962.910.340	1.498
	2008	219.511.983.524	209.523.135.041	4.550
	2009	186.186.177.408	238.754.102.642	28.234
	2010	226.471.115.390	272.280.875.238	20.228
	2011	292.382.047.250	310.670.903.268	6.255
	2012	321.303.749.090	354.757.395.555	10.412
	2013	347.139.775.048	405.343.219.208	16.767
	2014	385.681.949.172	463.466.526.334	20.168
MAPE (%)				**11.571**
Forecasting	2015		530.242.348.340	
	2016		607.063.964.170	
	2017		695.502.192.004	
	2018		797.382.240.590	
	2019		914.826.255.965	
	2020		1.050.198.174.596	

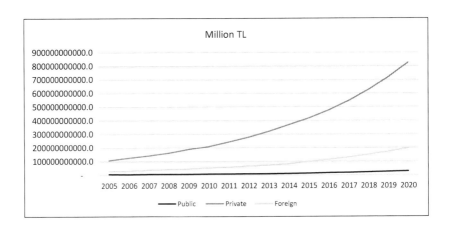

Tab. 4: Simulation and Forecasting of Export

	Years	Real Value of Export	Simulative and Forecasting Values	Absolute Percentage Error (%)
Simulation	2005	35.725.472	30.876.317	13.573
	2006	42.407.750	33.662.668	20.621
	2007	52.299.894	36.718.820	29.792
	2008	64.214.024	40.068.458	37.602
	2009	43.053.287	43.745.530	1.608
	2010	49.330.732	47.774.377	3.155
	2011	58.782.753	52.205.583	11.189
	2012	59.505.649	57.070.620	4.092
	2013	57.392.596	62.413.990	8.749
	2014	51.313.877	68.291.782	33.086
MAPE (%)				**16.347**
Forecasting	2015		74.753.007	
	2016		81.858.279	
	2017		89.692.705	
	2018		98.316.262	
	2019		107.812.051	
	2020		118.284.110	

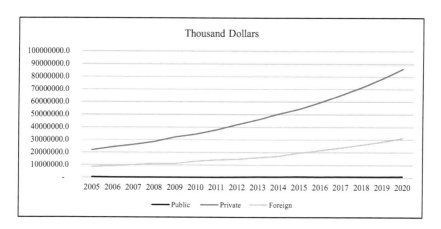

[2], interpreted the MAPE results as a convenient way to evaluate the accuracy of an estimate. According to this, MAPE value: If it is under 10%, it is a very accurate forecast, 10%–20% is a good estimate, 20%–50% is a reasonable estimate, and 50% is a wrong estimate. So the outcome is that the forecasting for the future of the findings will be healthy as well.

5 Conclusion

Forecasting of the economic data of firms operating in Turkish manufacturing sector is very important for firm managers and economic decision-makers in terms of the creation and effective implementation of policies. In addition, given the global economic problems and the ongoing political uncertainties in the region, analysis and accurate estimation of sales income and exports of firms are also important in determining new economic policies. In this study, grey estimation procedure was used to estimate the income and export amount of public, private, and foreign firms operating in Turkish manufacturing industry. According to the calculation results, this model shows that sales revenue and the export amount can be estimated.

According to the findings obtained, while the growth rate of foreign capital increases in terms of total exports in Turkish manufacturing industry, the growth rate of firms with private capital will decrease in terms of sales revenue. Growth rates of firms with public capital will decrease both in terms of export and sales revenue.

Bibliography

Hsu, L.-C. (2009). Forecasting the output of integrated circuit industry using genetic algorithm based multivariable grey optimization models. Expert Systems with Applications, 36(4), 7898–7903. doi: https://doi.org/10.1016/j.eswa.2008.11.004

Hsu, L.-C., & Wang, C.-H. (2009). Forecasting integrated circuit output using multivariate grey model and grey relational analysis. Expert Systems with Applications, 36(2), 1403–1409.

Lewis, C. D. (1982). *Industrial and business forecasting methods: A practical guide to exponential smoothing and curve fitting*. London: Butterworth-Heinemann.

Liu, S., & Forrest, J. Y. L. (2010). Grey systems: Theory and applications. Springer Science & Business Media.

Liu, S., & Yang, Y. (2017). Explanation of terms of grey forecasting models. Grey Systems: Theory and Application, 7(1), 123–128.

Wei, W., Yonghong, H., & Xin, D. (2007, 18–20 Nov. 2007). Application of grey system GM(1, N) model to predicting spring flow. Paper presented at the 2007 IEEE International Conference on Grey Systems and Intelligent Services.

Türkmen Taşer Akbaş and Bülent Arpat

The Relationship Between Demographic Variables and Work Safety Communication Attitudes of Managers: Example of Metal Industry in Denizli (Turkey)

1 Introduction

There are several risks that workers in the metal industry may be exposed to in terms of occupational health and safety (OHS). These risks in welding works; physical, chemical and ergonomic and social risks related to accidents (Karadağ, 2001: 30–31). In addition to these, ergonomics, technical and engineering methods and applications (Turan, 2015: 411–422, Eravcı and Taşçı, 2018) are needed to reduce these risks, as well as the contributions of disciplines such as medicine, law, education, communication, behavioural sciences and management sciences. Activities and practices related to the protection of employees from an occupational accident and health risks are among the duties and responsibilities of managers and the human resources management department at the workplace. One of the administrative tools to protect from OHS risks is the establishment of a safety climate in the workplaces and the development of a safety culture. Occupational safety attitudes of managers have a significant influence on the establishment of a safety climate in the workplaces and the development of a safety culture. Investigation of the attitude of safety communication, which is one of the dimensions of safety attitude, in the level of managers working in Denizli metal sector and related to demographic variables, may encourage many other types of research that contribute to organizational behaviour, management and organization and human resources management disciplines. Besides, this research may encourage several studies to provide practical contributions to the metal industry, enterprises and employees of the sector which historically played a role as much as the textile sector.

Purpose and Problem Statement of Research: The problem statement of this research: it has been established that there is a relationship between management safety talk and risk communication attitudes with employees and demographic variables of managers of metal sector enterprises. The study aims to explain the relationship between the safety communication aspects of the safety attitude: gender, marital status, education levels, the situation of experiencing work accident cases, age, managerial level, seniority as a manager and pre-managerial position.

Limitations of the Study: In this study, safety communication attitudes of the employees working in the managerial positions of Denizli province were analysed according to demographic factors. The nine dimensions of safety attitudes (Rundmo and Hale, 2003: 564–565), which are composed of a total of ten dimensions, are not included in the model of this study. Dimensions not included in the model of this study are: management safety commitment and involvement, fatalism concerning accident prevention, management attitudes towards rule violations, personal worry and emotion, powerlessness, priority of safety, mastery, hindrances and risk awareness.

2 Scope and Concepts of Research: OHS Communication Attitude

Today, organizational perception management aims to improve the interaction of managers with their internal and external environments. Most of the time, people are not evaluating facts according to their perceptions; in other words, according to how they perceive it, not according to reality itself. Organizational perception management ensures that the social responsibility and social sensitization activities of the organization are at the forefront of the organization while ensuring both the right work and doing the right work. It also requires effective management of all organizational and managerial activities. Safety communication is a useful tool for maintaining and protecting organizational reputation, organizational prestige and organizational attractiveness. In addition to maintaining the relationship between the organization and the environment in a healthy manner, it is imperative to communicate these relations and the prestige of organizational life (Tutar, 2008: 15). Within this framework, effective OHS communication within the organization is essential in terms of the fact that the managers have more real safety commitment.

It is possible to get people's time, muscle strength and physical presence on an hourly basis. However, employees' loyalty, commitment and ideas cannot be obtained through wages. The achievement of these can be possible with the success of the programs carried out within the organization. Within this framework, communication is a crucial tool in ensuring the participation of employees in work safety programs and the basis of social interaction in achieving these programs (Saari, 1998). People knowingly or unknowingly exchange information about their perceptions, thoughts, feelings, intentions and identities. They do this through direct contact, written or electronic means, words, expressions, gestures and signs (Hogg and Vaughan, 2005: 616). Relations in organizational structures are connections between people. An approach to analysing organizations, in terms of communication, defines organizations as information-processing systems (Roberts and O'Reilly, 1978: 283). Communication is the foundation of social interaction. If social systems are evaluated by organism metaphor, it can be said that communication has a function like vessels of an organism. Work safety communication: It is a phenomenon that has an impact on the occupational safety climate and safety culture and is associated with safety behaviours. Since communication is also negatively correlated (Tınaz, 2013: 46) with job stress, role conflict and role ambiguity, it can be said that OHS communication plays a crucial role in achieving the purpose of OHS practices and is an essential tool in preventing occupational accidents, occupational illnesses and work-related diseases.

Communication is the mutual transmission of signs and symbols. Communication is the process of creating meaning and sharing them mutually. Although people are now equipped with more information and communication technology, they are less interacting; and this is called the communication wall. The main purpose of communication is to create a behaviour change. Communication is a kind of mind orientation tool. The change in communication begins at the mental level first, then develops with belief and attitude and is then completed by behaviour. Communication in this direction is to create a material, emotional or intellectual change in the receiver. In terms of manager, it is aimed to make OHS communication, to have an opinion on OHS in receiver, to create an attitude in the receiver about OHS, to attract the attention of the receiver in OHS, to create a motivation in the receiver about OHS, to convince him about OHS and in this direction to conduct correct behaviours for OHS (Tutar, 2008: 30).

The behaviour of the manager who established the OHS communication can be explained by the situational theory of Grunig (1982). When people realize a problem, the higher their relationship with this problem and the more inadequate the information about how to behave, the more often they seek and process information. If a person is related to a particular situation, the motivation to communicate will increase as he will need the information to plan a behaviour related to the situation (Grunig, 1982: 168). The responsibilities of the executives are the management of OHS and are part of this management process. Management processes include responsibilities that cannot be left at the mercy of coincidences, chance or luck, uncontrolled development of situations, proactive interventions, planned activities and behaviours. For example, optimum coordination and cooperation between material and human resources, the personal authority of the manager, reaching the target through harmony, coherence and communication between the managers and the managed people, productivity, efficiency and profitability are among the features of management processes (Eren, 2003: 5–6). In terms of management process and communication, these explanations also clarify the basis of managers' communication attitudes within the context of OHS management. The relationship between OHS communication with occupational safety performance has been analysed in many studies of the literature.

It can be said that the effective OHS communication established between the managers and the employees has an essential role in achieving the OHS policies and objectives in the workplaces (e.g. in the development of safety climate, in the development of safety performance, in the development of safety behaviours) (Zohar and Polachek, 2014: 120; Alarcon et al., 2016; Kines et al., 2010; Li et al., 2015; Newnam et al., 2016; Törner, 2011; Tholen et al., 2013; Zin and Ismail, 2012; Fernando et al., 2008). The effects of several other factors, other than safety communication, such as *management, commitment to OHS, delegation of responsibilities in OHS practices, staff participation and engagement with staff empowerment, leading member interaction, perceived social support, safety perceptions and safety satisfaction*) are also investigated in literature (Cigularov et al., 2010: 1499; Hofmann and Morgeson, 1999; Mearns et al., 2003; Probst, 2004). OHS communication has a positive impact on employees' safety risks as well as the proactive perception of safety risks, and motivation to exhibit safety behaviours (Oah, Na & Moon, 2018: 428). OHS communication, the values of management, management and organizational practices are shown as essential components of the safety climate together with the participation of employees in health and safety activities; and it is stated that they have a reducing effect on accidents (Neal et al., 2000).

OHS communication has a crucial role for the establishment and maintenance of the safety culture as well as ensuring the continuity of OHS focus (Demirbilek, 2008: 5–6; Forest, 2012: 196–197; Kao et al., 2008: 146–150; Akalp and Yamankaradeniz, 2013: 108). The Safety Culture Policy of the United States Nuclear Regulatory Commission (www.nrc.gov, 2014) states that one of the elements of the positive safety culture is effective safety communication. Effective OHS communication consists of four elements, as described in this document: 1. All employees include OHS communication (complete, timely and frequently) to work activities (including between groups and shift changes). 2. Leaders report timely or justified reasons for operational and organizational decisions (encouraging them to ask questions about organizational change, resource allocation and more). 3. All employees voluntarily and openly communicate, provide information flow to all directions, supervisors and regulators within the organization (leaders must be honest, should not hinder feedback, listen with interest, follow all developments and share their evaluations with all employees). 4. Leaders continuously remind OHS of being one of the organization's top priorities (its relationship with strategies, its relevance to the operating budget, its relevance to human resources planning, its relevance to the reliability of the equipment, its relevance to business plans) and its expectations (www.nrc. gov, 2014).

OHS communication is a mutual conversation between managers and employees in terms of occupational safety, but the phenomenon of communication has a multi-faceted and layered structure that transcends verbal communication. OHS training and, the behaviours of managers in OHS issues (by identifying strategies and policies, exhibiting appropriate behaviours and being role models, awards and penalties, reporting and sharing of OHS-related incidents, accidents and near-miss incidents, exploration and analysis on accidents) are within the scope of OHS communication. Performing errors, performing OHS, OHS leadership practices, OHS training, etc. Many factors that play a role in the formation of safety climate and safety culture are strictly related to safety communication. One of these factors is the management commitment to job safety. According to Simard (1998), there is a relationship between employees' perceptions of senior management commitment to job safety and OHS motivation and safety behaviour. In other words, employees' safety behaviours may be affected by messages, symbols and values communicated in the organization (Brown et al., 2000: 447). Accordingly, a precursor of safety communication is the value and dedication that management assigns to job safety. The transfer of this value to the employees is ensured by safety communication. This relationship between the two variables was found in the study of Ocaktan (2009: 41). Effective communication positively affects the positive change in employees' perceptions of the organization and the nature of the safety culture and safety climate. The strong formation of OHS climate and culture in organizations is directly related to the effectiveness of safety communication (Şerifoğlu and Sungur, 2007: 47). They are the leading characteristics in organizations that have a positive safety culture: that the quality of communication is based on mutual trust, the perceptions shared by all members about the importance of occupational safety and the belief that preventive measures will be effective (Darby et al., 2005: 41). The effectiveness of safety communication is related to the direction and degree of the manager's attitude towards safety communication.

The importance of attitudes: Attitudes are a leading concept of behavioural sciences, as they provide a system that facilitates the adaptation of individuals to their environment, as well as a hidden power that directs the behaviour of individuals (Baysal and Tekarslan, 1996: 254). *Definitions of Attitude:* Highly organized, long-term feeling, belief and behavioural tendency is called attitude. These tendencies can be subject to: other people, groups, ideas, other regions or objects (Cüceloglu, 1997: 521). Other definitions of attitudes have also been made. For example, it is a tendency to react positively or negatively to any person, place or event (Kolasa, 1969: 431). Regarding one aspect of the individual's world (inner world), it is the process of enthusiasm and recognition depending on individual value judgements and beliefs (Eren, 2001: 173). It is a tendency that is attributed to an individual and regularly formed his thoughts, feelings and attitudes towards a psychological object (Kağıtçıbaşı, 1988: 84). The word "attitude", is derived from the Latin word "Optus" and means "suitable and ready for action" (South, 2009: 120).

Characteristics of Attitudes: a. Although beliefs both in terms of motivational and excitement are neutral, attitudes are either favourable (positive) or unfavourable (negative) (Krech and Crutchfield, 1980: 181). According to Güney (2009): b. Attitudes have a certain degree of strength. c. Attitudes have a certain degree of complexity. d. If there is consistency between physical, emotional and behavioural aspects, attitudes become stronger. e. As the number of attitudes in which an attitude is closely related, the probability of changing that attitude decreases.

Functions of Attitudes: According to Güney (2009), attitudes have some functions in terms of individuals. *These are:* a. Attitudes play a role in increasing the likelihood of individuals experiencing positive experiences, reducing negative experiences (energy saving). For example, managers ensure that OHS communication attitudes reduce occupational accidents and near-miss incidents. b. Attitudes are beneficial to people. For example, the OHS communication attitude of the managers causes the manager to prevent specific risks and to learn information that prevents them from experiencing specific problems. c. Attitudes have a function to ensure the harmony of the individual and culture and to be compatible with the individual with the social system. For example, managers with OHS communication attitudes can contribute to the formation of climate and culture of OHS, develop their organizations, making them more effective, healthy and resilient. In this respect, they can improve the compatibility of both themselves and their employees with the internal and external environment and systems. d. Attitudes have the function of protecting and explaining a person's self (self-esteem). For example, managers can make more accurate decisions through OHS communication attitudes, and they can achieve progress in their professional careers, gain the opportunity to be appreciated, develop their feelings of professional satisfaction and thus strengthen their defence mechanisms and develop their self. e. Attitudes have the function of providing information. For example; managers who have a positive attitudes towards occupational health and safety communication acquire both new information and reinforce their existing knowledge (management and leadership roles, communication, OHS management, OHS culture and climate, risk management, etc.) If the OHS attitudes of the manager are positive and high, the manager will feel a need to have more information about OHS, will increase their perceptions about OHS and will provide the basis for other attitudes related to safety communication. In terms of their duties and responsibilities, managers overcoming complex and challenging roles can use these attitudes.

The Elements of the Attitudes: The attitude of the managers on OHS communication can be explained in terms of three components (Cognitive, Emotional and Behavioural) (Kağıtçıbaşı, 1988: 84): 1. *Cognitive (opinion) dimension:* The fact that the managers of metalworks think that OHS communication is beneficial in reducing the work accidents and near-miss cases show that the manager's cognitive attitude is positive. The fact that he thinks that he is useless indicates that the manager's safety communication attitude is negative. 2. *Emotional dimension:* If the business managers of the metal sector enjoy safety communication, especially if safety communication makes the manager happy, this shows that the manager's safety communication attitude is positive. If the manager does not like safety communication, safety communication makes him feel bad; this indicates that the manager's safety communication attitude is negative. 3. *Behavioural dimension:* Managers in metal industry have switched to OHS, while continuing and repeating at certain times; and if they suggest lower level managers, top-level managers and other managers at the same level as them to switch to safety communication and encourage and also stimulate them on this basis, this indicates that the manager's safety communication attitude is positive. If the administrator does not establish, maintain or repeat safety communication, he/she advises others not to establish this communication, and if he/she discourages such communication, this indicates that the manager's attitude towards safety communication is negative.

Safety communication is a reflection of leadership processes. It can be foreseen that the leaders who use a flexible and rational approach to the three approaches (soft, rational and hard) used by the leader in the process of influencing their subordinates have more safety communication. The leaders who prefer to influence with a soft approach, emphasize the commitment of subordinates as well as the relationship between value systems and organizational goals while emphasizing the importance of new tasks, responsibilities and practices by using participatory decision-making and emotional language in the context of safety communication. Also, the flexible approach builds friendly relations with its subordinates, enhancing their integration and sensitivity to the leader's warnings and directives. Leaders who adopt a rational approach use strong language in safety communications. The effectiveness of safety communication will focus on the mutual benefits for the employee to do what is required under OHS. Leaders who adopt a rational approach to influence establish an OHS communication, which focuses on making an impact in favour of a reasonable one, rather than an employee's value system, on rational grounds (Clarke and Ward, 2006: 1176). Businesses with high OHS performance are not one-way communication channels in the process of solving problems related to work safety, but enterprises using bidirectional communication channels (Hale et al., 2010: 1033).

3 The Relationship of OHS Communication Attitude of the Managers with Demographic Factors

In the light of the propositions of Grunig (1982) in his theoretical work on communication behaviour, it can be said that the high level of awareness of the managers about the problems related to OHS is higher than the attitude and behaviour of safety communication. The effects of risk perceptions on attitudes and behaviours are included in several research models in the literature (Wu et al., 2017: 2). According to the suggestion of Grunig (1982), it is hypothesized that the top managers who consider themselves more responsible for the resolution of OHS problems are looking for more information than lower-level managers and therefore they have more safety communication attitude. In other words, assuming that higher level managers' awareness of OHS problems will be higher than lower level managers and they will consider themselves more responsible for solving the problems, it is hypothesized that OHS communication attitudes are higher. Another theoretical basis for the establishment of this hypothesis is that it is suggested that those with higher status (more knowledgeable) will have more communication than those with lower status (less knowledgeable) (Roberts and O'Reilly, 1979: 45). The executives are aware that they now manage a culture (Çağlar, 2013: 421). In this respect, safety communication, which is one of the necessary tools of creating and managing the safety climate and culture, is primarily and mostly the responsibility of the top managers; and this responsibility is a matter that the top managers are aware of.

Also, based on the assumption that the level of awareness of the managers of the older age group about the problems related to OHS and their level of individual responsibility will be higher than the younger age group, the hypothesis that they would show more frequent/more intense safety communication attitudes and behaviours, the safety communication attitudes would be relatively higher is established. Assuming that as the level of education increases, awareness of OHS will also increase, the hypothesis that the level of safety communication attitudes of the managers will be different according to the level of education is formed. As the level of awareness of the managers who had previously experienced work accidents and near-misses were higher, the hypothesis was created that they would exhibit a higher level of safety communication attitude than those who did not.

According to Grunig (1982) based on the suggestion that the higher the level of people seeing themselves as part of the processes, communication attitudes and behaviours will rise as well, it can be assumed that the levels of seeing themselves as a part of the process are higher than others for who are married executives, managers with higher education level, managers having previously experienced occupational accident cases, managers of middle age and above, senior executives, managers with higher working time, who have more working time in the sector than management it can be assumed that the levels of seeing themselves as a part of the process are higher than others. Accordingly, hypotheses have been developed that the level of safety communication attitudes of the managers with demographic characteristics is higher than the others.

The hypothesis of the study: H_1: The average safety communication attitudes of managers is statistically significantly different according to their gender. H_2: The average of employees' safety communication attitudes varies according to their marital status. H_3: The average of the safety communication attitudes of the managers is statistically significantly different according to their education level. H_4: Average of employees' safety communication attitudes is statistically significantly different compared to the cases of encountering work accident before. H_5: The average of managers' safety communication attitudes varies according to their age levels. H_6: The average of the managers' safety communication attitudes is statistically different compared to the managerial levels. H_7: The average of the managers' safety communication attitudes varies according to the working time in the managerial position. H_8: The average of the managers' safety communication attitudes differs according to the period of a non-executive career in the sector.

4 Method

In this study, relational screening model was preferred.

Population and Sample: In this research, managers working in the metal industry of Denizli Province constitute the working population of the study.

The sample of the study was formed by convenience sampling technique. In total, valid data from 226 executives were used in the analysis of this research.

Data Collection Tools: In this study, safety communication attitude dimension includes an analysis of the data collected using two of five items measuring the attitude of safety communication, which is included in the scale of ten-dimensional safety attitudes developed by Rundmo and Hale (2003). In this study, Likert's scale was used for the measurement of the occupational safety attitudes of the managers (1: I completely disagree, 2: I disagree, 3: I partially agree/partially disagree, 4: Agree, 5: I completely agree).

Analyses: In this research, descriptive statistics, t-test and ANOVA analyses were employed. Research, operating in the metal industry in the city of Denizli in Turkey was conducted with 226 managers. Firstly, descriptive statistical results regarding the participants' attitudes towards safety communication were reported. Then descriptive statistics on demographic variables of the sample were presented. The t-test analysis was conducted to determine the relationship between the gender of managers, the incidents of occupational accident incident and safety communication attitude. ANOVA analyses were conducted to determine the relationships between the education level of the managers and the managerial level and the attitude of safety communication.

According to the frequency table related to the demographic characteristics of the participants (Tab. 1), 87% of the managers are males, 73% are married, 40% of the age range 31–40, 67% of the undergraduate level and overtrained, 41% lower level and 20% upper-level managers and 54% of the participants are those who have never experienced a work accident.

The mean of the managers' safety communication attitudes was measured as 3,825; and the standard deviation was measured as 0,829 as shown in Tab. 2.

According to this result, it can be said that the average of the managers' OHS communication attitudes is high. In other words, the average level of managers' safety communication attitudes is not very high ("absolutely agree") or in intermediate level ("partly agree"), between 3,41 and 4,20 ("I agree").

The relationship between the gender of managers and work safety communication was analysed with the Independent Samples t-test, and according to the results H_1 was not supported. According to the results shown in Tab. 3, there was no statistically significant difference between the gender of managers and safety communication attitudes (p=0,075>0,05). According to this, there was no relationship between the gender of managers and the level of attitude of safety communication. In the study conducted by Ocaktan (2009: 43) with 710 managers and employees in an automotive factory, no significant difference was found in terms of safety communication in terms of gender.

Tab. 1: Frequencies Regarding Demographic Variables of Managers

Education Level	Frequency	%	Management Level	Frequency	%
Primary-Secondary-High School	55	24,3	Low	93	41,2
Bachelor's Degree and Higher	151	66,9	Middle	84	37,1
Unanswered	20	8,8	Top	45	20
Gender			Unanswered	4	1,7
Male	197	87,2	Encountering Work Accident		
Female	27	11,9	Yes	98	43,4
Unanswered	2	0,9	No	122	54
Age Level			Unanswered	6	2,6
18–30	68	30	Marital status		
31–40	90	40	Married	165	73
41–50	52	23	Single	53	23,5
51 and older	12	5,3	Unanswered	8	3,5
Unanswered	4	1,7			

Tab. 2: Descriptive Statistics of Managers on Measurement of OHS Communication Attitude

	N	Range	Min.	Max.	$\bar{x}$	SD
Manager's OHS Communication Attitude	226	4	1	5	3,825	0,829

Tab. 3: Relationship of Gender and Occupational Safety Communication Attitude

Gender	N	$\bar{x}$	SD	t	df	p
Male	196	3,8597	0,81773	1,786	221	0,075
Female	27	3,5556	0,91287			

The relationship between the marital status of the managers and safety communication was analysed by Independent Samples t-test, and H_2 was not supported. According to the results shown in Tab. 4, there was no statistically significant difference between the gender of managers and safety communication (p=0,343>0,05). According to this, there is no relationship between the

Tab. 4: Relationship Between Marital Status of Managers and Occupational Safety Communication Attitude

Marital Status	N	$\bar{x}$	SD	t	df	p
Married	165	3,8606	0,79746	0,949	216	0,343
Single	53	3,7358	0,93338			

Tab. 5: The Relationship Between Managers' Educational Status and Work Safety Communication Attitude

Educational Status	N	$\bar{x}$	SD	t	df	p
High School and lower	55	3,8818	0,83867	0,919	204	0,359
Bachelor's and higher degrees	151	3,7616	0,82832			

Tab. 6: Relationship Between Experiencing Occupational Accident and Occupational Safety Communication Attitude

Experiencing an Occupational Accident	N	$\bar{x}$	SD	t	df	p
No	122	3,7748	0,77700	-1,349	218	0,179
Yes	98	3,9235	0,85661			

marital status of the managers and the levels of the attitude of occupational safety communication. In a study carried out by Ocaktan in an automotive factory with 710 managers and employees (2009: 45), safety communications of singles are significantly higher than married people.

The relationship between the education status of the managers and the safety communication was analysed with the Independent Samples t-test, and H_3 was not supported. According to the results shown in Tab. 5, there was no statistically significant difference between the education level of managers and safety communication attitudes (p=0,359>0,05). According to this, there was no relationship between the education level of the managers and the attitude of safety communication. In a study carried out by Ocaktan in an automotive factory with 710 managers and employees (2009: 44), no significant relationship was found between education and occupational safety communication.

The relationship between experiencing work accident and safety communication attitude was analysed with the Independent Samples t-test, and H_4 was

Tab. 7: Relationship Between Age of Managers and Occupational Safety Communication Attitude

Descriptive Age	$\bar{x}$	Levene p	The Source of variance	Sum of Squares	df	Mean Square	F	p	Post-Hoc (Tamhane Test)
18–30	3,7313	0,032	Between Groups	4,745	2	2,373	3,676	0,027	18–30 and 41 and older
31–40	3,7611		Within Groups	140,712	218	0,645			(p=0,043) 31–40 and
41 and older	4,0703		Total	145,457	220	-			41 and older (p=0,033)

not supported. According to the results shown in Tab. 6, there was no statistically significant difference between work accident and safety communication of managers (p=0,179>0,05). According to this, managers experiencing occupational accident incidents do not have an impact on the attitude of safety communication.

The relationship between the age of managers and safety communication attitude was analysed by ANOVA, and H_5 was supported. According to the results shown in Tab. 7, there was a statistically significant relationship between the age of managers and safety communication (p=0,027<0,05). In order to determine the differentiated groups of safety communication, the Tamhane method was used from Post Hoc tests. According to the Tamhane test results, the difference is between 41 and over age groups and other age groups (18–30 and 31–40 years). According to this, there is an increase in the safety communication attitude as the managers' age. In other words, it can be said that there is a positive relationship between age and safety communication attitude. In this context, it is possible to say that 41 and over age group made a higher contribution to the development of safety climate and safety culture in comparison with other age groups. In a study carried out by Ocaktan in an automotive factory with 710 managers and employees (2009: 43), no significant difference was found between age groups in terms of safety communication. This result is different from the findings of Ocaktan (2009) in terms of age and safety communication attitudes.

The relationship between management level and safety communication was analysed by ANOVA method, and H_6 was supported. According to Tab. 8, there was a statistically significant relationship between the managerial level of the manager and safety communication (p=0,010<0,05). The Tamhane method was used in the Post Hoc tests to determine the groups in which safety communication was differentiated. According to the Tamhane test results, the difference is among

Tab. 8: The Relationship Between Managers' Position and Occupational Safety Communication Attitude

Descriptive Management Level	$\bar{x}$	Levene p	The Source of Variance	Sum of Squares	df	Mean Square	F	p	Post-Hoc (Tamhane Test)
Low	3,74	0,019	Between Groups	6,280	2	3,140	4,741	0,010	Top-Middle (p=0,008)
Middle	3,75		Within Groups	145,053	219	0,662			Top-Middle (p=0,002)
Top	4,16		Total	151,333	221	-			

Tab. 9: Relationship Between Managerial Tenure and Safety Communication Attitude

Descriptive Managerial Tenure	$\bar{x}$	Levene p	The Source of Variance	Sum of Squares	df	Mean Square	F	p
1 year	3,7353	0,614	Between Groups	2,942	3	0,981	1,558	0,201
2–10 years	3,8542		Within Groups	124,413	196	0,630		
11–20 years	4,0278		Total	126,355	199	-		
21 years and over	4,25							

the top management and other management groups. Accordingly, it is clear that top management has a more favourable opinion of safety communication and higher safety communication performance. In this context, it is possible for the upper management group to make a higher contribution than other managerial levels in the development of safety communication and related safety climate and safety culture. In a survey conducted by Ocaktan in an automotive factory with 710 managers and employees (2009: 46), it was reported that managers, experts, engineers and technicians had a higher level of safety communication than other employees. With the finding of this study, the finding of Ocaktan (2009) has the same results in terms of the relationship between managerial level and level of safety communication attitude.

The relationship between the managerial tenure and safety communication was analysed by ANOVA, and H_7 was not supported. According to the results shown in Tab. 9, there was no statistically significant relationship between the tenure of managerial position and safety communication (p=0,201>0,05).

Tab. 10: The Relationship Between Total Tenure in the Sector and Safety Communication Attitude

Descriptive		Levene	The Source of Variance	Sum of Squares	df	Mean Square	F	p	Post-Hoc (Bonferroni Test)
Total Tenure	$\bar{x}$	p							
1 year	3,58	0,279	Between Groups	5,420	2	2,185	4,20	0,016	1 year and 11 years and over (p=0,054)
2–10 years	3,7424		Within Groups	140,011	217	0,643			2–10 years and 11 years and over (p=0,062)
11 years and over	4,0104		Total	145,432	219	-			

Accordingly, the periods in the management position do not affect the attitude of safety communication.

According to the results analysed by the ANOVA on the relationship between the manager's total tenure including the time spent in the sector and safety communication attitude, H_8 was supported. According to the results shown in Tab. 10, there was a statistically significant relationship between the manager's total tenure and safety communication attitude (p=0,016<0,05). For the determination of the groups in which the different types of safety communication differed, the Bonferroni method was used from Post Hoc tests. According to the Bonferroni test results, the difference is between 11 years of total tenure and other groups. According to this, it is seen that those who have total tenure for more than 11 years have a more favourable safety communication attitude than the ones who have a total tenure of 10 years; and their safety communication attitudes are higher. In this context, it can be said that managers having 11 years and over total tenure will be more likely to contribute to the development of safety climate and culture than the other groups.

5 Conclusion

Our findings on the existence of the relationship between the level of tenure in the metal sector and the level of tenure before the management career in the metal sector and the safety communication attitudes can be explained with the theoretical perspective based on Grunig (1982). Considering the principle *"The person who does the job knows the best"*, it can be assumed that managers who have working experiences in the sector other than managerial career consider themselves more related to business processes, have more participation in business processes and have more information about business processes. In other words, it can be said that the managers who have working experiences in the sector before and after managerial position have higher awareness and more sensitivity to the dangers and risks. For these reasons, it can be said that the safety communication attitudes in the upper-level managers of the enterprises in the metal sector are higher than those of the lower level managers.

Again, in the same direction, the finding of the relationship between the age of managers and the safety communication attitude can be explained with this perspective. It can be said that this situation positively affects the communication attitudes of the employees with the employees regarding OHS, such as eliminating an obstacle for empathy. According to the findings of the study, the high level of management within the organizational hierarchy and the existence of a positive relationship between the safety communication attitude and the communication intentions were explained based on the theoretical background presented by Grunig (1982). It was observed that there was no relation between education level, marital status, gender, occupational accident incidents, management seniority variables and OHS communication attitude. In males, those with higher educational status, with more working time as managers, who are married and have previously encountered occupational accidents; assuming that the level of tendency to see themselves as a part of OHS processes would be higher, we hypothesized that the managers of these groups would have higher OHS communication attitudes. However, in terms of these demographic characteristics, the OHS communication attitudes of the managers did not differ from the level of OHS communication attitudes of the other groups.

Recommendations for implementation: 1. In promotions to executive positions, it can be considered as one of the preference criteria of the personnel who had previously worked in the sector at the operational level. 2. In the appointments to be made to the executive positions, the effect of higher age personnel on positive safety communication can be considered. 3. The teamwork related to the OHS can be used as the team leader from the first supervisors and mid-level managers who were working at the operational level in the sector and at an older age. 4. Ensuring the participation of employees in safety activities from the first- and middle-level managers who have operational experience at a more advanced age and in the sector can be used effectively. 5. In order to design and implement bidirectional communication of OHS, not one-way, necessary arrangements or changes can be made.

Suggestions for Researchers: Due to the relationship between the formation of safety culture in organizations and also safety climate improvement and safety communication in the organization, it can be suggested that the in-house communication processes and forms in metal industry business organizations should be explained more extensively, and the relationships should be analysed in depth with the help of some theoretical models to be developed. In future research, it can be suggested to conduct an extensive and comprehensive analysis of safety culture in metal sector enterprises, in terms of safety communication, and to make descriptive researches on the question of what kind of processes safety culture is formed in organizations by establishing organizational safety communication. These studies can also contribute to the development of a management model in Turkish culture.

Bibliography

Akalp, Gizem & Yamankaradeniz, Nurettin, (2013), "İşletmelerde Güvenlik Kültürünün Oluşumunda Yönetimin Rolü ve Önemi", **Sosyal Güvenlik Dergisi**, Vol. 3, N. 2, pp. 96–109.

Alarcon, Luis, F., Acuna, Diego, Diethelm, Sven & Pellicer, Eugenio, (2016), "Strategies for Improving Safety Performance in Construction Firms", **Accident Analysis and Prevention**, Vol. 94, September, pp. 107–118.

Baysal, A., Can & Tekarslan, Erdal, (1996), **İşletmeciler İçin Davranış Bilimleri**, 2. Basım, Avcıol Basım Yayın, İstanbul.

Brown, Karen, A., Willis, P. Geoffrey & Prussia, Gregory, E., (2000), "Predicting Safe Employee Behavior in the Steel Industry: Development and Test of a Sociotechnical Model", **Journal of Operations Management**, Vol. 18, N. 4, pp. 445–465.

Cigularov, Konstantin, P., Chen, Peter, Y. & Rosecrance, John, (2010), "The Effects of Error Management Climate and Safety Communication on Safety: A Multi-level Study", **Accident Analysis and Prevention**, Vol. 42, N. 5, pp. 1498–1506.

Clarke, Sharon & Ward, Katie, (2006), "The Role of Leader Influence Tactics and Safety Climate in Engaging Employees' Safety Participation", **Risk Analysis**, Vol. 26, N. 5, pp. 1175–1185.

Cüceloğlu, Doğan, (1997), **İnsan ve Davranışı**, 7. Basım, Remzi Kitabevi, İstanbul.

Çağlar, İrfan, (2013), **Küresel Normlu Çağdaş Değişim Yönetimi Aracı Olarak Örgüt Geliştirme**, 1. Basım, Nobel Akademik Yayıncılık Eğitim ve Danışmanlık Tic. Ltd. Şti., Ankara.

Darby-Farrington, Trudi, Pickup, Laura & Wilson, John, R., (2005), "Safety Culture in Railway Maintenance", **Safety Science**, Vol. 43, N. 1, pp. 39–60.

Demirbilek, Tunç, (2008), "İşletmelerde İş Güvenliği Kültürünün Geliştirilmesi", **Çalışma Ortamı**, Ocak-Şubat, Vol. 96, N. 2, pp. 5–7.

Eravcı Deniz, B. & Taşçı, Serhat, (2018), **Kaynak İşlerinde İş Sağlığı ve Güvenliği**, ÇASGEM (Çalışma ve Sosyal Güvenlik Eğitim Araştırma Merkezi), T.C. Aile, Çalışma ve Sosyal Hizmetler Bakanlığı, Ankara, Retrived from: http://www.casgem.gov.tr/dosyalar/yayinlar/834/dosya-834-936.pdf, (03.04.2019).

Eren, Erol, (2001), **Örgütsel Davranış ve Yönetim Psikolojisi**, 7. Basım, Beta Basım Yayım Dağıtım A.Ş., İstanbul.

Eren, Erol, (2003), **Yönetim ve Organizasyon**, 6. Basım, Beta Basım Yayım Dağıtım A.Ş., İstanbul.

Fernando, Yudi, Zailani, Suhaiza & Janbi, Luang, (2008), "The Determinant Factors of safety compliance At Petrochemical Processing Area: Moderator Effects of Employees Experience and Engineering Background", **Proceedings of the 9th Asia Pacific Industrial Engineering & Management Systems Conference (APIEMS)**, Proceeding Book, pp. 1442–1452, Bali, Indonesia. https://www.academia.edu/214013/The_Determinant_Factors_of_Safety_Compliance_at_Petrochemical_Processing_Area_Moderator_Effects_of_Employees_Experience_and_Engineering_Background

Forest, Jerry, J. (2012), "How to Evaluate Process Safety Culture", **Process Safety Progress** (American Institute of Chemical Engineers), Vol. 31, N. 2, pp. 195–197.

Grunig, James, E., (1982), "The Message-Attitude-Behavior Relationship: Communication Behaviors of Organizations", **Communication Research**, Vol. 9, N. 2, pp. 163–200.

Güney, Salih, (2009), **Sosyal Psikoloji**, 1. Basım, Nobel Yayın Dağıtım Tic. Ltd. Şti., Ankara.

Hale, Andrew, R., Guldenmund, Frank, W., Loenhout, P. L. C. H. & Oh, Joy, I. H., (2010), "Evaluating Safety Management and Culture Interventions to Improve Safety: Effective Intervention Strategies", **Safety Science**, Vol. 48, N. 8, pp. 1026–1035.

Hofmann, David, A. & Morgeson, Frederick, P., (1999), "Safety-Related Behaviour as a Social Exchange: The Role of Perceived Organizational Support and Leader-Member Exchange", **Journal of Applied Psychology**, Vol. 84, N. 2, pp. 286–296.

Hogg, Michael, A. & Vaughan, Graham, M., (2007), **Sosyal Psikoloji**, (İbrahim Yıldız, Aydın Gelmez, Trans.), 1. Basım, Ütopya Yayınevi, Ankara.

Kağıtçıbaşı, Çiğdem, (1988), "İnsan ve İnsanlar - Sosyal Psikolojiye Giriş", 7. Basım, Evrim Basım Yayım Dağıtım, İstanbul.

Kao, Chen-Shan, Lai, Wei, H., Chuang, Tien, F. & Lee, Jin-Chuan, (2008), "Safety Culture Factors, Differences, and Risk Perception in Five Petrochemical Plants", **Process Safety Progress** (American Institute of Chemical Engineers), Vol. 27, N. 2, pp. 145–152.

Karadağ, Kaan, (2001), "Kaynak İşlerinde İş Sağlığı ve Güvenliği", **Türk Tabipler Birliği, Mesleki Sağlık ve Güvenlik Dergisi**, Ekim, pp. 27–32. Ankara. Retrieved from: www.ttb.org.tr/dergi/index.php/msg/article/download/283/263, (03.04.2019).

Kines, Pete, Andersen, Lars, P. S., Spangenberg, Soren, Mikkelsen, Kim, L., Dyreborg, Johnny & Zohar, Dov, (2010), "Improving Construction Site Safety through Leader-Based Verbal Safety Communication", **Journal of Safety Research**, Vol. 41, N. 5, pp. 399–406.

Kolasa, Blair, J., (1969), **İşletmeler İçin Davranış Bilimlerine Giriş**, (K. Tosun, F. Aykar, T. Somay, M. Menteşe, Trans.) İstanbul Üniversitesi İşletme Fakültesi, Davranış Bilimleri Enstitüsü Yayınları: 1, Fatih Yayınevi, İstanbul.

Krech, David & Crutchfield, Richard, S., (1980), **Sosyal Psikoloji - Teori ve Problemler**, (Erol Güngör, Trans.), 3. Basım, Ötüken Neşriyat A.Ş., İstanbul.

Li, Heng, Lu, Miaojia, Hsu, Shu-Chien., Gray, Matthew & Huang, Ting, (2015), "Proactive Behavior-Based Safety Management Construction Safety Improvement", **Safety Science**, Vol. 75, June, pp. 107–117.

Mearns, Kathryn, Whitaker, Sean, M. & Flin, Rhona, (2003), "Safety Climate, Safety Management Practice and Safety Performance in Offshore Environments", **Safety Science**, Vol. 41, N. 8, pp. 641–680.

Neal, Andrew, Griffin, Mark, A. & Hart, Peter, M., (2000), "The Imact of Organizational Climate on Safety Climate and Individual Behaviour", **Safety Science**, Vol. 34, N. 1-3, pp. 99–109.

Newnam, Sharon, Goode, Natassia, Griffin, Mark & Foran, Cerdiwen, (2016), **Redefining Safety Communication in the Workplace: An Observational Study**, Monash University Accident Research Centre, ISCRR Institute for Safety, Compensation and Recovery Research, Research Report, Melbourne. Retrieved from: https://research.iscrr.com.au/__data/assets/pdf_file/0006/497706/defining-safety-communication-in-workplace.pdf, (03.04.2019).

Oah, Shezeen, Na, Rudia & Moon, Kwnagsu, (2018), "The Influence of Safety Climate, Safety Leadership, Workload, and Accident Experience on Risk Perception: A Study of Korean Manufacturing Workers", **Safety and Health at Work**, Vol. 9, N. 4, pp. 427–433.

Ocaktan, Mine, E., (2009), **Bir Otomotiv Fabrikasında Güvenlik Kültürünün Değerlendirilmesi**, Unpublished Doctoral Dissertation, Ankara Üniversitesi, Sağlık Bilimleri Enstitüsü, Ankara.

Probst, Tahira, M., (2003), "Development and Validation of the Job Safety Index and the Job Safety Satisfaction Scale: A Classical Test Theory and IRT Approach", **Journal of Occupational and Organizational Psychology**, Vol. 76, N. 4, pp. 451–467.

Roberts, Karlene, H. & O'Reilly III, Charles, A., (1978), "Organizations as Communication Structures: An empirical Approach", **Human Communication Research**, Vol. 4, N. 4, pp. 283–293.

Roberts, Karlene, H. & O'Reilly III, Charles, A., (1979), "Some Correlations of Communication Roles in Organizations", **The Academy of Management Journal**, Vol. 22, N. 1, pp. 42–57.

Rundmo, Torbjorn & Hale, Andrew, R., (2003), "Managers' Attitudes Towards Safety Accident Prevention", **Safety Science**, Vol. 41, N. 7, pp. 557–574.

Saari, Jorma, (1998), "Participatory Workplace Improvement Process", (Safety Policy and Leadership, 11. Chapter, Eds. Jorma Saari), **Encyclopedia of Occupational Health and Safety**, 4th Edition, ILO, Geneva.

Sawacha, Edwin, Noum, Shamil & Fong, Daniel, (1999), "Factors Affecting Safety Performance on Construction Sites", **International Journal of Project Management**, Vol. 17, N. 5, pp. 309–315.

Simard, Marcel, (1998), "Safety Culture and Management", (Safety Policy and Leadership, 4. Chapter, Eds. Jorma Saari), **Encyclopedia of Occupational Health and Safety**, 4th Edition, ILO, Geneva.

Şerifoğlu, Ulus, K. & Sungur, Elif, (2007), "İşletmelerde Sağlık ve Güvenlik Kültürünün Oluşturulması; Tepe Yönetiminin Rolü ve Kurum İçi İletişim Olanaklarının Kullanımı", **Yönetim**, Vol. 18, N. 58, pp. 41–50.

Tholen, Susanna, L., Anders, Pousette & Törner, Marianne, (2013), "Casual Relations Between Psychological Conditions, Safety Climate and Safety Behavior – A Multi-Level Investigation", **Safety Science**, Vol. 55, June, pp. 62–69.

Tınaz, Pınar, (2013), **Çalışma Yaşamında Örnek Olaylar**, 3. Baskı, Beta Yayınları, İstanbul.

Törner, Marianne, (2011). "The 'Social-Psychology' of Safety An Integrative Approach to Understanding Organizational Psychological Mechanisms Behind Safety Performance", **Safety Science**, Vol. 49, N. 8–9, pp. 1262–1269.

Turan, Ali, (2015), **Kaynak İşlerinde İş Güvenliği**, Kaynak Kongresi, IX. Ulusal Kongre ve Sergisi Bildiriler Kitabı, pp. 411–422. Retrived from: http://www1.mmo.org.tr/resimler/dosya_ekler/d44b9844b46e595_ek.pdf?tipi&turu&sube, (03.04.2019).

Tutar, Hasan, (2008), **Simetrik ve Asimetrik İletişim Bağlamında Örgütsel Algılama Yönetimi**, Birinci Basım, Seçkin Yayıncılık San. ve Tic. A.Ş., Ankara.

USNRC. (2014), **Effective Safety Communication**, Safety Culture Trait Talk, U.S. Nuclear Regulatory Commission, December, 6, pp. 1–4. Maryland. Retrived from: www.nrc.gov/docs/ML1500/ML15007A238.pdf, (11.03.2019).

Wachter, Jan, K. & Yorio, Patrick, L., (2014), "A System of Safety Management Practices and Worker Engagement for Reducing and Preventing Accidents: An Empirical and Theoretical Investigation", **Accident Analysis and Prevention**, Vol. 68, July, pp. 117–130.

Wu, Tungju, Wu, Yenchun, J., Tsai, Hsientang & Li, Yibin, (2017), "Top Management Teams' Characteristics and Strategic Decision-Making: A Mediation of Risk Perceptions and Mental Models", **Sustainability**, Vol. 9, N. 12, pp. 1–15.

Zhou, Zhipeng, Goh, Yang, M. & Li, Qiming, (2015), "Overview and Analysis of Safety Management Studies in the Construction Industry", **Safety Science**, Vol. 72, February, pp. 337–350.

Zin, Sulastre, M. & Ismail, Faridah, (2012), "Employers' Behavioral Safety Compliance Factors Toward Occupational, Safety and Health Improvement in the Construction Industry", **ASEAN Conference on Environment-Behavior Studies, Procedia Social and Behavioral Sciences**, Vol. 36, pp. 742–751, Indonesia: Bandung.

Zohar, Dov & Polachek, Tal, (2014), "Discourse-Based Intervention for Modifying Supervisory Communication as Leverage for Safety Climate and Performance Improvement: A Randomized Field Study", **Journal of Applied Psychology**, Vol. 99, N. 1, pp. 113–124.

Birol Erkan and Elif Tuğçe Bozduman

The Level of Innovation in Russia's Exports and Analysis of Global Competitiveness

1 Introduction

With the disintegration of the Soviet Union of Socialist Republics in 1991, Russia became the most important regional power. As Russia is one of the world's leading energy producers, the country's importance on the global platform is increasing day by day. Russia has the power to change the global energy sector as it has almost half of its current oil and gas reserves.

Russia is a major exporter in the field of energy because of its trade with other countries receives more. In this context, Russia, which is of strategic importance, wants to increase its share in the global economy. In this perspective, Russia has become an important force in the face of developed countries by taking part in BRICS countries.

In this study, analysis of export competitiveness of Russia between 2000 and 2017 was made. In this context, the general macroeconomic outlook of Russia has been put forward in the first chapter. In the second part, the indices used in competitive power analysis were explained. In the third part, Russia's export competitiveness was analyzed using these indices.

2 Macroeconomic Indicators of Russia

After the dissolution of the USSR, the countries that gained their independence started the process of transition to the market economy with the loss of the impact of socialism. This transition period has yielded different economic, political, and structural results in each country (Pashalieva & Kahriman, 2016). Russia has entered the process of transforming itself from the planned economy to market economy by aiming to attract foreign capital to its country (Bekcan, 2012). Russia carried out significant economic reforms in order to move from planned economy to market economy in 1992 (Duman & Samadov, 2003). Thanks to liberalization and reforms in foreign trade, Russia's basic economic indicators have improved rapidly since the early 1990s.

Russia is one of the few countries that have natural resources and manpower, the basis of a large economic entity. Due to the cold climate, the agricultural sector has lagged behind the industrial sector. The country's fuel, energy and

Tab. 1: Russia's Macroeconomic Indicators

	GDP (billion $)	GDP growth (%)	Inflation (%)	GDP per capita ($)	Unemployment (%)	Government debt (%of GDP)	Account balance (%of GDP)	Import (billion $)	Export (billion $)
2000	259	10	20.7	1 771	10.6	55.7	18	62	114
2001	306	5	21.4	2 100	9	44.3	11.1	74	113
2002	345	4.7	15.7	2 375	7.9	37.5	8.4	84	121
2003	430	7.2	13.6	2 975	8.2	28.3	8.2	102	151
2004	591	7.1	10.8	4 102	7.8	20.8	10.1	130	203
2005	764	6.3	12.6	5 323	7.1	14.8	11.1	164	268
2006	989	8.1	9.6	6 920	7.1	9.8	9.5	207	333
2007	1 299	8.5	8.9	9 101	6	8	5.9	279	392
2008	1 660	5.2	14.1	11 635	6.2	7.4	6.2	366	520
2009	1 222	-7.8	11.6	8 562	8.3	9.9	4.1	250	341
2010	1 524	4.5	6.8	10 674	7.3	10.6	4.7	322	445
2011	2 031	5.2	8.4	14 212	6.5	10.9	5.5	408	573
2012	2 170	3.6	5	15 154	5.5	11.8	3.5	447	594
2013	2 230	1.7	6.7	15 543	5.5	13.1	1.6	468	592
2014	2 063	0.7	7.8	14 125	5.2	15.6	3.1	426	558
2015	1 365	-2.8	15.5	9 329	5.6	15.9	5.1	281	391
2016	1 283	-0.2	7	8 748	5.5	17	1.8	263	329
2017	1578	1.6	5.3	10 749	5.2	13.5	2.1	326	411

Source: The World Bank Data (2019)

metallurgical production accounts for more than 35% of total industrial production (Keleş, 2017). Russia's GDP is the services sector with 62.8%, while the industry with 32.4%, and agriculture with 4.7%.

Russia has a serious economic dimension in terms of both national and foreign trade indicators. Russia, which has more than $1.5 trillion in national income, also has foreign trade and current surplus (Tab. 1). It can also be said that Russia is in a satisfactory position in terms of both unemployment and debt level. However, Russia is not at the level of developed countries in terms of per capita income levels.

3 Methodology

In this study, two international classifications were used for products exported while Russia's export competitiveness analysis was used. The first is the classification of exported products according to the factor density (Standard International Trade Classification) and the second is the classification according to technology equipment (International Standard Industrial Classification). Furthermore, in order to carry out a more detailed analysis on product basis, competitiveness of products that the country exports calculated was by using SITC Rev. 3 2 digit product classification.

There are many measurements that are used to calculate export competitiveness. The most important of these is Balassa Index (RCA). According to Balassa, RCA measures changes in relative price differences of production factors by measuring the relative trading performance of the country in certain commodities. It has been possible to identify which sectors have competitiveness through the use of the Balassa Index (Erkan & Bozduman, 2018).

The Balassa Index (RCA) is formulated as $(X_{ij}/X_j)/(X_{iw}/X_w)$ (Balassa, 1965):

In this formula, 'j' represents the country, 'i' product group, and 'w' represents the world. While the fractional share represents the domestic specialization in the mentioned form, the denominator also shows the world's specialization. The fact that the index value is greater than 1 shows the comparative advantage of the country's exports of that product, vice versa. If the RCA is between 1 and 2, it has a weak competitiveness; between 2 and 4 it has a competitiveness at medium level; and at 4 and above it has a strong competitiveness (Hinloopen & Marrewijk, 2000).

Since the RCA is between zero and infinity, it is asymmetric; and it needs to be adapted to another index conversion. This conversion is performed by the formulation of the RCA as (RCA-1)/(RCA+1) (Hossain, 2006). In this case, the name of the index is the Symmetric Revealed Comparative Advantage (RSCA) index (Kumar & Rani, 2016). Thus, the extreme values in the results will be less weighted and the results of these indices will be symmetrical by taking the value between +1 and -1 (Laursen, 2015). If the RSCA has positive value, the country has competitiveness in the export of a certain product (Erkan, 2012).

The Lafay Index (LI) measures the intra-industry trade and re-export flows by using either export or import data (Desai, 2012).

The LI is formulated as follows:

$$LI = 100 \left[\frac{X - M}{X + M} - \frac{\sum X - M}{\sum X + M} \right] \frac{X + M}{\sum X + M}$$

The index is between 50 and +50. If the LI is positive, the country has specialization in the foreign trade of the sector, vice versa (Reyes, 2014).

Tab. 2: Analysis Results of the Balassa Index (Based on Strong Superiority, 2000–2017)

Product Code	Product Name	Level of Superiority	RCA Coefficient	RCA ln	CV	Factor Intensity	Rate of Change (2000–2008; 2009–2017)
56	fertilizer	strong	10.16	2.32	25.9	raw material	↓
33	petroleum and products	strong	7.36	2.00	18.7	raw material	↓
24	cork and wood	strong	5.03	1.62	22.1	raw material	↓
32	coal/coke	strong	5.14	1.64	21.2	raw material	↑

Source: COMTRADE (2019)

4 Russia's Export Competitiveness Analysis

In the analysis section of the study, these indices related to Russia's export competitiveness are calculated by using both SITC Rev. 3 and ISIC Rev. 3 classifications.

4.1 An Analysis According to the Standard International Trade Classification

According to the Balassa (RCA) and the Symmetrical RCA Index scores, Russia has competitive advantage in exports of 12 out of 66 product groups (Tab. 2, Tab. 3). Four of these advantages are strong. In addition, three of the superiorities are moderate and five of the superiorities are weak. However, 8 of the 12 product groups in which the country has export competitiveness are raw material intensive, three are capital intensive, and one is R&D-based.

Russia has a strong competitive advantage of export product groups such as 'fertilizer, oil and petroleum products, wood and timber and stone coals' (Tab. 2). Russia is particularly competitive in fertilizer exports. However, the lack of variability coefficients (CV) of the RCA scores in Russia's mentioned products may be considered a sign of stability in the advantages.

When Russia's exports competitiveness of 12 product groups are examined on the basis of two periods (2000–2008, 2009–2017), it is observed that the competitiveness scores of eight product groups have decreased.

According to the analysis results of the Lafay Index, Russia has the competitiveness in the export of 16 product groups. However, 10 of the country's top

Tab. 3: Analysis Results of the Symmetrical RCA Index (2000–2017)

Product Code	Product Name	RSCA Coefficient	Factor Intensity	Rate of Change (2000–2008; 2009–2017)	Product Code	Product Name	RSCA Coefficient	Factor Intensity	Rate of Change (2000–2008; 2009–2017)
04	cereal	0.10	raw material	↑	32	coal/coke	0.67	raw material	↑
56	Fertilizer	0.82	raw material	→	35	electric current	0.06	capital	↑
33	petroleum and product	0.76	raw material	→	52	inorganic chemical	0.32	R&D-based (easy imitated goods)	↑
25	pulp and waste paper	0.23	raw material	→	68	non-ferrous metal	0.56	capital	→
27	crude fertilizer	0.25	raw material	→	23	crude rubber	0.44	raw material	→
24	cork and wood	0.68	raw material	→	67	iron and steel	0.41	capital	→

Source: COMTRADE (2019)

Tab. 4: Analysis Results of the Lafay Index (2000–2017)

Product Code	Product Name	Lafay Index Value	Factor Intensity	Product Code	Product Name	Lafay Index Value	Factor Intensity
04	cereal	0.27	raw material	32	coal/coke	1.24	raw material
56	fertilizer	1.11	raw material	35	electric current	0.09	capital
33	petroleum and products	27.30	raw material	52	inorganic chemicals	0.21	R&D-based (easy imitated goods)
25	pulp and waste paper	0.19	raw material	68	non-ferrous metal	2.92	capital
51	organic chemicals	0.14	R&D-based (easy imitated goods)	61	leather manufactures	0.01	labor
21	hide/skin/ fur raw	0.02	raw material	23	crude rubber	0.19	raw material
28	metal ores	0.09	raw material	34	gas natural	0.41	raw material
24	cork and wood	0.95	raw material	67	iron and steel	1.23	capital

Source: COMTRADE (2019)

product groups are raw material intensive, three are capital intensive, two are R&D-based, and one is labor intensive.

Both the RCA and the RSCA and the Lafay Index results show that Russia's export profile and superiority are mainly made up of raw material-intensive products. Moreover, even with a small number, Russia has the competitiveness in the export of high value-added product groups (organic and inorganic chemical products) (Tab. 4).

4.2 An Analysis According to the International Standard Industrial Classification

According to the Balassa Index (RCA) and the Symmetric RCA Index scores, Russia has the competitive advantage in the export of only low-medium-tech

Tab. 5: Analysis Results of the Balassa Index (2000–2017)

Product Groups	RCA Values					
	Average					
	2000–2008	2009–2017	Total	Min	Max	Average
Low Technology	0.39	0.50	8.04	0.36	0.69	0.44
Low-Medium Technology	4.80	4.07	79.82	3.23	5.49	4.44
Medium-High Technology	0.64	0.59	11.04	0.53	0.75	0.61
High Technology	0.24	0.19	3.88	0.12	0.43	0.21

Source: COMTRADE (2019)

product groups. However, the country has a competitive disadvantage, especially in the export of high-tech products. This shows that Russia's export profile is mainly composed of product groups with low R&D and innovation levels (Tab. 5).

When Russia's exports competitiveness is examined on the basis of two periods (2000–2008, 2009–2017), it is observed that the scores of the RCA and the RSCA of low-medium-tech, high-medium-tech, and high-tech products have decreased in the second period. In other words, Russia's competitive disadvantage in exports of high value-added products is deteriorating (Tab. 6).

According to the Lafay Index analysis results, unlike the RCA and the RSCA Index results, Russia has a competitiveness in the export of low-tech and low-medium-tech products (Tab. 7). In other words, Russia specialized in the foreign trade of these products groups (according to the Lafay Index results) although there is no competitiveness in the export of low-tech products (according to the RCA and the RSCA results).

Both the RCA and the RSCA and the Lafay Index scores show that Russia has no competitiveness in the export of high-tech products. In other words, Russia's export profile mainly consists of low-value product groups.

5 Conclusion

Russia, a member of the BRICS countries, which is said to be an important force on a global scale could not reflect its political power on the platform. Although Russia is an important political power, it is not an economic power that creates and exports technology. In this study, the global competitiveness of Russia was analyzed between 2000 and 2017.

Tab. 6: Analysis Results of the Symmetrical RCA Index (2000–2017)

Product Groups	RSCA Values					
	Average					
	2000–2008	2009–2017	Total	Min	Max	Average
Low Technology	-0.44	-0.33	-6.96	-0.47	-0.18	-0.39
Low-Medium Technology	0.65	0.60	11.31	0.53	0.69	0.63
Medium-High Technology	-0.22	-0.26	-4.34	-0.31	-0.14	-0.24
High Technology	-0.63	-0.68	-11.78	-0.79	-0.40	-0.66

Source: COMTRADE (2019)

Tab. 7: Analysis Results of the Lafay Index (2000–2017)

Product Groups	Lafay Values					
	Average					
	2000–2008	2009–2017	Total	Min	Max	Average
Low Technology	13.01	8.47	193.29	-2.23	17.60	11.12
Low-Medium Technology	0.37	3.89	38.36	-1.41	24.36	0.96
Medium-High Technology	-8.63	-6.72	-138.11	13.33	-4.84	-7.50
High Technology	-4.75	-5.64	-93.57	-8.80	-4.04	-5.05

Source: COMTRADE (2019)

Competitiveness analysis that is made according to SITC Rev. 3 and ISIC Rev. 3 classification shows that Russia has a competitive advantage in the export of raw material intensive and low-tech products. All of the indices related to the competitiveness measurement (the RCA, the RSCA, and the LI) used in the study show that the country has a competitive disadvantage in exports of high-tech and R&D-based products. In other words, Russia has no comparative advantage in the production and exportation of high value-added products. There is no doubt that Russia's inability to create added value in its production and exports will impede macroeconomic growth and foreign trade. In other words, it is likely that even if Russia increases its exports, the resulting income increase and competitive advantage will be low.

In this perspective, the country must produce and export products with high income flexibility in terms of both economic growth and improvement in foreign trade terms. In addition, Russia needs to be able to increase the level of innovation, research and development, and value added in its exports and to eliminate/reduce its foreign dependency in these products in order to become a stronger global actor. Only in this case, the country's global competitiveness will increase.

Bibliography

Balassa, B. (1965). Trade Liberalisation and "Revealed" Comparative Advantage. *The Manchester School of Economic and Social Studies, 33*(2), 99–123.

Balassa, B. (1977). Revealed Comparative Advantage Revisited: An Analysis of Relative Export Shares of the Industrial Countries 1953–1971. *The Manchester School, 45*(4), 327–344.

Bekcan, U. (2012). *Yeni Dünya Düzeninde Rusya-Çin İlişkileri.* Ankara: Ankara University Institute of Social Sciences Unpublished PhD Thesis.

COMTRADE. (2019). 07 04 2019, World Integrated Trade Solution: https://wits.worldbank.org/WITS/WITS/Restricted/Login.aspx.

Desai, F. P. (2012). Trends in Fragmentation of Production: A Comparative Study of Asia and Latin America. *Procedia – Social and Behavioral Sciences, 37*, 217–229.

Duman, M., & Samadov, N. (2003). Türkiye ile Rusya Federasyonu Arasındaki İktisadi ve Ticari İlişkilerin Yapısı Üzerine Bir İnceleme. *Kocaeli Üniversitesi Sosyal Bilimler Enstitüsü Dergisi,* (6), 25–47.

Erkan, B. (2012). BRIC Ülkeleri ve Türkiye'nin İhracat Uzmanlaşma ve Rekabet Düzeylerinin Karşılaştırmalı Analizi. *Ekonomik ve Sosyal Araştırmalar Dergisi,* 101–131.

Erkan, B., & Bozduman, E. T. (2018). A Research on Comparative Advantages in Germany's Technology-Intensive Exports. Ö. Özçelik (Ed.), *Studies on Interdisciplinary Economics and Business* (s. 59–74). Berlin: Peter Lang.

Hinloopen, J., & Marrewijk, C. v. (2000). On the Empirical Distribution of the Balassa Index. *Weltwirtschaftliches Archiv,* 1–26.

Hossain, M. B. (2006). Export Performance of Bangladesh's Fisheries Sector. *The Journal of Developing Areas,* 63–77.

Keleş, S. Ş. (2017). *Rusya Federasyonu Ülke Raporu.* İzmir: İzmir Ticaret Odası.

Kumar, N. R., & Rani, P. (2016). Status and Competitiveness of Fish Exports to European Union. *Fishery Technology,* 69–74.

Laursen, K. (2015). Revealed Comparative Advantage and the Alternatives as Measures of International Specialization. *Eurasia Business and Economics Society,* 99–115.

Pashalieva, M., & Kahriman, H. (2016). Bir Geçiş Ekonomisi Olarak Kırgızistan'da Doğrudan Yabancı Yatırımlar ve Orta Asya Ülkeleri ile Kıyaslanması. *Yönetim ve Ekonomi Dergisi*, 163–188.

Reyes, G. U. (2014). Examining the Revealed Comparative Advantage of the ASEAN 6 Countries Using the Balassa Index and Lafay Index. *Journal of Global Business and Trade, 10*(1), 1–12.

The World Bank Data. (2019). 13 05 2019, The World Bank: https://data.worldbank.org/.

Zuhal Önez Çetin

An Overview on E-Municipality Process in Turkey

1 Introduction

As to the Household Information Technologies Usage Survey (2018), the proportion of individuals using the Internet was 72.9% in Turkey. The use of computers and the internet was 59.6% and 72.9% in the 16–74 age groups in 2018, respectively. The computer and internet usage rates were 68.6% and 80.4% for males aged 16–74 and 50.6% and 65.5% for females, respectively. According to the results of the Household Information Technology Research of April 2018, 83.8% of the households had access to the internet from their home. This rate was 80.7% in the same month of 2017 (Turkish Statistical Institute/ TUIK, number 24862, 8 August 2018). In that regard, information technologies usage affected and changed the local citizens' demands and expectations from the central and local government institutions in Turkey. The innovations and developments at information and communication technologies and widespread usage of the internet also affected the public administration with respect to the provision of local services. E-government applications launched to be used with the target of responding to the increasing and diversifying needs of the citizens more efficiently and quickly and reducing the cost of public services (Arıkboğa, 2017: 1620). E-governance is mostly described as facilitating from information and communication technologies that passing beyond the previous information technology at government models (Heeks, 2001: 2).

The Project of e-state started with a Circular of Prime Ministry in the year of 2003 in Turkey (Yaman *et.al.*, 2003: 208). At the 9th Five Year Development Plan, it is also determined that e-government studies gathered in the E-Transformation Turkey Project and launched to execute in integrity (SPO, 2006: 59).[1] E-Government applications spreading and enabling theme took also part in 9th Five Year Development Plan, and the local governments' participation to that process has also been discussed with those clarifications as follows: "E-Government will be used as an effective tool in the restructuring of the public, and will support the establishment of a public administration structure, including local governments, which can provide flexible, high quality, effective, fast services, and adopt good governance principles" (SPO, 2006: 104).[2]

Moreover, by the effect of EU cohesion policy, e-Europe+ initiative in the 2000s onwards, Turkey also initiated e-government applications not only in the ground of central government but also in the basis of local government (Arıkboğa, 2017: 1620). Besides, local administrations are now confronted with lots of responsibilities with the changes at the local laws and regulations, and the realization of e-government transition, and it is pointed out that the local governments should meet with information technology, and those who met also need to develop their ability to use these technologies (Ergun, 2004: 140). In that context, e-municipality's necessity was clarified by the following themes: prospects of people and organizations from local governments; efficiency and effectiveness in local public services; more regular and healthy environment; regular traffic and roads; routing on roads; speed of subscriber transactions and payments; rapid, effective, and useful intervention in case of disaster; speed in zoning operations; and to explain the problems to the authorized persons (TBD/Türkiye Bilişim Derneği, 2004a cited Henden, 2005: 8). In this sense, the municipal administrations also including the metropolitan municipalities pursue the newly emerged e-government practices (e-municipality) in the provision of local services. By the usage of e-applications, the municipal administration can get an idea about the citizen's preferences concerning the public services, can reach to a wide section of the society, and can provide local services more easily and in a rapid way; on the other hand, citizens can reach to the information concerning the e-municipality services, and can take advantage of saving time (Hazman, 2005: 66–67). In the first part of the study, the concept of e-municipality, its functions, objectives, and stages have been examined. Secondly, the e-municipality initiatives' appearance has been analyzed in a historical perspective with the key projects and institutions in

---

1   For Details, see, Devlet Planlama Teşkilatı (State Planning Organization/SPO), (2006). 9th Five Year Development Plan, <www3.kalkinma.gov.tr/DocObjects/ Download/3577/oik676.pdf>, Item 314, p.59 (Accessed in 02.02.2019).

2   For Details, see, Devlet Planlama Teşkilatı (SPO), (2006). 9th Five Year Development Plan, <www3.kalkinma.gov.tr/DocObjects/Download/ 3577/oik676.pdf>, Item 705, p.104 (Accessed in 02.02.2019).

Turkey. Finally, the achievements and obstacles at the implementation process of e-municipality have been evaluated and some proposals have been developed on that dimension.

2 The Concept of E-Municipality

The e-government transformation, which is being carried out in all public institutions, is now being implemented by local governments in Turkey, municipalities are restructured, and they reflect local service provision to the electronic environment for the transition to e-municipality structure (Candemir and Kazançoğlu, 2009:196). In terms of local administrations, e-municipality is evaluated as the provision of the usage of information technologies in municipal administration at the local public services provision (Çoruh, 2009: 215, Erdal, 2002: 169). It is also determined that the concept of e-municipality should not be seen simply as the transition of municipal services to the electronic environment; this concept demonstrates a structure which is transparent, more effective and efficient, closer to the citizen, and more open to the citizens' participation. It is added that e-municipality includes a deeper transformation, such as the establishment of a customer-oriented service approach, the creation of a new administrative structure, and the development of human resources capable of understanding and using these technologies (Polat, 2006: 10).

E-municipality is determined to administer the information in regard to the urban spatial field via the support of innovative technology in order to enable the data in local citizens interest, and to provide it to the service of the citizens effectively (Bensghir and Akay, 2006: 33, Henden, 2005: 1), and that concept is also designated as the creation of a local government understanding, depending on the basis of service provision and transparency by using the developing technologies (Henden and Henden, 2005: 56). Moreover, e-municipality can also be identified as the use of the internet technologies at the registration of all services provided by the municipality, in all the decisions, plans, controls, and at these activities sharing with citizens and public institutions (Çoruh, 2009: 215).

Local governments are determined as the closest administrative units to the public that they have to perform a number of administrative (providing information and service to citizens) and political (being a democracy school) functions (Yıldız, 2001: 236). The purpose of e-municipality in the political sphere is pointed out as to perform better in areas such as transparency, accountability, and participation, through the usage of the internet and it is also added that the administrative

Chart 1: E-municipality's Functions in Terms of Municipalities and Citizens

E-municipality's functions in terms of municipalities	E-municipality's functions in terms of citizens
Efficiency and effectiveness in providing services	Better quality service
Ensuring tax justice	Citizen-oriented service
Performance measurement	7/24 service
Instrument for modernization and reform	Participation possibility in the design of services
Development of knowledge-based decision-making mechanisms	More transparent and accountable management

Polat (2006: 10–11)

dimension of internet usage in local administrations is more likely to occur as a web page creation activity in municipalities (Yıldız, 2001: 239–241). In a general sense, it is asserted that e-municipality is an e-government application that focuses on the following objectives (Trajkovik, 2013: 22–23):

- Service Transformation: The main idea is to make the local services more accessible, more affordable, cost-effective, more responsive, and participatory.
- Renovation of Local Democracy: The main purpose is to make assemblies more open, accountable, inclusive, and to able to manage communities. It is pointed out that governments will assist their citizens in accessing their political representatives and councils to discuss opportunities among themselves.
- Increasing Local Economic Viability: It is elucidated that modern communication infrastructure, skilled workforce, and effective promotion of e-business environment can help local and regional assemblies to promote employment in their respective fields and increase the employability of their citizens. It is also added that local government can use e-government services to achieve these benefits if there are facilitative services to improve the local economy.

Henden (2005: 7) clarified that "generally, by the e-municipal applications, it is targeted to make the local government services more democratic, easily accessible, and transparent. In a broad sense, local governments thanks to the e-municipal applications aimed to monitor their activities by the public, to promote the municipality at national and international scale with the lowest cost and in an effective way, to make accurate, reliable, and rapid data transfer to all press and broadcast organizations, to carry the municipality-citizens interaction to a higher ground by the usage internet technologies, to provide to monitor the urban agenda on the website, and to continue studies for the development of the data bank consisting of urban data", Consequently, the objectives of e-government applications in terms of local government units can be listed as to provide faster, high-quality, and easily accessible services; better usage of public resources (effectiveness and efficiency); and to increase the control and participation of the citizens in management and transparency (legislation, election results, tenders, budgets, and the declaration of council decisions) (Yıldız, 2019: 4).

2.1 The Stages of E-Municipality

At the usage of innovative technologies, local authorities came out as critical actors in offering the local services to the citizens. Local administrative units, especially the municipalities, try to accompany the new developments in technology within the context of e-municipality structuring process (the process of moving or transition to internet) at the municipality scale; and the process of moving to the internet in the municipality has three basic dimensions (Güler, 2006; Hazman, 2005: 67):

1) The provision of the automation of administrative processes such as financial, personnel, writing works, development planning, etc.
2) The realization of the services on the internet such as, taking the requests and complaints of the local people, requests for information concerning the issues under the jurisdiction of the local administration, making and realizing the licensing, permission, and application and the legal payment procedures on the internet,
3) The sharing of information and data of local government by ensuring the connection of the local governments with other public institutions.

As in any other organizations, there is a five-step process of the e-local goverment transformation:

1. Computerization phase, which refers to having a computer,
2. The process of automation as a system in which financial work, water fee, and tax collection is transferred to computer based on certain software, and the works are carried out in this environment,
3. Internet user stage as the provision of internet access rate with making an internet connection,
4. The stage of the network site presence that represents having a network site of local governments,

5. The transition of management to the internet in the base of the Urban Information System for municipalities (Güler, Akdoğan and Oktay, 2001).

As it is seen from the above clarifications, e-municipality transformation is examined through five-steps of computerization, automation, internet usage, website settlement, and carrying of management to the internet or transition to Urban Information System (Güler et al., 2001: 3). Additionally, e-municipality transformation (*e-belediyeleşme süreci*) on that dimension can be examined at three phases of unilateral information flow, reciprocal communication, and online processing (operations) (Polat, 2006: 12).

a) Unilateral Information Flow:
At this stage, it is pointed out that the municipality provides information and service to local citizens through web page with publishing press releases, announcements, and activity reports. This stage is mostly criticized as the provision of information away from the citizens' needs and expectations that pave the way for wasting of resources (Polat, 2006: 12).

b) Reciprocal Communication:
That stage of e-municipal process is more than offering general information in a one-way manner; the information is presented in a personalized way to the needs and demands of the person such as learning the water bill debt by specifying the subscriber number on the website and learning the sports facilities of the municipality in the neighborhood by giving the name of the district, participating in the municipal survey, and sending e-mail, it is expressed that the user at this stage gains the possibility to make his/her transactions (Polat, 2006: 12).

c) Online Processing (Operations):
At online processing stage of e-municipality, transactions such as payment of environment cleaning tax, participation to the municipal tenders, and registering or booking municipal sports facility can be made on municipal website (Polat, 2006: 12).

In this context, for the success of the e-municipality process and its stages, the conditions required for information technologies to function in local administrations are listed as follows (Uçkan, 2003: 53, cited in Yüksel, 2005: 255–256):

1. The use of information technologies should be continuous.
2. The update on the content should be performed regularly.
3. Human resources using these technologies should be created and managed.
4. Information technologies should be taken into account since they bring with them a number of risks and create a security problem. Although it is not

possible to completely eliminate the security risk in the electronic environ-ment, essential measures should be taken to minimize them, and the safety standards should be kept high.

5. Required precautions should be taken to protect personal and corporate pri-vacy meticulously, and the trust element should be ensured, which is required for the operation of information technologies to function.

6. Legal arrangements should be made on freedom of access to public informa-tion; public information outside sensitive ones should be made available to the knowledge and access of local people.

Furthermore, it is also emphasized that information technologies' provision of benefits to the local administrations depends on the interest of the public to that process. It is also pointed out that the rise at the interest and expecta-tion for local services through those technologies can lead the demand of citi-zens from central and local governments' allocation of more resources (Yıldız, 2004: 247).

2.2 The Usage Fields of Information Technologies by Municipal Administrations

Although e-municipality service headings of each municipality are different, the following services can be listed generally: map, zoning application, and cadastral operations; city/region planning; technical infrastructure services and coordination; construction and management services of park-garden and green areas; crisis management; urban management/supervision; technical and social infrastructure management and control; transportation systems; traffic/address information system; subscriber system; zoning status/building license/building permit; tax and fees; public health; education; defense and security; trade and industry; and tourism and service desks (Türkiye Bilişim Derneği, 2004a cited in Tosun Karakurt, 2008: 76). In that context, some of the e-municipal system's online services can be listed as (Çoruh, 2008: 154 cited in Çoruh, 2009: 216):

• Learning the zoning status of the land by entering the plot, island, or parcel no. information,
• Learning whether the license has been issued according to the registration number for construction applications,
• Determination of the amount of parking for the construction and payment of the fee,
• Real estate (building, land) tax notification, tracking, and to be paid if desired,

- To be able to learn the amount of water debt and to be paid if requested,
- Complaint application and follow-up,
- Application to the Directorate of Science Affairs,
- Access to local government activities and laws, filling and following the application form for obtaining information,
- Declaration of environmental cleaning tax, payment, and follow-up,
- Drinking water subscription contracts and monitoring of payments,
- To obtain information about tenders,
- Opening and working license application,
- Form and follow-up license for sewer connection,
- To determine days from marriage office,
- Sharing of municipal council decisions with citizens,
- Traffic and weather information,
- Pharmacy information on duty,
- Municipal budget and project information and realizations,
- Land and building value of square meters,
- Wear rates according to building age,
- Sea and air pollution measurement information,
- Ability to upload required documents (doc, gif, jpg files) for all applications,
- Payment of debts related to services by credit cards on the internet.

3 The Appearance of E-Municipality in Turkey

"Local Governments Research and Training Center" was established in 1989 within the structure of TODAIE (Public Administration Institute for Turkey and the Middle East) in order to organize education and working program at the national level for the local employees in local administrations, to contribute to the development, and effective and efficient functioning of local administrations, and Local Net (YEREL-Net Portal) has established what is called as local government network that enables the meeting of local administrations in Turkey (Hazman, 2005:70). The local portal implicates the information related with the local laws and regulations, legislative developments, administrative, political, and local development; concerning the local governments in Turkey (Alodalı, Usta, Güneş, 2010: 469). "Local Net Project" is developed by the cooperation of TODAIE and State Planning Organization (SPO) with the target of setting up a website sharing network for enabling easy access to information in respect to the areas of municipality, special provincial administration, and villages; and thanks to that network, an environment for local governments in sharing their experiences is also aimed to be provided (Arıkboğa, 2017: 1626). In that context,

Güler et al. (2001: 3) also expressed that the necessity to share the experience of a large number of local governments in a common communication pool started to be provided with Local Net Project. It is also determined that difficulties faced by people working in the area of local governments in accessing relevant numerical data, Local Net Project is pointed out to set up to provide those related data (Altınok and Bensghir, 2005: 699).

The Ministry of the Interior's General Directorate of Local Authorities had also an initiative to have a database on the Internet and as a result on April 4, 2001, "Local Information Project" came to the forefront to facilitate data exchange between local government and central government (Hazman, 2005: 70). That project was launched by a signed protocol by TODAIE and Ministry of Interior and transferred to Ministry of Interior in 2001. The key objective of that project is to collect all data related to local governments in electronic environment and to gather these data to assist the policy development and decision-making process (Şahin, 2007: 175). Within the context of this project, it is pointed out that all legal, political, economic, geographic, and cultural data related to municipalities are compiled and entered to the data (TBD, 2004b cited in Çukurçayır and Sipahi, 2010: 455).

Moreover, TBB Municipal Information System Project (BELBİS)'s main target is designated as to develop compatible application software for the provision of the municipal services through the use of information technologies, and carrying it to a certain standard. The scope of the project is to make the analysis of the functioning of the municipality and design of workflows, to form the basic application software database standards, to develop basic application software, to make testing and documentation work, to provide training, and to assist e-municipal integration studies for the e-government gate (Taşkan, 2013: 22). Software applications developed for e-municipality in Turkey are listed as Budget and Accounting Application Software, Portable Application Software, Staff Application Software, Document Tracking Application, and Income Module (Taşkan, 2013: 22).

At "National E-government Strategy and Action Plan," 2016–2019, there are significant expressions towards the local government e-government applications such as (T.C. Ulaştırma, Denizcilik ve Haberleşme Bakanlığı: 2019):

• Local administrations' data sharing criteria with central government will be determined, and technical capacity for e-transformation will be supported in local governments where needed. (p. 13)
• It is determined that IT competence and technical infrastructures are generally weaker in local governments than central government. In particular, it is

necessary to overcome the difficulties experienced in general resource procurement and competence development, especially in human resources for
e-transformation in local governments. (p. 25)
- E-transformation efforts in central government units and local governments
  will be carried out in accordance with national e-government policies. (p. 26)
- Investment projects for innovative approaches will be supported in the work
  and operations of central government units and local governments. (p. 29)
- Providing training and guidance services to the central government and local
  governments is required especially for project and procurement management
  processes related to e-government studies. (p. 36)
- Identifying the common practices that can be used for similar services offered
  by local governments, determining the needs, developing the applications, and
  disseminating the developed practices in all local government units. (p. 80)

Some legal regulations on e-government applications are also available in local
governments. In that regard, it is clarified that the local government laws keep
the issue of e-government in terms of local governments in a limited way only
touching upon geographical and urban data system (In the article 14th of the
Municipal Law No. 5393 dated 2005; In the article 7th of the Metropolitan
Municipalities Law No. 5216 dated 2004). In this sense, the laws such as Law on
the Right to Information No. 4982 dated 2003, the Electronic Signature Law No.
5070 dated 2004, and the Universal Service Law No. 5369 dated 2005 are evaluated as the legal basis for local governments in Turkey (Şat, 2012: 9).

Consequently, the e-municipal projects carried out in our country are determined as significant projects that will lead to the contribution of the municipalities to the development of the country, in that regard, e-municipality applications
are designated as city and region planning, development application and cadastral operations, technical infrastructure services, green area construction and
management services, urban audit/management, taxes and fees, crisis management, transportation, traffic, public transport, trade and industry, tourism, education, community health, address numeration information system, and service
tables (Hazman, 2005: 70–71).

4 The Achievements and Obstacles of E-Municipality in Turkey

Kesgin (2011: 82) clarified that "one of the most fundamental innovations at
e-municipality is as its alleviation of the vertical state of the hierarchical structure
in the management levels. The development of information technologies has also
influenced the power distribution and has included new actors in the system in
accordance with the logic of governance, e-municipality can reduce the distance

barrier in participation and makes institutions more comfortable and quickly reached for the public." Moreover, Henden and Henden (2005: 54–55) also listed the benefits by the following issues listed below:

- To reduce the intensity of bureaucratic documents,
- To reduce the intensity of the employees due to the freedom of citizens to receive some information in the electronic environment,
- To save time for both employees and citizens on the basis of transactions to be made,
- To ensure the strengthening of municipality-citizen relations,
- To ensure employee satisfaction due to a certain amount of decrease in work intensity,
- To be able to ensure that the urban agenda is easily monitored,
- To be able to gather information about city data more easily,
- To be able to learn the expectations, demands, and complaints of the public more easily thanks to the surveys on the internet.

In that regard, Şahin (2007: 168) also determined the expected benefits from e-municipality as follows: "organizing and presenting local services according to the needs of local people, reducing costs in local services, access to local services that can be transferred to the internet in 7 days 24 hours, supervision of municipal services and actions and decisions of municipal administration, monitoring municipal activities and agendas from everywhere, equal provision of services to local people living in different neighborhoods, more active participation of local citizens in municipal activities and democratic processes, preventing bribery and corruption in activities such as reconstruction, parcel, tender, etc., reducing bureaucratic processes by transferring more local services to the internet, accountable and more transparent municipal administration, establishing a municipal administration that can respond to the demands and complaints of local people in a short time, the elimination of obstacles between citizens and local government, setting up an effective network structure between central government and local governments, and mutual exchange of information."

Some obstacles have also emerged in terms of small-scale municipalities; it is elucidated that the high cost of information technology at the establishment phase creates problems for the municipalities having limited resources, and it is also pointed out that the metropolitan municipalities have more advantages in terms of sufficient financial resources, trained manpower, and information infrastructure (Negiz and Saraçbaşı, 2012: 44).

The problems and obstacles at e-municipality process have been determined by many scholars with different dimensions. At that point, many of the e-municipality networking sites are determined as not user-friendly, sites are pointed as not to be prepared and functioned with the focus of public or public officials; and it is also added that it is very rare to see the municipal budget and final accounts on network sites (Güler, Akdoğan, Oktay, 2001: 5). Moreover, the other obstacles are the high initial investment costs (at the establishment phase) of information technologies, lack of financial resources, the resistance of the internal staff to change, the unwillingness of the managers to change due to the lack of information and training, and the lack of technical personnel and informatics experts (Saraçbaşı, 2010: 89). In that regard, cautious approach to e-transformation policies and projects, restructuring programs due to lack of knowledge in local government levels, the resistance of personnel to new technology applications, the need of education and communication, and bureaucratic obstacles are also counted as problems at the usage of information technologies in state institutions and municipalities (Tosun Karakurt, 2008; 77–78).

Critically, in a study, 10 general factors and 50 sub-factors related to successful e-municipality were determined, and those factors are listed as (Siegfried *et.al.*, 2003: 452–453): the formation of required vision and strategy for the e-municipality applications, the modernization necessity of the administrative framework for the e-municipality facilitators, e-municipality applications (these are determined as the core elements), the calculation of the cost and benefit, the appropriate usage of technology and technical equipment, the skilled and trained personnel necessity, e-municipality adoption and acceptance, the collaborative understanding of stakeholders (public-private cooperation), the appropriate time interval and required budget, and e-municipality legal knowledge.

At that point, Nur Şat (2008: 275) listed the following themes at the solution of e-municipality problems as follows: municipal programs and service programs of other public institutions should be harmonized; strong resources in the budget should be directed for the processes related to the purchase, maintenance, updating, and efficient use of computer hardware and software in municipalities; and the necessary renewal of the municipality legislation should always be carried out in parallel with the developments in the IT sector. Moreover, Turkish Informatics Association (Türkiye Bilişim Derneği, 2004b: 8 cited in Şat, 2012: 4) evaluated the success factors of e-municipality applications from the administrative and legal point of view by the following clarifications:

• To meet the financial resource requirement,
• To pay attention to equality in the provision of services by municipal administration and employees,
• To create a coordinated structure in order to facilitate the communication of the district's municipalities and big city,

- To monitor and follow the urbanization in the rapidly growing and developing cities,
- To establish the Urban Information Systems in order to determine, plan, and meet the needs of people,
- To provide the share of information between relevant institutions, to facilitate information exchange between public institutions,
- To ensure confidentiality of personal information,
- To use the identification number in all business and transactions,
- To carry out all transactions with a common number since the birth of the person.

5 Conclusion and Proposals

In this sense, local citizens in Turkey have no similar technological habits owing to age, education, occupation, social, and economic factors. Some sections of the society can reach to those e-municipal services easier than the other sides that the central and local government units should take the required precautions in order to eliminate the gaps at the use of those e-municipality applications and access to information technologies through numerous tools such as free training courses. At the other side, the security at the online transactions of the municipality has vital importance for the e-municipality users; a strong security policy (data security) has to be adopted by municipal institutions; and the legal basis of the e-municipality applications must be set up on that dimension. The municipalities should have skilled and trained staff in order to reach the expected results from the e-municipality applications; the local public officials should have the technological capability to analyze, use, and orient those innovative applications. The required budget should be allocated to not only the investment to the infrastructure of technology but also to the other related departments of the municipality having ties at the success of e-municipality process. The municipal administrations should set up standardization and cooperation among them at the application of e-municipality applications. Consequently, there is a need for more research and case study concerning e-municipality to highlight the obstacles and achievements of e-municipality applications in Turkey.

Bibliography

Alodalı, M. Fatih Bilal, Usta, Sefa, and Güneş, İsa, (2010). *Türkiye'de Yerel Yönetimlerde E-Belediyecilik Uygulamaları ve İl Belediyelerinin Karşılaştırmalı Analizi*, Bursa: Dora Yayın.

Altınok, Ramazan and Bensghir, Türksel Kaya,, (2005). "Türk Kamu Yönetiminde E-Dönüşüm Yerel Boyutu", Hüseyin Özgür ve Muhammet Kösecik (Ed.), *Yerel Yönetimler Üzerine Güncel Yazılar-1*, 1.Baskı, pp. 675–715, Ankara: Nobel Yayın.

Arıkboğa, Ülkü, (2017). "Belediye Hizmetlerinin Elektronik Ortamda Sunumu: İstanbul Büyükşehir Belediyesi E-Belediye Uygulamalarının Analizi", *Süleyman Demirel Üniversitesi İktisadi ve İdari Bilimler Fakültesi Dergisi*, C. 22, Kayfor 15 Özel Sayısı, pp. 1619–1644.

Bensghir, Türksel Kaya, and Akay, Aslı, (2006). "Bir Kamu Politika Aracı Olarak Coğrafi Bilgi Sistemleri (CBS): Türkiye'de Belediyelerin CBS Uygulamalarının Değerlendirilmesi", *Çağdaş Yerel Yönetimler*, Vol. 15(1), pp. 31–46.

Bensghir, Türksel Kaya, and Altınok, Ramazan ve Türksel, (2005). "Türk Kamu Yönetiminde E-Dönüşüm Yerel Boyutu", H. Özgür ve M. Kösecik (Ed.), *Yerel Yönetimler Üzerine Güncel Yazılar-1*, 1.Baskı, pp. 675–715, Ankara: Nobel Yayın.

Candemir, Aykan, and Savaşçı Kazançoğlu, İpek, (2009). "E-Belediye Çerçevesinde Ege Bölgesi Kıyı Belediyelerinin Web Sitelerinin İçerik Analizi Yöntemiyle Değerlendirilmesi", *Uluslararası Bilgi, Ekonomi ve Yönetim Kongresi Bildiriler Kitabı*, 7.

Çoruh, Mustafa, (2008). *Bilişim Teknolojisi, Ekonomisi ve Toplumu. Evde, Okulda, İşyerinde ve Kentte Yaşantımız Nasıl Değişiyor?*, İstanbul: Kitap Matbaacılık.

Çoruh, Mustafa, (2009). "Kent Bilişim Sistemi ve e-Belediye", *9. Akademik Bilişim Konferansı Bildiriler Kitabı*, 11–13 Şubat 2009 Şanlıurfa: Harran Üniversitesi, pp. 213–219.

Çukurçayır, M. Akif, and Sipahi, Esra, (2010). "Türkiye'de Yurttaş Başkana Ulaşabiliyor mu? İl Belediyeleri Üzerinde Periyodik Bir İnceleme", Bekir Parlak (Ed.), *Yerel Yönetimler Yerel Siyaset ve Kentsel Politikalar*, Bursa: Dora Yayın, pp. 451–465.

Devlet Planlama Teşkilatı (SPO), (2006). Dokuzuncu Kalkınma Planı (2007–2013). Ankara: DPT Yayını.

Erdal, Murat, (2002). "Elektronik Bilgi Çağında Kamu Yönetimi ve Bir Yerel Yönetim Uygulaması: İstanbul Büyük Şehir Belediyesi", *1. Bilgi ve Ekonomi Kongresi Bildiri Kitabı*, İzmit: Kocaeli Üniversitesi, pp. 165–180.

Ergun, Turgay, (2004). *Kamu Yönetimi Kuram Siyasa Uygulama*, Ankara: TODAİE.

Feenberg, Andrew, and Bakardjieva, Maria, (2002). "Community Technology and Democratic Rationalization", *The Information Society*, Vol. 18, pp. 181–192.

Güler, Birgül Ayman, Akdoğan, Argun, and Oktay, Hakan, (2001). "Yerel Yönetimler ve İnternet Paneli", Türkiye'yi İnternete Taşımak Konferansı, İstanbul, 2. 11. 2001, <www.inet.tr.org.tr/inetconf7/Sunum/yerelyonetim. docoturumlar/yerelyonetimler.doc>. (Accessed in 10.01.2019).

Güler, Birgül Ayman, (2006). "Yerel Yönetimler ve İnternet", <http://inet-tr.org. tr/inetcont7/sunum/yerelyonetim.doc>. (Accessed in 15.01.2019).

Hazman, Gülsüm Güler, (2005). "Afyonkarahisar Belediyesinde E-Belediye Uygulamaları ve Yerel Farkındalık", Afyon Kocatepe Üniversitesi, İİBF Dergisi, C.VII, pp. 65–84.

Heeks, Richard, (2001). "Building e-Governance for Development: A Framework for National and Donor Action", Institute for Development Policy and Management, pp. 1–33, <http://unpan1.un.org/intradoc/groups/public/ documents/NISPAcee/UNPAN015485.pdf>. (Accessed in 22.01.2019).

Henden, H. Burçin, (2005). "Katılımcı Yerel Yönetim Anlayışında E-Belediyeciliğinin Yeri ve Önemi", Uluslar arası İnsan Bilimleri Dergisi, Vol. 1(1), pp. 1–13.

Henden, H. Burçin, and Henden, Rıfkı, (2005). "Yerel Yönetimlerin Hizmet Sunumlarındaki Değişim ve E-Belediyecilik", Elektronik Sosyal Bilimler Dergisi, Güz 2005, Vol. 4, pp. 48–66.

Kesgin, Bedrettin, (2011). "E-Dönüşüm ve E-Belediyecilik: Katılma ve Yönetişim Sorununda Yoksullar", Yalova Sosyal Bilimler Dergisi, Vol. 2, April 2011, pp. 77–85.

Negiz, Nilüfer, and Saraçbaşı, Yasemin, (2012). "Demokratik Yönetişim Sağlanmasında e-Belediye ve Uygulamaları: Akdeniz Bölgesi Örneği", Bilgi Ekonomisi ve Yönetimi Dergisi, Vol. VII, I, pp. 42–52.

Polat Karakaya, Rabia, (2006). "Yerel Yönetim Vatandaş Etkileşimi", Stratejik Rapor, (Ed.), TASAM, Türkasya Stratejik Araştırmalar Merkezi, Ekim: E-Belediyecilik Kılavuzu.

Saraçbaşı, Yasemin, (2010). "Türkiye'de E-Belediyecilik Uygulamalarında Belediye Vatandaş İlişkisi: Malatya Belediyesi Örneği", Yayınlanmamış Yüksek Lisans Tezi, Süleyman Demirel Üniversitesi Sosyal Bilimler Enstitüsü Kamu Yönetimi Anabilim Dalı.

Siegfried, Tina, Grabow, Busso, and Druke, Helmut, (2003). "Ten Factors for Succes for Local Community e-Government", R. Traunmuller (Ed.), EGOV (International Conference on Electronic Government), pp. 452–455.

Şahin, Ali, (2007). "Türkiye'de E-Belediye Uygulamaları ve Konya Örneği", Erciyes Üniversitesi İktisadi ve İdari Bilimler Fakültesi Dergisi, Vol. 29, pp. 161–189.

Şat, Nur, (2008). "Demokrasi İçin Bir Araç: E-Belediye", Yayınlanmamış Doktora Tezi, Marmara Üniversitesi, İstanbul.

Şat, Nur, (2012). "Yerel Yönetimlerde E-Devlet Uygulamaları", *E-devlet Kamu Yönetimi ve Teknoloji İlişkisinde Güncel Gelişmeler*, Nobel Yayınları, Ankara, pp. 235–262.

Taşkan, Kerim, (2013). "Türkiye'de E-Belbis İşlemleri, E-İmza ve Belbis Projesi", TBB İller ve Belediyeler Dergisi, Vol. 783–784, Temmuz-Ağustos 2013, pp. 17–24.

TBD (Türkiye Bilişim Derneği), (2004a). "E-Belediye Taslak Rapor-I", *II. Türkiye Bilişim Şurası*, <http://www.bilisimsurasi.org.tr/e-turkiye/docs/e-belediye_taslak_raporu_1-5.doc>. (Accessed in 17.02.2019).

TBD, (2004b). "E-Belediye Raporu", *Türkiye Bilişim İkinci Şûrası*. Ankara. 2004. <http://www.bilisimsurasi.org.tr/e-turkiye/docs/e-belediye14042004.doc>. (Accessed in 17.01.2019).

T. C. Ulaştırma, Denizcilik ve Haberleşme, Bakanlığı, (2019). Ulusal E-devlet Stratejisi ve Eylem Planı, 2016–2019, <http://www.edevlet.gov.tr/wp-content/uploads/2016/07/2016-2019-Ulusal-e-Devlet-Stratejisi-ve-Eylem-Plani.pdf>. (Accessed in 25.01.2019).

The Metropolitan Municipalities Law No. 5216, Date of Official Gazette 23.07.2004, No. 25531.

The Municipal Law No. 5393, Date of Official Gazette 13.07.2005, No. 25874.

Tosun Karakurt, Elif, (2008). "Türkiye'de E-belediyecilik Uygulamaları: Bursa-Nilüfer-Osmangazi-Yıldırım Belediyelerinin Web Sitelerinin Analizi", *Çağdaş Yerel Yönetimler Dergisi*, Vol. 17, No. 2, pp. 71–94.

Trajkovik, Vladimir, (2013). "Yerel Yönetimler için Bilgi ve İletişim Teknolojileri BİT: Standartlar, İlkeler ve En İyi Uygulamalar", T.C. Marmara Belediyeler Birliği Yayını, Yayın No: 81 <http://marmara.gov.tr/ UserFiles/ Attachments/2017/04/13/49a1a60c-8a17-43d4-833f-968749b43802.pdf>, p. 23. (Accessed in 25.01.2019).

Turkish Statistical Institute/ TUIK, (2018). "Hanehalkı Bilişim Teknolojileri (BT) Kullanım Araştırması, 2018", Number 24862, 8 August 2018, <http:// www.tuik.gov.tr/PreHaberBultenleri.do?id=27819> (Accessed 15.01.2019).

Uçkan, Özgür, (2003). *E-Devlet, E-Demokrasi ve Türkiye*, Literatür Yayınları, İstanbul.

Yaman, Kemal, Aşgın, Sait, and Ece KAYA, (2013). "Comparative Analysis of the e-Municipality Applications in Turkey: The Case of Western Black Sea Region, *Yönetim ve Ekonomi*, Vol. 20, No. 1, pp. 207–220.

Yıldız, Mete, (2001). "Yerel Yönetimlerde İnternet Uygulamaları ve E-Devlet", Bekir Parlak ve Hüseyin Özgür (Ed.), Avrupa Birliği ile Bütünleşme Sürecinde Yerel Yönetimler, Alfa Yayınları.

Yıldız, Mete, (2004). "Yerel Yönetimlerde İnternet Uygulamaları ve E-Devlet", (http://www.bilgiyonetimi.org/ cm/pages/). (Accessed in 25.01.2019).

Yıldız, Mete, (2019). Bilgi Toplumu ve Kamu Yönetimi, 11. Hafta Dersi, Yerel Yönetimlerde E-devlet, Hazırlayan Mete Yıldız. <http://www.acikders.org.tr/mod/resource/view.php?id=2777>, pp. 1–11, (Accessed in 25.01.2019).

Yüksel, Fatih, (2005). "Bilgi Teknolojileri ve Yerel Yönetimler", *Selçuk Üniversitesi İİBF Sosyal ve Ekonomik Araştırmalar Dergisi*, 5(10), pp. 247–259.

Pınar Evrim Mandacı[1] and Özge Bolaman Avcı

Long and Short-Term Relationships Between Islamic Indexes and Their Conventional Counterparts: Is There an Opportunity of Diversification?

1 Introduction

There exists a plethora of studies examining the relationship among stock markets within the World. While most of these studies argue that stock markets of developed countries are mostly integrated (such as Taylor and Tonks, 1989; Kasa, 1992; Bekaert and Harvey, 1995; Narayan and Smyth, 2005; Baele, 2005; Goetzmann et al., 2005; Lafuente and Ordonez, 2007; Evrim Mandacı and Çağlı, 2016, etc.), majority part of them argue that those of developing countries are mostly segmented indicating potential diversification benefits for international investors (see, for instance, Kwan et al., 1995; DeFusco et al., 1996; Choudhry, 1997; Linne, 1998; Bekaert et al., 2005; Evrim Mandacı and Torun, 2007, etc.). On the other hand, there exist a few studies indicating that the integration between the stock markets of developed and developing countries increases during the financial crises' periods (see for instance Arshanapalli and Doukas 1993; Ratanapakom and Sharma, 2002; Yang et al.; 2004; Yunus, 2013, etc.). Islamic stocks have gained importance during the last global financial turmoil because of their low correlations with the conventional counterparts during that period. These markets are of interest to investors and practitioners since the Islamic indexes can be viewed as safe havens. There is a strong need to enhance the understanding of the directions of information transmission across the conventional and Islamic indexes to help investors to create successful trading strategies and to maximize the benefits of diversification (Hkiri et al., 2017: 215).

Islamic equity investments have Sharia-based screens that restrict investment in certain industries and favor growth and small cap stocks. By contrast, conventional stock markets prefer value and mid-cap stocks, and do not have investment screens (Ajmi et al., 2014: 214). Islamic stocks differ from

---

their conventional counterparties in terms of the role of Shariah[2] (Islamic law) screening. The Shariah screening has provided general rules to evaluate whether a particular firm is halal (lawful) or haram (unlawful) for investment (Derigs and Marzban, 2008). The Shariah rules do not allow businesses related to immoral activities (e.g., liquor, gambling), and the most distinct feature of Islamic firms would be the limit of leverage using interest-based debt. The filtering criteria will consequently remove large noncompliant firms from the pool of investable equities, leaving the remaining Shariah compliant investable universe to become smaller and portray more volatile returns (Hussein and Omran, 2005). As a result, Islamic equity markets are less diversified consisting of lower leverage and smaller size stocks of firms. In terms of the real sector grounded Islamic markets, they tend to show traces of reduced exposure in some crises owing to low leverage effect, while the less diversified portfolio nature increases vulnerability in other crises (Rizvi et al., 2015: 315). Because of their different features when we compare them with their conventional counterparts, the relationship between them might be low, which indicates the opportunities of diversification benefits. Therefore, it is valuable to examine the relationship between the Islamic stocks and their conventional counterparts.

If stock markets are completely integrated, identical securities could be priced identically in these markets. Therefore, international investors cannot benefit from arbitraging opportunities. The main aim of this study is to examine the relationship between Islamic Equity Markets and their conventional counterparts to investigate whether diversification benefits exist for global investors and portfolio managers. We examine the relationship between the Broad Market Islamic Indices and their conventional counterparts to determine whether international investors can provide diversification benefits through investing Islamic stocks in different regions. Dow Jones Islamic Market Index (DJIM), which is a Sharia-based equity index, is used to represent the Islamic stock markets. This index includes shares of companies whether located in Muslim or non-Muslim countries as long as they are Sharia-compliant (i.e., they have to pass a set of rules-based screens). The Broad Market indices that we use in this study consist of DJIM World, DJIM Developed Countries, DJIM Emerging Markets,

---

2   (i) A company's debt financing is not more than 33% of its capital, (ii) interest-related income of a company is not more than 10% of its total income, and (iii) the composition of account receivables and liquid assets (cash at banks and marketable securities) compared to total assets is minimum at 51% while a few cite 33% as an acceptable ratio.

DJIM Europe, DJIM Asia Pacific, and DJIM GCC[3] indices. Nature of integration among Islamic markets and conventional markets particularly attracts attention of investors who intend to diversify their portfolios. In this study, we employ Gregory Hansen Test to examine long-term relationship between Islamic indices and conventional indices. In contrast with most of the studies which have not found cointegration between variables, we prove existence of cointegration. Because of that reason we have applied causality via error correction model rather than standard Granger Causality Test. Our study is essential since it aims to contribute the limited literature on Islamic indices. According to our results, no diversification opportunity exists in the long term.

The chapter is organized as follows: following introduction, Section 2 provides the summary of the existing studies, Section 3 provides methodology, Section 4 gives data and empirical results, and the last section concludes the chapter.

2 Literature Review

We observed many studies examining the relationship between the Islamic and conventional stock markets and also among the Islamic stock markets. Most of these studies focused on the spillover effects and the impact of financial crises on these relationships. However, there are just a few studies examining the long-run relationship by employing cointegration techniques. The aim of this study is to fill this gap in Islamic finance literature.

Among the studies considering the spillover effect, Hammoudeh et al. (2013) examined the spillover between the conventional and Islamic equity markets and investigated how global crises affected Islamic markets (USA, Europe, and Asia). They used threshold and Markow-Swiching models and found that conventional stock prices responded positively to changes in Islamic equity markets. However, Dania and Mathotra (2013) found a positive and statistically significant return spillover from conventional to Islamic returns for the markets including North America, Europe, Far East, and Asia. They also found similar evidence for asymmetric volatility spillover.

Kassab (2013) used a GARCH model to investigate the persistence of volatility of the DJIM and conventional (i.e., S&P 500 index) markets. They found a strong volatility persistence of both markets, with the DJIM index being less volatile than the conventional index in the long run and exhibiting less risk at crisis periods. Akhtar et al. (2013) investigated the volatility linkages between Islamic

---

3   Gulf Cooperation Council.

and conventional assets including equities, bonds, and bills. They argued that including at least one Islamic asset lowers the volatility spillovers by up to 7.17%. They stated that the particularities of Islamic finance assets lower the degree of the dynamic linkages between Islamic markets and their conventional counterparts. Majdaub and Mansour (2014) used a sample of five countries including Turkey, Indonesia, Pakistan, Qatar, and Malaysia and investigated their relationship with the US market employing three multivariate GARCH models namely GARCH BEKK, CCC, and DCC using MSCI Islamic and conventional indices. The estimation results of the three models showed that the US and Islamic emerging equity markets are weakly correlated over time. Additionally, no complete evidence is found to support the US market spillovers.

On the other hand, Nazlioglu et al. (2015) analyzed volatility spillovers between the DJIM index and three conventional stock markets for the USA, Europe, and Asia during the sample periods, and the pre- and post-GFC sub-periods. Using the Hafner and Herwartz (2006) causality-in-variance test, they provided strong evidence of risk transfers between these apparently different stock markets, indicating a contagion between them. Furthermore, they found evidence that the volatility structure is changing during the pre- and post-global financial crises sub-periods. El Alaoui et al. (2015) studied co-movement dynamics of Dubai financial market index returns with some regional Islamic index returns (Dow Jones indices of GCC, developed markets and Sukuk) from April 1, 2008 to March 23, 2011. They employed wavelet analysis and found that the closer markets tended to exhibit a contagion effect.

In a most recent study, Hkiri et al. (2017) examined volatility spillovers across nine regional Islamic stock indexes and their conventional counterparts, using the generalized vector autoregressive framework. They used daily data covering the period 1999 to 2014 including various financial crises and found that global financial crises strongly affect the cross-market volatility. Although the contagion hypothesis was evident for both Islamic and conventional indexes, the findings also suggested the presence of a decoupling of the Islamic indexes from their conventional counterparts during turbulent periods.

Among the studies examining cointegration and causality between them, Hakim and Rashidian (2002) employed the multivariate cointegration to examine the causality linkage between the Islamic and conventional markets represented by the Dow Jones Islamic Market Index (DJIM) and the US Wilshire 5000 Index, respectively, and found nı statistical significant causality relationship between these markets. Abd Majid and Haj Kassim (2010) examined the integration among five Islamic stock markets including Malaysia, Indonesia, Japan, the UK, and the USA. They found that investors can gain benefits by diversifying in different economic grouping countries such as developed and developing. Hussin et al. (2013) used VAR estimation technique to study integration among Islamic stock markets in Malaysia, Indonesia, and the World and found cointegration among them. Similarly, Saiti et al. (2014) investigated whether Islamic stock prices provide potential diversification benefits for US-based investors. Using the DCCGARCH model, they found that Islamic indices offer better diversification opportunity compared to the Far East countries.

On the other hand, Abdul Karim et al. (2010) investigated the effects of global financial crises on the integration and co-movement of Islamic stock markets. They used cointegration techniques from February 12, 2006 to December 31, 2008. They divided the period into two as before and after the financial crises. They found that the markets are cointegrated in both before and after the crises. They argued that 2007 subprime crises did not affect the long-run co-movements among Islamic stock markets. Similarly, Dewandaru et al. (2013) used international CAPM model and found that there was a steady increase in the integration of Islamic country's stock markets over the last decade while the developed stock markets had a steady high integration with the global market.

Dewandaru et al. (2014) investigated the contagion during nine major crises and measured the integration in Islamic and conventional equity markets across different regions (such as Asia Pacific, the USA, Eurozone, and the UK) for the period 1996–2012. They employed wavelet decomposition and found incomplete stock market integration with relatively higher fundamental integration for Islamic markets which may be attributable to their real sector allocation nature. Additionally, Islamic markets showed traces of reduced exposure to the most recent global crisis because of their lower leverage nature. They found a weaker short-term integration for Islamic index pairs of the EU and UK, as well as developed and emerging markets. In contrast, most of the Islamic index pairs portray stronger fundamental integration before 2006, driven by the progress of trade openness across regions. From this year onwards, both Islamic pairs and conventional pairs exhibit almost complete long-term integration. Similarly, Rizvi et al. (2015) investigated the co-movements in Islamic and mainstream equity markets across the USA and Asia Pacific by using daily data of Dow Jones Islamic Market indices and Dow Jones Global indices from January 1, 1996 till December 31, 2014. They employed wavelet decomposition and argued that Islamic markets tended to show traces of reduced exposure in the recent financial crises due to their low leverage nature; however, the less diversified portfolio nature increases vulnerability in other crises.

On the other hand, Majdaub et al. (2016) examined both the long- and short-run integration between Islamic and conventional counterparts for France, Indonesia, the UK, and the USA from September 8, 2008 to September 6, 2013. They used the cointegration procedures of Johansen (1988), and Gregory and Hansen (1996) to examine the long-run co-movements and the multivariate Asymmetric Generalized Dynamic Conditional Correlation GARCH (AGDCC-GARCH) approach of Cappiello, Engle, and Sheppard (2006) to evaluate the short-run market integration between stock prices. They found long-run relationships between them other than the UK. They argue that the Islamic finance industry in the considered economies (except the UK) does not seem to be compliant to Islamic law's rules, which reduces benefits of international diversification and hedging. On the other hand, they found weak linkages between the Indonesian market and the developed markets for both conventional and Islamic stock prices. However, they observed a strong linkage between the Islamic and conventional indices of developed markets.

Ajmi et al. (2014) used heteroscedasticity-robust linear Granger causality and nonlinear Granger causality tests to examine the links between the Islamic and global conventional stock markets, and between the Islamic stock market and several global economic and financial shocks. They used daily data of Dow Jones Islamic Market (DJIM) index and the S&P stock market indices for the USA, Europe, and Asia, respectively, from January 4, 1999 to October 8, 2010. They found the existence of significant linear and nonlinear causality between the Islamic and conventional stock markets, but more strongly from the Islamic stock market to the other markets.

El Alaoui et al. (2015) investigated the co-movement dynamics of different time scales and horizons of Islamic Dubai financial market index returns with their counterpart regional Islamic indices returns such as GCC index, Asean index, developed countries index, emerging markets index, and Global Sukuk index between 2006 and 2011 using wavelet methodology. Additionally, they measured the lead-lag relationship between them. They found that investors should move from Dubai to Asian Islamic stock market during the bearish periods and might fly from stock to Sukuk market when time horizon of investment is eight days. They found that Dubai Islamic market is positively correlated with the GCC and Saudi. It was following GCC and Leading Sukuk market.

Abbes and Trichilli (2015) investigated the dynamic integration between the Islamic developed and emerging markets to explore whether there exist potential diversification benefits. They used 27 developed and emerging markets and found long-run integration for only similar economies. Their Vector Error Correction Model provided a lowest level of short-run integration among

European and Asian emerging markets, MENA-Latin American and European-Latin American Islamic stock markets. The integration and causality relations among Islamic stock markets tended to change overtime, especially during the financial crises.

In their study, Yılmaz et al. (2015) analyzed ten major Dow Jones Islamic equity sector indexes by implementing the novel methodologies of dynamic conditional correlation (DCC) and dynamic equicorrelation (DECO) on Dow Jones Islamic Market sector indexes. They found that prior to the financialization period, firm fundamentals and real economic factors had an important role in driving the Islamic equity prices; however, this role seemed to weaken in the last decade with the global financialization, leading to highly integrated Islamic equity sectors just as in the case of the conventional financial sectors.

3 Methodology

In the empirical part of this study firstly Gregory Hansen Cointegration Test is applied. By this way, existence of a long-term relationship between Islamic indexes and their conventional counterparts is questioned. In the next step, causality relationship between variables is examined by using Granger Causality Test which is applied via Error Correction Model.

Residual-based technique of Gregory and Hansen (1996) tests the null hypothesis of no cointegration against the alternative hypothesis of cointegration with a single structural break of unknown date in the long-run parameters of the equations. There are three models that are suggested by Gregory and Hansen (1996): cointegration with level shift (C), cointegration with level shift and trend (C/T), and cointegration with regime shift (C/S). Equations of Gregory Hansen Cointegration Test are reported as:

Model = Level Shift (C)
$$y_{1t} = \mu_1 + \mu_2 \varphi_t + \alpha^T y_{2t} + e_t \quad t = 1, \ldots, n$$
Model = Level Shift with Trend (C/T)
$$y_{1t} = \mu_1 + \mu_2 \varphi_{t\tau} + \beta t + \alpha^T y_{2t} + e_t \quad t = 1, \ldots, n$$
Model = Regime Shift (C/S)
$$y_{1t} = \mu_1 + \mu_2 \varphi_{t\tau} + \alpha_1^T y_{2t} + \alpha_2^T y_{2t} \varphi_{t\tau} + e_t \quad t = 1, \ldots, n$$

Standard Granger Causality approach entails estimating vector autoregression in the first difference form. Nonetheless according to Engle and Granger (1987), if cointegration exists, results from this approach could be misleading since the system does not represent the cointegration properties among variables. In

Tab. 1: Indexes

Broad Market Islamic Index		Conventional Counterpart (Benchmark) Index	
Name	Code	Name	Code
Dow Jones Islamic Market World Total Return Index	DJIM	S&P Global BMI (US Dollar) Gross Total Return	S&P-G
Dow Jones Islamic Market Developed Markets Total Return Index	DJIM-DM	S&P Developed BMI (US Dollar) Gross Total Return	S&P-D
Dow Jones Islamic Market World Emerging Markets Total Return Index	DJIM-EM	S&P Emerging BMI (US Dollar) Gross Total Return	S&P-Em
Dow Jones Islamic Market Europe Total Return Index	DJIM-E	S&P Europe BMI (US Dollar) Gross Total Return	S&P-EU
Dow Jones Islamic Market Asia/ Pacific Total Return Index (USD)	DJIM-A/P	S&P Asia Pacific BMI (US Dollar) Gross Total Return	S&P-A/P
Dow Jones Islamic Market GCC Total Return Index (USD)	DJIM-GCC	S&P GCC Composite Total Return Index in US Dollar	S&P-GCC

such a case, VECM is required to be estimated. Equation which shows Granger Causality test that is applied upon VECM is given as:

$$\Delta Y_t = \alpha_0 + \sum_{i=1}^{p-1} \alpha_{1i}\Delta Y_{t-i} + \sum_{i=1}^{p-1} \alpha_{2i}\Delta X_{t-i} + \varphi_1 ECT_{t-1} + \varepsilon_{1t} \tag{1}$$

$$\Delta X_t = \beta_0 + \sum_{i=1}^{p-1} \beta_{1i}\Delta Y_{t-i} + \sum_{i=1}^{p-1} \beta_{2k}\Delta X_{t-i} + \varphi_2 ECT_{t-1} + \varepsilon_{2t} \tag{2}$$

Here ECT indicates residuals of the long-run cointegration relationship, whereas is the error correction term. Granger Causality test based on VECM allows testing not only short-run but also long-run causality. Short-run Granger non-causality from X to Y is tested by the use of Wald (F-test) specified as $H_0 : \alpha_{2i} = 0$ in equation (1). The long-run Granger causality is tested by the t-statistic on ECT_{t-1} in each equation where a significant t-value indicates existence of long-run Granger causality. In this study, only results of short-run Granger Causality Test is reported.

Tab. 2: Islamic Indexes

Broad Market Islamic Index	Number of Countries
Dow Jones Islamic Market World Total Return Index	58
Dow Jones Islamic Market Developed Markets Total Return Index	24
Dow Jones Islamic Market World Emerging Markets Total Return Index	34
Dow Jones Islamic Market Europe Total Return Index	16
Dow Jones Islamic Market Asia/Pacific Total Return Index (USD)	15
Dow Jones Islamic Market GCC Total Return Index (USD)	6 (Saudi Arabia, Qatar, United Arab Emirates, Kuwait, Bahrain, and Omar)

Tab. 3: Cointegration Relationship Between Dow Jones Islamic Market World Total Return Index and S&P Global BMI (US Dollar) Gross Total Return Index

Model	Test Stat.	Break Date	Critical Value (%5)	Critical Value (%1)
C	-11.96068	2017Jan	-4.61	-5.13
C/T	-12.00031	2017Jan	-4.99	-5.45
C/S	-11.97739	2017Jan	-4.95	-5.47

Tab. 4: Cointegration Relationship Between Dow Jones Islamic Market Developed Markets Total Return Index and S&P Developed BMI (US Dollar) Gross Total Return

Model	Test Stat.	Break Date	Critical Value (%5)	Critical Value (%1)
C	-11.97920	2017Feb	-4.61	-5.13
C/T	-11.98303	2017Feb	-4.99	-5.45
C/S	-11.99041	2017Jan	-4.95	-5.47

4 Data and Empirical Results

In this study monthly data is used for the periods between September 2008 and October 2018. Logarithm of all indices are used as return. Six Islamic indices and six conventional counterparts that we include in our data set is given in Tab. 1.

Tab. 5: Cointegration Relationship Between Dow Jones Islamic Market World Emerging Markets Total Return and S&P Emerging BMI Gross Return Index

Model	Test Stat.	Break Date	Critical Value (%5)	Critical Value (%1)
C	-6.453825	2013m6	-4.61	-5.13
C/T	-6.478876	2013m4	-4.99	-5.45
C/S	-9.652509	2017m2	-4.95	-5.47

Tab. 6: Cointegration Relationship Between Dow Jones Islamic Market Europe Total Return Index and S&P Europe BMI (US Dollar) Gross Total Return

Model	Test Stat.	Break Date	Critical Value (%5)	Critical Value (%1)
C	-7.555209	2013m2	-4.61	-5.13
C/T	-7.545982	2011m1	-4.99	-5.45
C/S	-7.631819	2010m4	-4.95	-5.47

Tab. 7: Cointegration Relationship Between Dow Jones Islamic Market Asia/Pacific Total Return Index (USD) and S&P Asia Pacific BMI (US Dollar) Gross Total Return Index

Model	Test Stat.	Break Date	Critical Value (%5)	Critical Value (%1)
C	-10.47334	2010m2	-4.61	-5.13
C/T	-10.65901	2013m12	-4.99	-5.45
C/S	-10.54577	2011m3	-4.95	-5.47

Tab. 8: Cointegration Relationship Between Dow Jones Islamic Market GCC Total Return Index (USD) and S&P GCC Composite Total Return Index in US Dollar

Model	Test Stat.	Break Date	Critical Value (%5)	Critical Value (%1)
C	-11.04355	2012m10	-4.61	-5.13
C/T	-11.34511	2011m5	-4.99	-5.45
C/S	-10.98436	2012m10	-4.95	-5.47

Tab. 2 presents the number of countries in Islamic indexes included in our data set.

Tab. 9: Causality Relationship Between Dow Jones Islamic Market World Total Return Index and S&P Global BMI (US Dollar) Gross Total Return

	Test Statistics		
Null Hypotheses	**Chi-square**	**Probability**	**Conclusion**
Dow Jones Islamic Market World Total Return Index does not Granger Cause S&P Global BMI (US Dollar) Gross Total Return Index	4.102529	0.5348	Fail to Reject Ho
S&P Global BMI (US Dollar) Gross Total Return Index does not Granger cause Dow Jones Islamic Market World Total Return Index	3.155793	0.6760	Fail to reject Ho

4.1 Results of Gregory Hansen Test

Gregory Hansen Test Results are given through Tab. 3 to Tab. 8. By this way long-term relationship between Islamic indices and their conventional counterparts is questioned.

As it is obvious in the tables, all Islamic indices have cointegration relationship with their conventional counterparts. In other words, a long-term relationship exists between Islamic indices and counterparts. Existence of cointegration means that there is not an opportunity of diversification in the long term.

Since existence of cointegration is proved, causality relationship is examined via VECM.

4.2 Results of Causality Test

Results are presented through Tab. 9 to Tab. 14.

According to Granger Causality test which is applied via VECM, causality relationship could not be detected between three Islamic indices and their conventional counterparts such as Dow Jones Islamic Market World Total Return Index and S&P Europe BMI (US Dollar) Gross Total Return, Dow Jones Islamic Market Developed Markets Total Return Index and S&P Developed BMI (US Dollar) Gross Total Return, and Dow Jones Islamic Market GCC Total Return Index (USD) and S&P GCC Composite total return index in US dollar. This means there is not a short-run relationship between variables which may create an opportunity of diversification in the short run. Bidirectional causality relationship is found between two Islamic indices and conventional counterparts such as Dow Jones Islamic Market

Tab. 10: Causality Relationship Between Dow Jones Islamic Market Developed Markets Total Return Index and S&P Developed BMI (US Dollar) Gross Total Return

	Test Statistics		
Null Hypotheses	**Chi-square**	**Probability**	**Conclusion**
Dow Jones Islamic Market Developed Markets Total Return Index does not Granger Cause S&P Developed BMI (US Dollar) Gross Total Return Index	3.645394	0.6015	Fail to Reject Ho
S&P Developed BMI (US Dollar) Gross Total Return Index does not Granger cause Dow Jones Islamic Market Developed Markets Total Return Index	3.064456	0.6900	Fail to reject Ho

Tab. 11: Causality Relationship Between Dow Jones Islamic Market Emerging Market Total Return and S&P Emerging Market BMI Gross Return Index

	Test Statistics		
Null Hypotheses	**Chi-square**	**Probability**	**Conclusion**
Dow Jones Islamic Market Emerging Markets Total Return Index does not Granger Cause S&P Emerging Market BMI (US Dollar) Gross Total Return Index	15.75188	0.0063	Reject Ho
S&P Emerging Market BMI (US Dollar) Gross Total Return Index does not Granger cause Dow Jones Islamic Market Emerging Markets Total Return Index	17.96438	0.0151	Reject Ho

Emerging Market Total Return and S&P Emerging Market BMI Gross Return Index, Dow Jones Islamic Market Asia/Pacific Total Return Index (USD) and S&P Asia Pacific BMI (US Dollar) Gross Total Return Index. A unidirectional causality relationship is detected from S&P Europe BMI (US Dollar) Gross Total Return Index to Dow Jones Islamic Market Europe Total Return Index indicating that conventional stock market leads the Islamic stock market for Europe.

Tab. 12: Causality Relationship Between Dow Jones Islamic Market Europe Total Return Index and S&P Europe BMI (US Dollar) Gross Total Return

Null Hypotheses	Test Statistics		
	Chi-square	Probability	Conclusion
Dow Jones Islamic Market Europe Total Return Index does not Granger Cause S&P Europe BMI (US Dollar) Gross Total Return Index	11.08777	0.0857	Fail to Reject Ho
S&P Europe BMI (US Dollar) Gross Total Return Index does not Granger cause Dow Jones Islamic Market Europe Total Return Index	13.69492	0.0332	Reject Ho

Tab. 13: Causality Relationship Between Dow Jones Islamic Market Asia/Pacific Total Return Index (USD) and S&P Asia Pacific BMI (US Dollar) Gross Total Return Index

Null Hypotheses	Test Statistics		
	Chi-square	Probability	Conclusion
Dow Jones Islamic Market Asia/Pacific Total Return Index does not Granger cause S&P Asia Pacific BMI (US Dollar) Gross Total Return Index	13.33711	0.0380	Reject Ho
S&P Asia Pacific BMI (US Dollar) Gross Total Return Index does not Granger cause Dow Jones Islamic Market Asia/Pacific Total Return Index	13.32615	0.0381	Reject Ho

5 Conclusion

In this study, we examine the long- and short-run relationship between Islamic indices and their conventional counterparts by using Gregory Hansen Cointegration Test and Granger Causality Test, which is applied via VECM. Based on the results of Gregory Hansen, there is not an opportunity of diversification in the long run. However, three of six Islamic indexes (DJIM World Total Return Index, DJIM Developed Markets Total Return Index, and DJIM GCC Total Return Index) do not have causality relationship with their counterparts, which may show an opportunity of diversification in the short run. Nonetheless,

Tab. 14: Causality Relationship Between Dow Jones Islamic Market GCC Total Return Index (USD) and S&P GCC Composite Total Return Index in US Dollar

Null Hypotheses	Test Statistics		
	Chi-square	Probability	Conclusion
Dow Jones Islamic Market GCC Total Return Index does not Granger cause S&P GCC Composite Total Return Index	5.4303480	0.4899	Fail to Reject Ho
S&P GCC Composite Total Return Index does not Granger cause Dow Jones Islamic Market GCC Total Return Index	4.653073	0.5890	Fail to Reject Ho

since short-run relationships exist between these Islamic indices and their conventional counterparts, it can be concluded that benefit from diversification vanishes in the long run. Our results are in consistence with Majdoub et al. (2016), whereas it contrasts with Hakim and Rashidian (2002). Despite the growing interest in exploring the relation between conventional indices and Islamic indices, there is still a limited number of studies, which in turn makes our study essential. For further study, relationship within Islamic Indices could be investigated. Moreover, Turkish Islamic Indices (Participation 30 Index, Participation 50 Index) that have been rarely examined in empirical studies so far could be investigated.

Bibliography

Abbes, M. B., and Trichilli, Y. (2015). "Islamic stock markets and potential diversification benefits", *Borsa Istanbul Review*, 15(2), pp. 93–105.

Abd Majid, M. S., and Haj Kassim, S. (2010). "Potential benefit across global Islamic equity markets", *Journal of Economic Cooperation and Development*, 31(4), pp. 103–126.

Abdul Karim, B., Akila Mohd. Kassim, N., and Affendy Arip, M. (2010). "The subprime crisis and Islamic stock markets integration", *International Journal of Islamic and Middle Eastern Finance and Management*, 3(4), pp. 363–371.

Ajmi, A. N., Hammoudeh, S., Nguyen, D. K., and Sarafrazi, S. (2014). "How strong are the causal relationships between Islamic and conventional finance systems?", *Journal of International Financial Markets*, Institutions and Money, 28, pp. 213–227.

Akhtar, S. M., Jahromi, M., John, K.Moise, C. E. (2013). Intensity of Volatility Linkages in Islamic and Conventional Markets. AFA 2012 Chicago Meetings

Paper. Available at SSRN: http://ssrn.com/abstract=1782220 or http://dx.doi.org/10.2139/ssrn.1782220.

Arshanapalli, B., and Doukas, J. (1993). "International stock market linkages: evidence from the pre- and post- October 1987 period", *Journal of Banking and Finance*, 17, pp. 193–208.

Baele, L. (2005). "Volatility spillover effects in European equity markets", *Journal of Financial and Quantitative Analysis*, 40(02), pp. 373–401.

Bekaert, G., and Harvey, C. R. (1995). "Time-varying world market integration", *Journal of Finance*, 50(2), pp. 403–444.

Bekaert, G., Harvey, C. R. and Ng, A. (2005). "Market integration and contagion", *Journal of Business*, 78, pp. 39–69.

Cappiello, L., Engle, R. F., and Sheppard, T. (2006). "Asymmetric dynamics in the correlations of global equity and bond returns", *Journal of Financial Econometrics*, 4, pp. 537–572.

Choudhry, T. (1997). "Stochastic trends in stock prices: evidence from Latin American markets", *Journal of Macroeconomics*, 19, pp. 285–304.

Dania, A., and Malhotra, D. K. (2013). "An empirical examination of the dynamic linkages of faith-based socially responsible investing", *The Journal of Wealth Management*, 16, pp. 65–79.

Defusco, R. A., Geppert, J. M., and Tsetsekos, G. (1996). "Long-term diversification potential in emerging stock markets", *Financial Review*, 31, pp. 343–363.

Derigs, U., and Marzban, S. (2008). "Review and analysis of current Shariah-compliant equity screening practices", *International Journal of Islamic Middle Eastern Finance and Management*, 1(4), pp. 285–303.

Dewandaru, G., Rizvi, S. A. R., Bacha, O. I., and Masih, M. (2013). "An analysis of stock market efficiency: developed vs Islamic stock markets using MF-DFA". *In: Presented at 15th Malaysian Finance Conference*, p. 2013.

Dewandaru, G, Rizvi, S. A. R., Masih, R., Masih, M., and Alhabshi, S. O. (2014). "Stock market co-movements: Islamic versus conventional equity indices with multi-timescales analysis", *Economic Systems*, 38, pp. 553–571.

el Alaoui, A., Dewandaru, G., Rosly, S., and Masih, M. (2015). "Linkages and co-movement between international stock market returns: case of Dow Jones Islamic Dubai Financial Market index", *Journal of International Financial Markets*, Institutions and Money, 36, pp. 53–70.

Engle, R. F., and Granger, C. W. J. (1987). "Cointegration and error correction: Representation, estimation and testing", *Econometrica*, 55, pp. 251–276.

Evrim Mandacı, P. and Torun, E. (2007). "Testing integration between the major emerging markets", *Central Bank Review*, 1, pp. 1–12.

Evrim Mandacı, P., and Çağlı, E. Ç. (2016). "Who drives whom? Investigating the relationship between the major stock markets", *Financial Studies*, 2, pp. 6–24.

Goetzmann, W. N., Li, L., and Rouwenhorst, G. K. (2005). "Long-term global market correlations", *Journal of Business*, 78(1), pp. 1–38.

Gregory, A. W., and Hansen, B. E. (1996). "Residual-based tests for cointegration in models with regime shifts", *Journal of Econometrics*, 70, pp. 99–126.

Hafner, C. M., and Herwartz, H. (2006). A Lagrange multiplier test for causality in variance. *Economics Letters*, 93(1), 137–141.

Hakim, S., and Rashidian, M. (2002). "Risk and Return of Islamic Stock Market Indexes", Paper Presented at the Economic Research Forum Annual Meetings (Sharjah, UAE).

Hammoudeh, S., Jawadi, F., and Sarafrazi, S. (2013). "Interactions between conventional and Islamic stock markets: A hybrid threshold analysis", Mimeo: Drexel University.

Hkiri, B., Hammoudeh, S, Aloui, C., Yarovayae, L. (2017). "Are Islamic indexes a safe haven for investors? An analysis of total, directional and net volatility spillovers between conventional and Islamic indexes and importance of crisis periods", *Pacific-Basin Finance Journal*, 43, pp. 124–150.

Hussein, K., and Omran, M., (2005). "Ethical investment revisited: evidence from Dow Jones Islamic indexes", *Journal of Investing*, 14(3), pp. 105–124.

Hussin, M. Y. M., Yusof, Y. A., Muhammad, F., Razak, A. A., Hashim, E., and Marwan, N. F. (2013). "The integration of Islamic stock markets: does a problem for investors?", *Labuan e-Journal of Muamalat and Society*, 7, pp. 17–27.

Johansen, S. (1988). "Statistical analysis of cointegration vectors", *Journal of Economic Dynamics and Control*, 12, pp. 231–254.

Kasa, K. (1992). "Common stochastic trends in international stock markets", *Journal of Monetary Economics*, 29, pp. 95–124.

Kassab, S., (2013). "Modeling volatility stock market using the ARCH and GARCH models: comparative study index (SP Sharia VS SP 500)", *European Journal of Banking and Finance*, 10, pp. 72–77.

Kwan, A. C., Sim, A. B., and Cotsomitis, J. A. (1995). "The causal relationships between equity indices on World exchanges", *Applied Economics*, 27, pp. 33–37.

Lafuente, J. A., and Ordóñez, J. (2007). "The effect of the EMU on short and long-run stock market dynamics: new evidence on financial integration", *International Journal of Financial Markets and Derivatives*, 1(1), pp. 75–95.

Linne, T. (1998). "The Integration of the Central and Eastern European Equity Markets into the International Capital Markets: A Co-Integration Analysis", Institut Für Wirtschaftsforschung, 1, pp.1-16.Majdoub, J., and Mansour, W. (2014). "Islamic equity market integration and volatility spillover between emerging and US stock markets", *The North American Journal of Economics and Finance*, 29, pp. 452–470.

Majdouba, J., Mansourb, W., and Jamel, J. (2016). "Market integration between conventional and Islamic stock prices", *North American Journal of Economics and Finance*, 37, pp. 36–457.

Narayan, P. K., and Smyth, R. (2005). "Cointegration of stock markets between New Zealand, Australia and the G7 economies: searching for co-movement under structural change", *Australian Economic Papers*, 44, pp. 231–247.

Nazlioglu, S., Hammoudeh, S., and Gupta, R., (2015). "Volatility transmission between Islamic and conventional equity markets: evidence from causality-in-variance test", *Applied Economics*, 47(46), pp. 4996–5011.

Ratanapakom, O. and Sharma, S. C. (2002). "Interrelationships among regional stock indices", *Review of Financial Economics*, 11, pp. 91–108.

Rizvi, S. A. R., Arshad, S., and Alam, N. (2015). "Crises and contagion in Asia Pacific–Islamic v/s conventional markets", *Pacific-Basin Finance Journal*, 34, pp. 315–326.

Saiti, B., Bacha, O. I., and Masih, M. (2014). "The diversification benefits from Islamic investment during the financial turmoil: the case for the US-based equity investors", *Borsa Istanbul Review*, 14(4), pp. 196–211.

Taylor, M. P. and Tonks, I. (1989). "The internationalization of stock markets and the abolition of U.K. exchange control", *Review of Economics and Statistics*, 71, pp. 332–336.

Yang, J., Kolari, J. W. and Sutanto, P. W. (2004). "On the stability of long-run relationship between emerging and US stock markets", *Journal of Multinational Financial Management*, 14, pp. 233–248.

Yilmaz, M. K., Sensoy, A., Ozturk, K., and Hacihasanoglu, E. (2015). "Cross-sectoral interactions in Islamic equity markets", *Pacific-Basin Finance Journal*, 32(2015), pp. 1–20.

Yunus, N. (2013). "Contagion in international financial markets: a recursive cointegration approach", *Journal of Multinational Financial Management*, 23, pp. 327–337.

H. Işıl Alkan and Bora Alkan

The Issue of Gender Pay Gap: How to Combat?

Introduction

Women all over the world are less likely to be involved in labour markets than men, and when they find an opportunity to involve, they face the problem of gender pay gap. Although women's participation in labour markets is high in developed countries, women may be paid less than men. In other words, wage inequality does not appear to be directly related to the level of development or level of income of the countries. The existence of this problem even in the prominent countries in terms of gender equality reveals that this problem is difficult to cope with. The determinants of gender pay gap are various and are varying by the country. The aim of this study is to examine the global gender pay gap issue and to underline the methods of struggle. In this framework, firstly, the definition and determinants of wage gap will be discussed and secondly, extent and recent trends will be examined in the study. Thirdly, as an important subject the motherhood pay gap will be observed. The study concludes with the conclusion section which deals with the methods of combating the problem.

1 The Definition and the Determinants of Gender Pay Gap

Gender pay (wage) gap is a concept which has various definitions in the literature. According to OECD, it is the difference between median earnings of men and women relative to median earnings of men (OECD, 2019a). For Platenga and Fransen, it is the difference between women's earnings and men's earnings mostly based on differences in gross hourly wages. The wage gap can be calculated as the ratio of the average gross hourly wage of the woman to the average gross hourly wage of the man (2010, p. 415). According to the definition of International Labour Organization (ILO), the pay gap[1] is the difference between male and female average earnings as a percentage of the male earnings, and it can be calculated based on the average or median value. The pay gap consists of "explained" and "unexplained" portions. Differences in educational levels, qualifications, work experience, occupational category and hours worked compose the "explained" part whereas the discrimination creates the "unexplained" portion (ILO, 2019a, p. 2).

---

1 The definition of ILO will be taken into account in this study.

The explained and unexplained parts are of importance as they help to investigate the main determinants of gender pay gap. The chief determinants of gender wage gap can be summarized under five main headings as below:

1. Human capital
2. Gender role theory
3. Occupational segregation
4. Undervaluation of women's work
5. Discriminatory behaviour

Human capital can be expressed as the sum of the knowledge and skills included by the labour force (Kaynak, 2007, p. 303). According to the neoclassical human capital model, which is one of the discrimination theories in the labour market, human capital is the main factor that increases productivity and gains (Blau, Ferber& Winkler, 2006, p. 160). According to Becker, human capital is a broad concept that represents individuals' abilities, education and health. Education and courses pave the way for higher human capital[2] and hence increase productivity (1993, pp. 15–25). In the literature, various studies verify the positive relationship between human capital attainment and wage differentials[3].

According to the human capital model, men and women are not substitutes in the labour market. Even if the levels of intelligence and education are approximate, considering the work experience it is assumed that the woman's human capital is lower than that of the male. Women take place in the labour market for shorter periods than men, so there is a difference in productivity between men and women. The difference in labour force participation changes the quality of the workforce, and wage differences explain the qualitative nature between men and women labour (Blau & Jusenius, 1976, p. 185).

Gender roles adopted from a very early stage lead to different ways/choices for women and men in the field of education and employment. However, the mentioned choices, shaped by social pressure and elections, are often not very conscious choices. As a result, different paths in education and employment lead to significant differences in earnings (Brynin, 2017, p. 16).

---

2 Polachek and Xiang (2014: 3) assert that actual human capital investments are difficult to observe because data concerning human capital usually consist years of schooling and actual work experience; however, other important determinants such as quality of schooling and types of on-the-job-training are rarely available. Thus, access to precise measures of human capital is not easy.
3 Please see: Verner (2000), Mincer (1970), Schady (2001), İsmail et.al. (2014), Lopez-Bazo and Motellon (2009), Mincer (1991).

Occupational segregation is the other fact contributing to gender wage gap. Although women have been increasingly participating in the labour market in recent years, occupational segregation is quite intense across the world. And high level of segregation creates inequality between men's and women's earnings. Occupational segregation is quite common in all parts of the world, including the European Union. According to the stated segregation, women and men are disproportionately concentrated in specific occupations. In detail, women concentrate on care-related jobs and services, while men concentrate on "heavy" professions which are associated with machinery, craft, trade, skilled agriculture and fishery. While men occupy the legislative and managerial occupations at a great extent, women are concentrated in lower-level jobs. On the other hand, while males rarely take part in non-standard jobs, such as part-time, women work more intensively in such flexible work (Grybaite, 2006, pp. 88–89).

Another contributor of gender pay gap is undervaluation of women's work. Grimshaw and Rubery assert that two kinds of undervaluation emerge in terms of women's work. Firstly, women are paid less than men in the same job for the same efficiency, and secondly, women are generally employed in jobs which are undervalued. In such cases, either the woman's potential is not sufficiently utilised, or the woman will be charged under what she deserves (2007, p.V).

Discriminatory behaviour is the other determinant of gender pay gap. Discriminatory behaviour manifests itself in three different forms in the labour market: employer discrimination, employee discrimination and customer discrimination. In employer discrimination, the employer discriminates against women in the labour market and wants to hire a woman if her wages are lower than that of a man (Blau et.al, 2016: 219). Employee discrimination is based on personal prejudice, and employees do not want to take orders from a female chief, nor do they want to share the responsibility of a job with a female employee. Another type of discrimination based on personal bias is customer discrimination. In this type of discrimination, customers do not want to be served by female employees. In particular, people want to receive services that require high responsibility, especially from men (for instance, pilot). Women can concentrate on jobs requiring less qualifications (for example, stewardess). Because jobs that require less qualifications are low, women are imprisoned in low-paid jobs (Ehrenberg & Smith, 2000, p. 438–439).

It should be underlined that the mentioned above are the main determinants because certain micro- and macro-factors also affect the gap. For instance, a study examining the gender wage gap for a sample of 53 economies for 1995–2010 period reveals that a higher female share in the industry sector widens the pay gap. The result is valid for both developed and developing countries, and

Tab. 1: Employment to Population Ratio by Regions (15+) (%) (ILOSTAT, 2019a)

	Male	Female
World	71,4	45,3
Africa	68,1	50,3
Americas*	69,3	49,6
Arab States	72,8	15,5
Asia and the Pacific	74,6	43,6
Europe and Central Asia	62,1	47

*Including Latin America and the Caribbean and North America

consistent with the other studies in the literature. Unorganized labour unions for female workers is seen as the main reason (Terada-Hagiwara et. al, 2018, p. 17). According to another study, coupled with the tertiary education, population growth and government expenditure impacts gender income inequality in the selected Sub-Saharan African countries (Busayo and Olufunmilayo, 2013, p. 83).

2 Extent and Recent Trends in Gender Pay Gap

While the employment rate of women and men in the world varies in terms of regions, the employment rate of women in the world average is less than the rate of men. In other words, there is an employment gap between both sexes globally (ILOSTAT, 2019a). Although women's participation in labour markets has increased in recent years in many regions, women are less employed than men globally; and the employment gap is significant in the Arab States when examined worldwide (Tab. 1).

Unequal division of labour in the household and limited access to paid employment create pay gaps worldwide. Women perform most of the unpaid household chores and care work as a result of unequal division of labour in household, thus they have more limited opportunity to reach high-quality paid work in comparison with men. According to the results of the time-use surveys, women work more hours than men when their unpaid labour is taken into account (ILO, 2019b, p. 19). However, it should be underlined that the work of the woman is often invisible and unpaid. In high-income countries, women prefer to work part-time, whereas in middle- and low-income countries women seeking wage employment are directed towards informal employment, thus these tendencies directly affect the pay gap (ILO, 2019b, p. 20).

Table 2 reveals that gender pay gaps using monthly wages are higher than the gaps using hourly wages across the world in all income levels. The main

Tab. 2: Gender Pay Gap Using Hourly and Monthly Wages in Several Countries, the Latest Years (ILO, 2019b, pp. 24–25)

Countries	Gender pay gap using hourly wages	Gender pay gap using monthly wages
	Median gender pay gap	*Median gender pay gap*
High Income	**15,7**	**24,9**
Republic of Korea	36,0	36,0
United Kingdom	20,6	35,2
United States	18,4	25,7
Switzerland	18,1	37,5
Spain	14,4	21,9
Sweden	12	17,5
Norway	9,8	21,3
Netherlands	10,6	40,3
Italy	6,2	16,9
Hungary	2,0	6,5
Upper-Middle Income	**17,3**	**20,2**
Russian Federation	24,5	30,6
China	20	20
Brazil	10,8	20,8
Turkey	5	19,2
Bulgaria	1,9	2,1
Lower-Middle Income	**14,8**	**22,3**
Pakistan	47,2	62,5
Indonesia	21,9	28,6
Vietnam	7,7	8,9
Mongolia	4	16,7
Low Income	**22,7**	**31,7**
Nepal	34,5	44,7
Tanzania	25	25
Gambia	12,5	28
Malawi	10,7	31,9
World	**16,6**	**21,8**

reason for this situation is that the working hours of women and men are different and that part-time work is more specific to women. Moreover, in the form of part-time work, wages are generally less and working conditions are of less quality (Fagan et. al., 2014: 55). ILO verifies the stated assertion because according to ILO database, part-time work is more widespread among women in most countries in varying proportions, for instance, 72% of women but 26% of men employees work as part-time workers in Netherlands (ILO, 2019a, p. 23). However, it should be noted that part-time work is not very desirable for women in many countries, as it is determined that women in Bulgaria, Italy, Romania, and Spain choose to work as part-time unwillingly (ILO, 2016). Another element that obliges women to work in part-time is that women are largely responsible for domestic work and care work (ILO, 2018).

High prevalence of informal employment in the developing countries and women's concentration in informal employment also deepens the wage gap in the developing regions. Yahmed (2016: p. 26) determines that gender wage gap is higher in informal jobs (13%) compared to formal jobs (5%). Akar et al. also reveal that firm-size wage gap is greater for informal employment than formal employment in Turkey (2013, p. 1). In many emerging economies of the world, including Turkey, women's informal employment in the agriculture sector is intense compared to men's; moreover, women's hourly and daily wages are significantly lower than the wages of men's in the stated sector (Alkan, 2019, pp. 44–86; FAO, 2011: p. 18, FAO, 2010, pp. 16). Briefly, it is enunciable that one of the prominent reasons for gender pay gap is the high prevalence of part-time work among women (especially in high-income countries) and the more intensive participation of women in informal employment (especially in low-income countries). Hence, the lack of full-time and invulnerable employment opportunities in all countries condemns women to unequal wages.

OECD statistics reveal that the gender pay gaps are in a decreasing trend in recent years in most OECD countries. The statistics determine that the gender gap in median earnings decreased in 32 of the 35 OECD countries between 2006 and 2016. In this regard, Austria, Belgium, Greece, Switzerland and Japan are the prominent countries realizing improvements because the stated countries achieved more than 8 percentage points decrease concerning the gap. On the other hand, Hungary, Latvia and Chile witnessed at least nine percentage points increase. Additionally, Hungary, Mexico and Turkey are the countries seeing increases since 2010 (OECD, 2019b).

3 Motherhood Pay Gap

While the gender pay gap is being examined on a global basis, another factor that needs to be explored is the motherhood pay gap. This gap measures the gap between mothers and non-mothers and also between mothers and fathers.

Tab. 3: Motherhood and Fatherhood Gaps in Several Countries for Latest Years (ILO, 2019b, 80).

Countries	Motherhood gap	Fatherhood gap
Argentina	10,50	-0,30
Australia	5	-7,30
Brazil	7,70	-7
Canada	1,2	-3,40
China	10,40	0,10
Korea (Rep. of)	12,60	-26,00
Mexico	5,80	-3,40
Turkey	29,60	2,40
United States	4,30	-18,80
Russia	14,70	2

According to Budig and England, there are several reasons why mothers earn less than other women. Firstly, their professional experience decreases with the motherhood; secondly, their productivity at work decreases; thirdly, they are discriminated by employers and lastly, they tend to choose mother-friendly jobs which trade-off higher wages (2001, pp. 204).

ILO data reveals that, while the stated gap is less than 1% in Canada, it is around 30% in Turkey. In short, mothers are paid less. Factors such as disruption in labour force participation and the decrease in working hours lead to low wages according to ILO. Moreover, family-friendly policies also bring low wages. On the other hand, promotion opportunities are more limited for mothers (ILO, 2019b, XVII).

Tab. 3 shows motherhood and fatherhood gaps for various countries. The motherhood gaps are calculated by comparing the hourly wages of non-mothers to the hourly wages of mothers, while the fatherhood gap compares the hourly wages of non-fathers to the hourly wages of fathers. A positive motherhood (or fatherhood) gap indicates that mothers (or fathers) earn less than non-mothers (or non-fathers) (ILO, 2019b, 79).

This gap is higher in developing countries when compared with the developed ones. Motherhood pay gap is increasing as the number of children of the woman increases. Having one child has a more limited impact on the relevant gap, while having two children in particular three children significantly raises the gap (Grimshaw & Rubery, 2015, p.V). As can be seen in Tab. 3, the motherhood gap is higher in developing countries and highest in Turkey where the patriarchal structure is sovereign.

Conclusion (or Ways to Tackle the Gender Pay Gap)

According to the United Nations, gender pay gap is difficult to close due to four main reasons: 1) Gender segregation is a substantial problem, women's domestic responsibilities restrict their access to labour market. 2) Legislations "for equal pay for work of equal value" are limited and usually not effective. 3) Gender inequalities may be seen in new forms if women change the concentrated occupations. 4) Increasing inequalities and reduced regulation obstruct gender equality (UN, 2019). However, how difficult it may be, there are various ways of dealing with this problem.

First of all, increasing the education level of women is of importance especially in developing countries as education allows the rise of women's human capital. However, education alone is not sufficient both in developing and developed countries as scientific studies refer. Particularly, education in high-income countries impacts gender pay gap less than 1%, so, education is not an explanatory variable for gender pay gap for developed countries; because in many cases, the education level of women in high-income countries is higher than that of men. In this case, the first factor explaining the pay gap is the lower wage paid to women for equal work. Women receive lower wages than men, even if they are more educated in many countries. Therefore, "equal pay for equal work" has to be the first target to achieve. Additionally, the domestic responsibilities of women have to be lessened for their high labour market participation. Female employment has to be encouraged by the help of various social policies especially in specific regions where women's labour force participation is marginal, in other words the employment gap between sexes is higher.

The second factor explaining the gender pay gap in all countries is the undervaluation of women's work in heavily feminized professions as wages are lower in feminized professions. In this regard, women's work has to be fully evaluated and wages should be increased in feminized professions. Besides, the concentration of women in certain professions should be alleviated and the number of women should be increased in sectors where men are concentrated (in some instances, by the help of employment quotas). Moreover, prejudices against women employees should be minimised; in other words, discrimination of employers, employees and customers should be prevented both with various measures and awareness raising practices.

The third significant factor is the motherhood pay gap. As stated in the previous section, mothers are paid less and they have less promotion opportunities in labour markets. To overcome the motherhood pay gap, services providing child and elderly care should be increased, work in the household should be distributed equitably and policies encouraging the return of women should be implemented. Especially, encouraging the return of women can prevent the long-term detachment of women from the labour market. On the other hand, since the factors that reveal the pay gap differ according to the countries, it is imperative to reduce the gap with country-specific measures. Healthy sectoral data is deficient but essential in developing countries. Additionally, policies to reduce the share of women in informal economy will narrow this gap especially in the developing world where the informality is extensive (ILO, 2019b, 89–98).

Although the participation of women in the labour force is increasing in recent years, increasing participation does not narrow the pay gap. Even some Scandinavian countries, which are at the top of gender equality, face this problem. Pay gap is a difficult problem to tackle due to stated facts above; thus, the problem requires differentiated measures on country basis. However, there are policies that can be implemented jointly in all countries. These are: equal pay for equal work, combating discrimination and narrowing the informal economy scale. As a result, living in a world having less inequality should not be a dream which can never be realized.

Bibliography

Akar, G., Balkan, B., Tümen, S., 2013. Overview of Firm-Size and Gender Pay Gaps in Turkey: The Role of Informal Employment. Ekonomi-tek, 2(3): September / Eylül 2013, 1–21.

Alkan, I., 2019. Tarım Sektöründe Kadın Emeği. 2. Baskı, Ankara: Gazi Kitabevi.

Becker, G., 1993. Human Capital, a Theoretical and Emprical Analysis with Special Reference to Education. Chicago and London: The University of Chicago Press.

Blau, F., Ferber, M., Wrinkler, A., 2006. The Economics of Women, Men and Work. USA: Pearson Prentice Hall, pp: 160–219.

Blau, F., Jusenius, C., 1976. Economists' Approaches to Sex Segregation in the Labour Market. An Appraisal, Signs Journal, 1(3): 181–199.

Brynin, M., 2017. The Gender Pay Gap. Equality and Human Rights Commission Research Report Series, Institute for Social and Economic Research, University of Essex, Manchester.

Budig, M. J., England, P., 2001. The Wage Penalty for Motherhood. American Sociological Review, 66(2): (Apr., 2001), pp. 204–225.

Busayo, A., Olufunmilayo, S., 2013. Determinants of Gender Income Inequality in Selected Sub Saharan African Countries. Journal of Economics and Sustainable Development, 4(16): pp. 73–84.

Ehrenberg, R., Smith, R., 2000. Modern Labor Economics: Theory and Public Policy, USA: Addison Wesley Longman, pp. 438–442.

Fagan, C., Norman, H., Smith, M., Gonzalez Menendez, M. C., 2014. In Search of Good Quality Part-time Employment. Conditions of Work and Employment Series No. 43, Geneva: International Labour Office.

FAO, 2010. Gender Dimensions of Rural and Agricultural Employment: Differentiated Pathways Out of Poverty, FAO & IFAD & ILO Publications, pp. 7–92, Rome.

FAO, 2011. Women in Agriculture, Closing the Gender Gap for Development, FAO Publications, pp. 7–115.

Grimshaw, D., Rubery, J., 2007. Undervaluing Women's Work, Working Paper Series No. 53, European Work and Employment Research Centre University of Manchester, Manchester.

Grimshaw, D., Rubery, J., 2015. The Motherhood Pay Gap: A Review of the Issues, Theory and International Evidence, Conditions of Work and Employment Series No. 57, Geneva: ILO.

Grybaite, V., 2006. Analysis of Theoretical Approaches to Gender Pay Gap. Journal of Business Economics and Management, 7(2), pp. 85–91.

ILO, 2016. World Employment and Social Outlook: Trends for Youth. Geneva: International Labour Office.

ILO, 2018. Care Work and Care Jobs for the Future of Decent Work. Geneva: International Labour Office.

ILO, 2019a. Pay Equity, a Key Driver of Gender Equality. (Date Accessed: 24/04/2019). https://www.ilo.org/wcmsp5/groups/public/@dgreports/@gender/documents/briefingnote/wcms_410196.pdf.

ILO, 2019b. Global Wage Report 2018/19. (Date Accessed: 27/04/2019). https://www.ilo.org/wcmsp5/groups/public/---dgreports/---dcomm/---publ/documents/publication/wcms_650553.pdf.

ILOSTAT, 2019a. ILO Labour Statistics. (Date Accessed: 04/06/2019). https://www.ilo.org/ilostat/faces/oracle/webcenter/portalapp/pagehierarchy/Page3.jspx?MBI_ID=7&_afrLoop=538618573921115&_afrWindowMode=0&_afrWindowId=7n33c41sm_1#!%40%40%3F_afrWindowId%3D7n33c41sm_1%26_afrLoop%3D538618573921115%26MBI_ID%3D7%26_afrWindowMode%3D0%26_adf.ctrl-state%3D7n33c41sm_172.

Ismail, R., Saukani, R., Abubakar, N. T., 2014. Human Capital and Regional Wage Differentials in Malaysia. Actual Problems of Economics, 155(5): 328–338.

Kaynak, M., 2007. Kalkınma İktisadı. 2. Baskı, Ankara: Gazi Kitabevi.

Lopez-Bazo, E., Motellon, E., 2009. Human Capital and Regional Wage Gaps. Research Institute of Applied Economics, Working Papers 2009/24, Barcelona.

Mincer, J., 1970. The Distribution of Labor Income: A Survey with Special Reference to Human Capital Approach. Journal of Economic Literature, 8: 1–26.

Mincer, J., 1991. Human Capital, Technology and the Wage Structure: What Do Time Series Show?, National Bureau of Economic Research, Working Paper No. 3581, Cambridge.

OECD, 2019a. Gender Wage Gap. (Date Accessed: 24/04/2019). https://data.oecd.org/earnwage/gender-wage-gap.htm.

OECD, 2019b. Gender Pay Gaps, Key Findings. (Date Accessed: 04/06/2019). https://www.oecd.org/els/LMF_1_5_Gender_pay_gaps_for_full_time_workers.pdf.

Plantanga, J., Fransen, E., 2010. The extent and the origin of the gender pay gap in Europe. (in) The International Handbook of Gender and Poverty, Concepts, Research, Policy (ed: S. Chant), Edward Elgar Publishing, UK.

Polachek, S. W., Xiang, J., 2014. The Gender Pay Gap Across Countries: A Human Capital Approach, IZA Discussion Papers, No. 8603, Bonn: Institute for the Study of Labor (IZA).

Schady, N. R., 2001. Convexity and Sheepskin Effects in the Human Capital Earning Function: Recent Evidence for Filipino Men. Policy Research Working Paper 2566, World Bank (Date Accessed: 03/05/2019). http://documents.worldbank.org/curated/en/603651468775518234/pdf/multi0page.pdf.

Terada-Hagiwara, A., Camingue-Romance, S. F., Zveglich, J. E., 2018. Gender Pay Gap: A Macro Perspective, ADB Economics Working Paper Series, No.538, Asian Development Bank, Philippines.

UN, 2019. Tackling the Gender Pay Gap: From Individual Choices to Institutional Change. (Date Accessed: 03/06/2019). http://www.unwomen.org/en/digital-library/publications/2016/3/the-persistence-of-the-gender-pay-gap.

Verner, D., 2000. Wage and Productivity Gaps: Evidence from Ghana. World Bank. (Date Accessed: 03/05/2019). http://citeseerx.ist.psu.edu/viewdoc/download?doi=10.1.1.203.4525&rep=rep1&type=pdf.

Yahmed, S. B., 2016. Formal But Less Equal. Gender Wage Gaps in Formal and Informal Jobs in Brazil. Discussion Paper No. 16-085 (Date Accessed: 04/05/2019). http://ftp.zew.de/pub/zew-docs/dp/dp16085.pdf.

Sadiye Oktay, Serdar Bozkurt, and Kübra Yazıcı

The Concept of Professional Skepticism in Auditing: Content Analysis for Databases

1 Introduction

The financial information produced by the accounting information system can be expressed as the window of the organizations to the external environment; so accurate, reliable, complete, timely, transparent, understandable, and comparable presentation is essential and vital for the parties concerned. Many institutions, such as investors, government, credit institutions, and trade unions, benefit from the information produced by the accounting information system. The number of institutions that benefits from this information has increased considerably due to the rapid developments in the Information Age. Within the global economic system, the decisions taken by the relevant parties based on this information affect the whole society in certain aspects. The reliability of the information provided by the organizations is essential in terms of public disclosure. The audit mechanism ensures safety in the public disclosure of information. The security of unaudited details will always remain of low quality, and its accuracy will be open to questioning. The safety of the audit process depends on the conduct of the audit under national and international principles and standards. The audit activity is a technical issue as well as a social phenomenon. Therefore, auditing standards, which serve as a general guideline, are utilized in the conduct of the process. Auditing standards are a set of general principles that help the auditor in fulfilling his/her professional responsibility and shed light on it.

To be considered appropriate and valid, the auditor must suit with the principles stipulated in the rules. Standards contain guidance and explanatory information for auditors. The concept of "professional skepticism" is among the most prominent issues in many standard items. Some of the main objectives of the auditors are to prevent errors or frauds in the financial statements and to prevent misregistration of the data. The concept of professional skepticism also implies that the auditors approach the events in a questioning manner to avoid such negativities. Professional skepticism may also be referred to as an approach or attitude that includes a critical evaluation of audit evidence. Professional skepticism can be regarded as one of the most essential and indispensable elements of auditing.

The importance of professional skepticism has been emphasized many times in auditing standards. International auditing standards recognize that the auditor should act within the framework of professional skepticism. The notion of professional skepticism was first introduced in 1977 in the audit standard No. 16 entitled "The Independent Auditor's Responsibility for the Detection of Errors or Irregularities" (Ray, 2015). The content of many standards published since then emphasizes the concept of professional skepticism. Professional skepticism, which has an essential place in the theory and implementation of the audit profession, should be applied correctly. The critical and questioning point of view, which is the core of professional skepticism, is essential for influential audits and should be used by each auditor in all audit areas and stages (Ciolek, 2017: 34).

The importance of the professional skepticism approach is emphasized continuously both in the audit standards, in the audit literature, and by the national and international competent authorities. From this point of view, it can be said that there is a global consensus on the significance of the role of professional skepticism in auditing practices. The audit profession is the only profession that explicitly encodes the phenomenon of professional skepticism and states it as a legal requirement (Hurtt et al., 2003: 10). Within this scope, the goal of this study is to analyze the researches about this concept, which is extremely important for the audit profession, by the content analysis method. No investigations have been conducted on this subject using the content analysis method. In this respect, our study differs from other studies. There are many studies on professional skepticism in other countries; however, there are not enough studies in our country yet. For this reason, the results of our research are essential in terms of shedding light on the studies planned on this subject in the future and supporting a guiding function for them.

2 Professional Skepticism

The concept of skepticism and suspicion first appeared in the science of philosophy. Then, the idea of scientific skepticism, which includes a critical point of view, emerged. Finally, the concept of skepticism that is specific to each job, namely the concept of professional skepticism, has started to be discussed.

Suspicion is "the state of being unable to decide to hesitate about the accuracy of something" (Cevizci,1999: 532). The phenomenon of suspicion, not contented with the explanation presented, is a tendency to think and question that things can be otherwise than they are. On the other hand, skepticism comes from a Greek verb to investigate and question (Dimitrova & Sorova, 2016: 3). Skepticism is "the view that the human mind cannot reach certain and positive truths in knowledge, that precise and correct information is not possible, and that humanity cannot reach reality by going beyond appearances" (Cevizci, 1999: 533).

The concept of skepticism, which is considered from different points, has a vital status in the audit operations. The phases of the audit process consist of customer operation selection and recruitment, planning the audit, conducting the audit program, and preparing audit reports. At all these stages of the audit, the auditor always acts with a skeptical approach. In this process, the skepticism attitude of the auditor contributes to the improvement of the quality of the audit and the achievement of the objective expected from the audit. For such reasons, the auditor should be sufficiently skeptical and act with a questioning approach and without prejudice while conducting the audit. Accordingly, it is widely accepted that professional skepticism is one of the professional qualifications that auditors should have (Ashari et al., 2013:7).

There is no generally accepted description of the concept of professional skepticism, which forms an essential part of modern auditing. However, numerous definitions of professional skepticism have been made by various individuals and institutions. These definitions focus around "the presumptive-doubt perspective" and "the neutral perspective" (Quadackers et al., 2014:639). *The presumptive-doubt approach* is based on the assumption that those responsible for the preparation of financial statements are negligent, inadequate, or dishonest at a certain level (Dimitrova & Sorova, 2016:6). *The neutral approach* auditors suppose that the business management is not completely honest but, at the same time, the auditors believe that the business management is reliable (Porter et al., 2003:62, Güredin, 2014: 132).

After all these explanations, some definitions in the audit literature and made by the regulatory authorities are as follows: Professional skepticism can be expressed as an approach or manner that involves a questioning mind and being alert to circumstances that could potentially cause misstatements of financial statements due to errors or fraud. In other words, audit evidence in professional skepticism is evaluated critically. Professional skepticism is behavior that involves a questioning mental approach (Karahan & Çukacı, 2019; Karahan, 2018; Azgın, 2018). Professional skepticism is a fact that guides the professional judgment of the auditor during the audit. Thus, the auditors become more sensitive to possible faulty and fraudulent transactions. In this context, professional skepticism can be expressed as critical evaluations that reinforce the auditor's independence (Türedi et al., 2018:9).

Professional skepticism is an examination of the accuracy of the auditor's audit evidence. At this point, the auditors assess whether the evidence contradicts the disclosures of management, other information, and documents. That is to say, auditors assess whether the evidence contradicts management disclosures and other information and documents through professional skepticism in a critical point of view (Karahan, 2018: 192; Cömert et al., 2013).

According to Hurtt (2010) professional skepticism is to provide more support from other auditors and to make an alternative explanation. Nelson (2009) defines professional skepticism as the attitude of the auditor to disbelieve the management's arguments and the customer's declarations and claims until they obtain sufficient evidence to eliminate the doubts. Kadous (2000) expressed that professional skepticism means that the auditor can act independently of the customer demands and that the service to the public is superior to the service to the customer. Shaub and Lawrence (1996) defined professional skepticism as a professional auditor's preference to perform the duties of a professional auditor to prevent or reduce the harmful consequences of another person's behavior. According to the McMillan and White (1993) professional skepticism is sensitivity to audit evidence that declines the risk of fraud and error in the financial statements.

The concept of professional skepticism in the glossary of the International Standards on Auditing is expressed as behavior involving a questioning mind and critical evaluation of audit evidence (Dalkılıç & Oktay, 2011:65). The International Auditing and Assurance Standards Board (IAASB) defines professional skepticism in auditing standards as being alert to situations that indicate possible misleading statements resulting from errors and fraud. At the same time, professional skepticism defines behaviors as a questioning attitude in the critical evaluation of audit proof. Professional skepticism according to INTOSAI (International Organization of Supreme Audit Institutions) is an attitude that includes a questioning point of view, being alert to the conditions that indicate possible false reporting due to error or fraud, and critical evaluation of the evidence. According to the CAQ (Center for Audit Quality), professional skepticism is the behavior that constitutes a questioning mind and judgment until it receives enough evidence. Professional skepticism develops awareness against risk and by nature is an enemy of fraud.

American Institute of Certified Public Accountants (AICPA) Statements on Auditing Standards (SAS) 1 defines professional skepticism as a manner that involves having a questioning mind and a critical evaluation of audit evidence. According to Public Company Accounting Oversight Board (PCAOB), professional skepticism is a behavior that involves a questioning mental attitude in the critical evaluation of audit evidence required for effective audits. According to Public Oversight, Accounting and Auditing Standards Authority Turkish

Standards on Auditing (TSA) 200, professional skepticism is expressed as an attitude which includes being careful against mistakes in the financial statements due to errors or fraud and evaluating audit evidence carefully (KGK, 2017:7). In the No: 22 Independent Audit Communiqué published by the Capital Markets Board of Turkey (CBM), professional skepticism can be expressed as an approach or attitude that interrogates independent audit evidence, regularly judges whether the independent audit evidence shows a significant risk of fraud, and critically evaluates the independent audit evidence (SPK Series X, Communiqué No: 22, Section 6, i.8). According to the definitions, it is seen that the questioning mental attitude and behavior form the basis of professional skepticism. Therefore, it can be said that professional skepticism is necessary for effective and high-quality audits. Each auditor must apply the professional skepticism approach throughout the audit process and also in every aspect of the audit process (Ciolek, 2017:34).

3 Models of Professional Skepticism

There are different approaches in the literature about defining the concept of professional skepticism. The fact remains that, the studies focus on "presumptive-doubt perspective" and "neutral perspective." In light of these approaches, The Nelson Professional Skepticism Model and The Hurtt Professional Skepticism Model have emerged. The fact remains that, although there is no consensus as to which of these two models is best suited for auditing practices, the Hurtt Professional Skepticism Model is more prominent.

3.1 Nelson Professional Skepticism Model

In the Nelson professional skepticism model, a possible suspicion approach is adopted. The model shown in Fig. 1 is based on the integration of the existing literature on professional skepticism into the central trio of skeptical judgment, suspicious behavior, and audit evidence (Nelson, 2009:5).

The main focus of the model is that the skeptical judgment and suspicious behavior should be evaluated separately. In general, suspicious behavior stems from doubtful perception. However, it cannot be said that every dubious sense becomes a suspicious behavior (Nelson, 2009: 5). While skeptical decisions depend on the auditor's cognition abilities and mood, suspicious behavior is a feature of auditor performance (Grenier, 2010: 6). In the model (Fig. 1), skeptical judgment is presented as the primary determinant of suspicious behavior. As a result, suspicious behaviors arise when the auditor acts based on the underlying dubious sense (Nelson, 2009: 5).

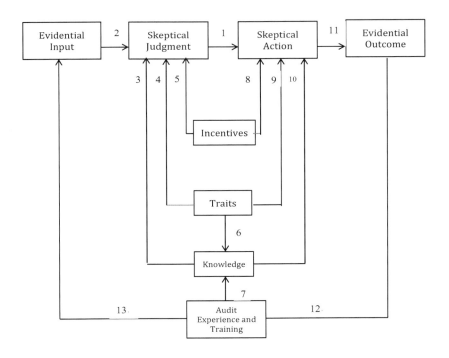

Fig. 1: Nelson Professional Skepticism Model. Source: (Nelson, 2009: 5)

The evidential inputs in the model provide an essential contribution to the skeptical judgment process. Evidential data are information collected and evaluated during the audit process. While the initial evidential inputs affect the planning of the audit, then the evidential contributions included in the model may affect the auditor's opinion. The information (is an output of experience and personal characteristics), own features, and motives in the model are shown as determinants of skeptical judgment and skeptical behavior. Evidential outcomes become part of the auditor's experience and are used as input for the next decision process in the future. This model is cyclical because audit evidence is both input and output in the auditor's decision-making process (Nelson, 2009:6–13).

3.2 Hurtt Professional Skepticism Model

Hurtt et al. (2003) created a model of professional skepticism by combining philosophical skepticism perspectives, professional emphasis on suspicion in audit standards, and issues proposed by previous audit research. In the model shown in Fig. 2, the concept of professional skepticism is defined as a multidimensional structure that includes six different characters grouped under three main factors. In this structure, it is stated that professional skepticism includes both a personal trait (a relatively constant, permanent aspect of a person) and a situation (a temporary state caused by situational variables) (Hurtt, 2010:149).

Hurtt (2010) stated that these characteristics are determined through rigorous screening of audit standards and review of research on skepticism in the fields of audit, psychology, philosophy, and consumer behavior. The first three characteristics of professional skepticism (questioning mind, suspension of the judge, and search for knowledge) is associated with the examination of evidence. All three show that the auditor is willing to investigate and thoroughly examine the evidence before making a decision. That is, an auditor who exhibits professional skepticism must wait for any judgment and not be satisfied with less than convincing evidence (Hurtt et al., 2003: 12–13, Hurtt, 2010: 152). The fourth feature, interpersonal understanding, reveals the need to consider the human aspects of the audit when evaluating evidence. This feature explains the knowledge of evidence providers. As stated in audit standards, the auditor should be able to identify the factors that create incentives/pressure on individuals in a way that causes corruption. Also, the auditor should be able to determine very well the opportunities that an individual may use to justify fraudulent action or the possibility of corruption. The auditor should bear in mind that even statements from individuals he/she considers to be reliable can contain errors and fraud (Dalkılıç & Oktay, 2011: 70; Hurtt, 2010: 152). Besides, self-confidence and self-determination characteristics address the individual's ability to work and act on the information obtained. Self-confidence: it enables auditors to oppose the assumptions of others and to evaluate their insights at least as much as others' insights. Self-determination: it is associated with the ability of an auditor to decide individually when enough information is obtained to satisfy him/her personally (Hurtt et al., 2003: 15–16). Each feature consists of elements that affect the level of professional skepticism of auditors. Skeptical behaviors arise according to the level of professional skepticism. These behaviors include the search for broader information, the search for more outliers, the evaluation of more alternatives, and the questioning of resource security. An auditor with a high level of professional skepticism is expected to undertake further research to obtain a sufficient basis for audit decisions (Hurtt et al., 2003: 16–19).

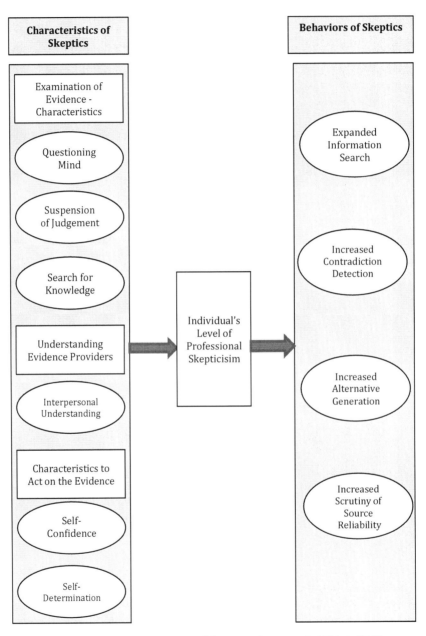

Fig. 2: Hurtt Professional Skepticism Model. Source: (Hurtt et al., 2003: 1–35, Kopp et al., 2003: 26)

4 The Importance of Professional Skepticism in Auditing

The audit operations consists of several successive phases. This process starts with the receipt of the work, continues with the execution of the audit works, and ends with the preparation and disclosure of the audit report. It is essential that the audit can serve the expected purpose; therefore, at each stage of the process, the auditor should demonstrate his/her professional skepticism to the extent required by the work. This is one of the principal responsibilities of the auditor in the work of audit. It can be easily stated that it is one of the essential elements of the audit profession.

Regulatory authorities and practitioners agree on the importance of professional skepticism in auditing practices. The critical role played by professional skepticism is often emphasized both in many national and international auditing standards and in the audit literature.

Professional skepticism is a critical constituent of every accomplished audit (Farag & Elias, 2016:124). If the auditors act in contradiction with the professional skepticism approach, audit firms may face many detrimental situations such as audit failures-indicates that an audit activity was performed incorrectly and that there are mistakes in company accounts-, various lawsuits and loss of reputation (Main sources of finding customers are acceptance) in the medium and long term (Karahan, 2018: 41). The massive company scandals in the world in the early 2000s, the research and investigation reports published by the competent authorities at various times, and the studies in the audit literature confirm these findings. For example, it is possible to say that the Enron scandal is a significant audit failure due to insufficient professional skepticism by audit firm partners and auditors (Benston & Hartgraves, 2002: 126–127). In the past, these and similar scandals have been very costly for the audit sector. This cost can be calculated not only in terms of monetary dimension but also as a loss of reputation and investors' trust in capital markets (Carpenter et al., 2002: 1).

United States Securities and Exchange Commission (SEC) conducted a study covering the ten years between 1987 and 1997 on the investigation of causes related to against the auditors on fraud incidents in the financial statements. According to the research, an inadequate level of professional skepticism by auditors ranks third among the ten audit deficiencies that are cited as fraudulent reporting reasons resulting from audit failure (Beasley et al., 2001:65). The issue of insufficient audit evidence at the top of the list is directly related to the concept of professional skepticism

(Dalkılıç & Oktay, 2011: 64). Alkan (2018) carried out a study related to administrative fines imposed on audit firms because of conduct contrary to ethical principles by the Capital Markets Board of Turkey. Noncompliance with the policy of professional skepticism in the study covering the period between 2008 and 2018 is one of the three reasons in the second place. Also, Alkan's (2018) study is similar to the results of the survey conducted in the United States.

According to the results of another study conducted by FRC (2010) in the United Kingdom, in the audits of Equitable Life Assurance Society, London International Group, Independent Insurance, TransTec, Wickes, and ERF Holdings, professional skepticism was not applied sufficiently. Besides, the results of the same research revealed that there were problems such as over-reliance on the statements of customer business' managers, obtaining the data without the necessary investigations, and not receiving sufficient confirmations from the third parties. In the 2016 global fraud report, ACFE cites assets abuse, corruption, and fraudulent financial reporting as the cause of the comprehensive economic loss of approximately $ 3.7 trillion. Many studies conducted in the field of audit on the origins of these cases, which are also associated with audit failures, show the lack of professional skepticism in the first place (Göçmen, 2018:523). Zhao et al. (2006) examined the ten most significant audit failures in the United States. According to the study results; bribery, the auditor's independence problem, and lack of professional skepticism and care are listed as causes of audit failures.

As a result, it can be stated that professional skepticism, which is accepted as an essential part of modern auditing, constitutes the main point of verification. If the auditors carry out their audit activities in a professional skepticism approach, audit failures will decrease. Audit failure is a global phenomenon that causes serious harm to states, societies, audit institutions, and the audit profession (Kayrak, 2015: i). Decreasing audit failures increases quality and efficiency in audit and provides audit firms superiority in competition. Furthermore, the reduction of audit failures increases public confidence in the audit mechanism.

5 Research Methodology

5.1 Research Problems

The research is designed to determine the point where the studies in the literature come from the content aspect of the concept of professional skepticism. In this way, the perspective of professional skepticism, which is a fundamental concept in the field of accounting and auditing, can be put forth. In this context, the following research questions have been formulated:

How is the distribution of the studies on the concept of professional skepticism according to:

- The year of publication?
- Journal names?
- Sample sizes?
- Types of research (qualitative, quantitative, mixed)?
- Data collection tools and data analysis methods?

5.2 Purpose and Importance of Research

Professional skepticism is a critical concept in accounting and especially in the field of auditing. This study aspires to determine the direction of the studies related to the concept of professional skepticism, which is one of the most important tools of effective auditing.

This study aims to explore the content of the professional skepticism studies conducted in the literature with content analysis. In this way, it is thought that the evaluations about the level of emphasis on the researches about professional skepticism can be made more accurately. Also, this study will be an awareness of the literature. Thus, it is thought that the literature on this subject will be enriched in the following periods.

5.3 Scope of the Research

Content analysis method, which is one of the qualitative data analysis techniques, was used in the study designed to determine the position of professional skepticism in the literature. Within the scope of this research, the studies on the concept of professional skepticism in EBSCO, Wiley, Sage, and JSTOR databases were examined. Studies in related databases, the type of the study, the year of the study, the name of the journal, sample size, research methodology, data collection tool, analysis technique, and the issues related to this concept were evaluated. The sample of the study consists of 48 research papers available in the literature until April 2019.

5.4 Data Analysis

Content analysis, one of the most frequently used methods in the social sciences, is a research technique in which objective and precise results from the text are presented after a series of procedures (Weber, 1989: 5; Stone et al., 1966: 213).

In this study, the articles related to the concept of professional skepticism in the databases were examined through content analysis.

The content analysis aimed at defining data is carried out with a four-stage process. This process, which begins with the coding of the data, continues with the discovery of themes. Then, codes and issues are edited, and the findings are defined and interpreted (Yıldırım & Şimşek, 2006). In this context, content analysis was carried out by determining the concept of "professional skepticism" as a selection criterion.

5.5 Results

In this study, 48 articles related to the concept of professional skepticism were analyzed in EBSCO, Wiley, Sage, and JSTOR databases until April 2019. In this context, it was determined that the first study on the subject in the related databases was made in 1993. Moreover, it is observed that there is an increase in professional skepticism studies, especially after 2015 (7 articles; 15 percent). Considering this increase, it can be stated that the number of publications about the concept of professional skepticism will increase in the coming years. Tab. 1 exhibits the distribution of articles in regard to the year of the study.

Table 2 demonstrates the distribution of articles in regard to the name of the journal. The professional skepticism articles are mostly seen in journals about accounting and auditing. Besides, the fact that the concept of professional skepticism is examined frequently in journals related to ethics shows that the issue is not only theoretically but also very important in social life.

When the size of the sample used in the studies about the concept of professional skepticism are examined, it is seen that 5 of the articles have less than 50 sampling (16 percent), 12 of them have 50–100 sampling (38 percent), 10 of them have sampling between 101–249 (31 percent), and 5 of them have 250 and more (16 percent) sampling (Tab. 3). This shows that the sample size is quite important in the studies conducted on the concept of professional skepticism. It can be thought that the progressive studies on this subject will be carried out with a large number of samples.

Tab. 4 shows the distribution of articles in regard to research types. According to this table, quantitative research constitutes 30 of selected items on professional skepticism according to research types (63 percent). This order is followed by qualitative, mixed, and theoretical research types (Tab. 4). In this context, quantitative studies related to the subject of professional skepticism have been realized more. Moreover, it may be thought that the emphasis on qualitative, mixed, and theoretical types of research will contribute to the literature.

Tab. 1: Distribution of Articles in Regard to Publication Year

Year of Publication	F	%
1981	1	2
1993	1	2
2009	2	4
2010	1	2
2011	3	6
2013	4	8
2014	3	6
2015	7	15
2016	7	15
2017	8	17
2018	10	21
2019	1	2
Total	48	100

F=frequency

Tab. 2: Distribution of Articles in Regard to Journal Names

Name of Journal	F	%
Auditing: A Journal of Practice & Theory	6	13
Accounting, Organizations and Society	5	10
Journal of Business Ethics	4	8
Managerial Auditing Journal	3	6
The Accounting Review	3	6
Behavioral Research in Accounting	2	4
Issues in Accounting Education	2	4
Others*	23	46
Total	48	100

* Journals who had published only one article about this topic are evaluated together

Considering the distribution of studies in regard to data collection tools, in 26 of the 48 articles (74 percent), a survey was used as a data collection tool (Tab. 5). This shows that the most frequently used data collection tool in the studies on professional skepticism is the survey.

Tab. 3: Distribution of Articles in Regard to Sample Sizes

Sample Sizes	F	%
Less than 50	5	16
50–100	12	38
101–249	10	31
250 and above	5	16
Total	32*	100

*Six articles related to theoretical context were not comprised in the research

Tab. 4: Various Types of Research in the Articles

Types of Research	F	%
Qualitative	7	15
Quantitative	30	63
Mixed (Qualitative and Quantitative)	5	10
Theoretical	6	13
Total	48	100

Tab. 5: Distribution of Data Gathering Tools

Data Collection Tools	F	%
Survey	26	74
Interview	4	11
Case Study	2	6
Experiment	2	6
Live Simulation	1	3
Total	35	100

* Multiple data collection tools were used in some of the articles at the same time

Up to this section, the content analysis research results related to professional skepticism are mentioned. After this stage, the conclusion, suggestion and discussion section will be started.

6 Discussion and Conclusion

With globalization, the information published by organizations has become more important for the society. Apart from providing information to organizations, the accuracy of the information provided is also critical. In this context, the concept of professional skepticism is of excellent importance in the audit of financial data.

In this study, content analysis method was used in order to examine the antecedents' literature of the concept of professional skepticism. The articles reached by examining four different databases (EBSCO, Wiley, Sage, and JSTOR databases) are between 1981 and April 2019. The articles which reached were evaluated in regard to publication years, journal names, sample sizes, research types, and data collection tools.

As a result of the research, it is seen that there is an increase in articles about professional skepticism after 2015. Therefore, the interest of researchers is increasing day by day. The articles are published in journals covering ethics and organizational behavior as well as journals in accounting. This shows that the concept is related to multiple disciplines. Generally, studies are quantitatively weighted and are concentrated in the sample of 50–250. In subsequent studies, it may be useful to expand the study by including these and different databases.

Bibliography

ACFE, (2016). *Report to the Nations on Occupational Fraud and Abuse: 2016 Global Fraud Study*, https://www.acfe.com/rttn2016/docs/2016-report-to-the-nations.pdf, (02.07.2019).

AICPA, (1997). *SAS No.1 AU Section 230: Due Professional Care in the Performance of Work*, https://www.aicpa.org/content/dam/aicpa/research/standards/auditattest/downloadabledocuments/au-00230.pdf, (12.07.2019).

Alkan, G. İ. (2018). Etik Teoriler Işığında Bağımsız Denetim ve BİST'de Bir Araştırma. *Muhasebe Bilim Dünyası Dergisi, 20*, 129–149.

Ashari, A., Masruri, M. & Zahro, N. I., (2013). "Corruption awareness, ethical sensitivity, professional skepticism and risk of corruption assessment: exploring the multiple relationship in Indonesian case", *Proceedings of 3rd Asia-Pacific Business Research Conference*, 25 – 26 February 2013, Kuala Lumpur, Malaysia, pp. 1–20. https://studylib.net/doc/13327127/proceedings-of-3rd-asia-pacific-business-research-conference, (12.07.2019).

Azgın, N. (2018). *Denetçinin Mesleki Şüpheciliğinin Denetim Kalitesine Etkisi,* (Unpublished Doctoral Dissertation), Anadolu University, Eskişehir, Retrieved from https://tez.yok.gov.tr/UlusalTezMerkezi/tezSorguSonucYeni.jsp, (12.07.2019).

Beasley, M. S., Carcello, J. V. & Hermanson, D. R. (2001). Top 10 audit deficiencies. *Journal of Accountancy, 19* (1), 63–66.

Benston, G. J., & Hartgraves, A. L. (2002). Enron: what happened and what we can learn from it. *Journal of Accounting and Public Policy, 21* (2), 105–127.

Carpenter, T., Durtschi, C. & Gaynor, L. M., (2002). "The role of experience in professional skepticism, knowledge acquisition, and fraud detection", *Accounting Workshop at Florida State University*, http://citeseerx.ist.psu.edu/viewdoc/download?doi=10.1.1.598.3570&rep=rep1&type=pdf, (29.06.2019).

CAQ, (2010). *Deterring and Detecting Financial Reporting Fraud: A Platform for Action*, https://www.thecaq.org/wp-content/uploads/2019/03/deterring-and-detecting-financial-reporting-fraud-a-platform-for-action.pdf, (12.07.2019).

Cevizci, A. (1999). *Paradigma Felsefe Sözlüğü*, İstanbul: Paradigma Yayınları, Retrieved from https://tr.scribd.com/document/354667086/Ahmet-Cevizci-Felsefe-Sozlu%C4%9Fu-pdf, (12.07.2019).

Ciolek, M. (2017). Professional skepticism in auditing and its characteristics. *Global Challenges of Management Control and Reporting, 474*, 33–41.

Cömert, N., Kardeş-Selimoğlu, S., Uzay, Ş. & Uyar, S. (2013). *Uluslararası Denetim Standartları Kapsamında Bağımsız Denetim*, Sakarya: SAÜSEM, Retrieved from http://www.dt-audit.com/dosyalar/Egitim/Denetim/1.Hafta/2.BLMDENETIMDEGENELILKELERVESORUMLULUKLAR.pdf, (12.07.2019).

Dalkılıç, A. F. & Oktay, S. (2011). Uluslararası Denetim ve Güvence Standartlarında Mesleki Şüphecilik. *İSMMMO Mali Çözüm Dergisi, 103*, 63–78.

Dimitrova, J. & Anica, S. (2016). The role of professional skepticism in financial statement audit and its appropriate application. *Journal of Economics, 1* (2), 1–17.

Farag, M. S. & Elias, R. Z. (2016). The relationship between accounting students' personality, professional skepticism and anticipatory socialization. *Accounting Education, 25* (2), 124–138.

FRC, (2010). Auditor Scepticism: Raising the Bar, https://library.croneri.co.uk/misc201008auditor-scepticism, (02.07.2019).

Göçmen, F. D. (2018). Bağımsız Denetçinin Mesleki Şüpheciliği. *Akademik Sosyal Araştırmalar Dergisi, 82*, 522–540.

Grenier, J. H. (2010). *Encouraging Professional Skepticism in the Industry Specialization Era: A Dual-Process Model and An Experimental Test* (Unpublished Doctoral Dissertation), University of Illinois at Urbana-Champaign, Urbana, Illinois, Retrieved from https://pdfs.semanticscholar.org/3dcc/fadb9be35758e5430cab321e0cea48c5b29e.pdf, (12.07.2019).

Güredin, E. (2014). *Denetim ve Güvence Hizmetleri SMMM ve YMM'lere Yönelik İlkeler ve Teknikler*, İstanbul: Türkmen Kitabevi.

Hurtt, K. (2010). Development of a Scale to Measure Professional Skepticism. *Auditing: A Journal of Practice & Theory, 29* (1), 149–171.

Hurtt, K., Eining, M. M. & Plumlee, D. (2003). *Professional Scepticism: A Model with Implications for Research, Practice, and Education.* Working paper, University of Wisconsin, https://studylib.net/doc/7579385/professional-skepticism--a-model-with-implications-for-pr..., (28.06.2019).

IAASB, (2009). ISA 200: *Overall Objectives of the Independent Auditor, and the Conduct of an Audit in Accordance with International Standards on Auditing,* https://www.ifac.org/system/files/downloads/a008-2010-iaasb-handbook-isa-200.pdf, (12.07.2019).

INTOSAI, (2009). ISSAI 1003: *Glossary of Terms from the Handbook of International Standards on Auditing and Quality Control,* http://www.issai.org/issai-framework/4-auditing-guidelines.htm, (12.07.2019).

Kadous, K. (2000). The effects of audit quality and consequence severity on juror evaluations of auditor responsibility for plaintiff losses. *The Accounting Review, 75* (3), 327–341.

Karahan, A. (2018). *Bağımsız Denetçinin Mesleki Şüpheciliğinin Denetim Satandartları Bağlamında Denetim Kalitesine Etkisi ve Bir Araştırma.* (Unpublished Doctoral Dissertation), İnönü University, Malatya, Retrieved from https://tez.yok.gov.tr/UlusalTezMerkezi/tezSorguSonucYeni.jsp (12.07.2019).

Karahan, A. & Çukacı, Y. C. (2019). Bağımsız Denetçinin Mesleki Şüpheciliğinin Denetim Satandartları Bağlamında Denetim Kalitesine Etkisi ve Bir Araştırma. *Avrasya Sosyal ve Ekonomi Araştırmaları Dergisi, 6* (2), 1–27.

Kayrak, M. (2015). Denetim Başarısızlığı Kavramı: Nedenleri, Sonuçları ve Çözüm Önerileri. *Niğde Üniversitesi İktisadi ve İdari Bilimler Fakültesi Dergisi, 8* (1), 91–103.

KGK, (2017). BDS 200: *Bağımsız Denetçinin Genel Amaçları ve Bağımsız Denetimin Bağımsız Denetim Standartlarına Uygun Olarak Yürütülmesi,* http://www.kgk.gov.tr/Portalv2Uploads/files/Duyurular/v2/BDS/bdsyeni25.12.2017/BDS%20200-Site.pdf, (02.07.2019).

Kopp, L., Lemon, W. M. & Rennie, M. (2003). A Model of Trust and Professional Skepticism in the Auditor-Client Relationship, *School of Accountancy Seminar Series,* University of Waterloo, http://citeseerx.ist.psu.edu/viewdoc/download?doi=10.1.1.515.8784&rep=rep1&type=pdf, (29.06.2019).

McMillan, J. J. & White, R. A. (1993). Auditors' belief revisions and evidence search: the effect of hypothesis frame, confirmation bias, and professional skepticism. *The Accounting Review, 68* (3), 443–465.

Nelson, M. W. (2009). A model and literature review of professional skepticism in auditing. *Auditing: A Journal of Practice & Theory, 28* (2), 1–34.

PCAOB, (2017). *Auditing Standards of the Public Company Accounting Oversight Board*, https://pcaobus.org/Standards/Auditing/Documents/PCAOB_Auditing_Standards_as_of_December_15_2017.pdf, (02.07.2019).

Porter, B., Simon, J. & Hatherly, D. (2003). *Principles of External Auditing*, Chichester: John Wiley & Sons, Ltd.

Quadackers, L., Groot, T. & Wright, A. (2014). Auditors' professional skepticism: neutrality versus presumptive doubt. *Contemporary Accounting Research, 31* (3), 639–657.

Ray, T. (2015). Auditors still challenged by professional: recommendations for firms, standards setters, and regulators, *The CPA Journal, 85* (1), https://www.questia.com/magazine/1P3-3634171961/auditors-still-challenged-by-professional, (12.07.2019).

Shaub, M. K. & Lawrence, J. E. (1996). Ethics, experience and professional skepticism: a situational analysis. *Behavioral Research in Accounting, 8*, 124–157.

SPK, (2006). *Sermaye Piyasasında Bağımsız Denetim Standartları HakkındaTebliğ* (Series: X, Number: 22), http://spk.gov.tr/Sayfa/Dosya/590, (02.07.2019).

Stone, P. J., Dunphy, D. C. & Smith, M. S. (1966). The General Inquirer: A Computer Approach to Content Analysis. *Revue philosophique de Louvain, 66.*

Türedi, H., Ala, T. & Tepegöz, Ş. M. (2018). Uluslararası Denetim Standartları Açısından Kurumsal Yönetim Sürecinin Değerlendirilmesi. *Muhasebe ve Finansman Dergisi, 78*, 1–16.

Weber, R. P. (1990). *Basic Content Analysis* (No. 49). Sage Publications, London.

Yıldırım, A. & Şimşek, H. (2006). *Sosyal Bilimlerde Nitel Araştırma Yöntemleri* (5th ed.). Ankara: Seçkin Yayıncılık.

Zhao, S-D., Chen, L-P. & Hua, L. (2006). Study of American audit failure. *Journal of Modern Accounting and Auditing, 2* (6), 64–70.

Murat Koçyiğit and Murat Çakırkaya

A Research on Evaluating the Effect of Interactive Communication on Consumer-Based Brand Equity in Terms of Social Media Marketing

1 Introduction

Consumers traditionally used the internet basically to read, watch, and buy products and services. However, the consumers began to increasingly use the platforms such as content sharing sites, blogs, social networks, and wikis to create, modify, share, and discuss internet content. All of these platforms are social media tools that can significantly impact a company's reputation, sales, and even survival. However, many executives are either passing it up or ignoring this media format. Because they do not understand what it is, how it can take various forms, and how to interact with it (Kietzmann et al., 2011:241).

Today, marketing communication evolves into event marketing, online viral marketing, eWOM (Electronic Word of Mouth), and Social Media Marketing approaches beyond the traditional marketing communication. The goal is to create integrated marketing campaigns that will strengthen various online and offline channels, enabling at least one of these channels to be seen by targeted consumers wherever they go (Alameddine, 2013: 15). Compared to changeable market quotations and similar communication models, the use of social media has become a new and effective approach that firms can use to provide value to their customers (Zauner et al., 2012: 688).

Today, brands are the most valuable assets of the company that add economic and strategic value to their owners, and brands are seen as the second most important assets of a company following the customers. The concept of brand equity first entered the marketing literature in the 1980s, and it attracted great interest from both scientists and marketing practitioners in the 1990s. In connection with this, numerous articles and books on the subject have been produced and this trend continues increasingly. The main reasons for this are: brands with strong brand equity gain more share from the market, increase brand awareness, increase marketing communication activities, and have many advantages such as loyalty. Additionally, it is known that having a high brand equity leads to high consumer choice and purchase intent (Alhaddad, 2015: 74). In the following part, related literature will be examined and a conceptual framework will be shared on the relationship between brand equity and interactive communication with regards to social media marketing.

2 Conceptual Framework

2.1 Social Network Sites and Social Media Marketing

The development of the Web 2.0. technology has made the emergence of user-generated content possible. This made the distinction between amateur and professional content even more difficult. The social interactions that develop around the content play a key role in understanding the importance of user-generated content. The ability to vote, comment, criticize, and write answers in this new world of media enhances the attraction of the new media and ensures its continuity. The basic feature of the new generation is that they want to share their experiences, present them to the evaluation of friends and other community members, and allow them to build their reputation through these comments. Therefore, key concepts of social software in the new world of Web 2.0 are mentioned as: identity, dialogue, relationship, sharing, reputation, and group (Jin et al., 2009: 1172–1174).

In summary, various definitions were made in the literature on social media marketing, which can be defined as the use of social media tools in the promotion of the organization, brand, or product (Barefoot and Szabo, 2010: 13). For example, Weinberg (2009: 3) defined social media marketing as a process that allows individuals to advertise their websites, products, brands, and services through online social channels that increases their awareness, and that allows communication and interaction with large masses that were not possible to reach with traditional advertising channels. Gunelius (2011: 10), on the other hand, named all kinds of direct or indirect marketing activities that increase awareness and reputation, that enable the brand, institution, product, or individual to take action, and that are performed with social networking tools such as blogs, microblogs, social networks, social marking and content sharing, as social media marketing. Eley and Tilley (2009: 4) considered social media marketing as telling a tale or story, or communicating a message. If this story or message is interesting, shocking, or funny, the interest it attracts will be much higher. On the other hand, this message can be a video, photo, blog entry (spot), and Twitter or Facebook message. Another definition of social media marketing belongs to Tuten (2008: 19). Tuten defined social media marketing as an online advertising environment in which social communities, including social networks, virtual worlds, social news sites, and social opinion sharing sites, are used in a cultural context in order to realize communication objectives and ensure branding. Social media marketing, which allows products, services, and brands to increase their reputation and visibility online, is complementary to interactive marketing and to interactive communication as well (Kelly, 2007: 148–149; Bajpai and Pandey, 2012: 206).

Today, social media marketing is becoming a standard in promoting products and services of the companies. The use of social media has a unique quality that allows organizations to develop relationships of dialogue and interaction with the consumer (Krajenke, 2014: 10). Succeeding in social media marketing depends on applying the right strategy. The three basic steps of social media marketing are: the follow-up of existing conversations, simplification of these conversations, and finally popularization in terms of the participants (As cited in: Bergh and Behrer, 2013: 212; Ross et al., 2009: 579).

2.2 Interactive Communication on Social Media Platforms

Two kinds of interaction can be mentioned that are mediated by technology. These are: functional interaction and situationality interaction. A functional interaction is basically the ability to have a dialogue or exchange of information between users and their interfaces. This includes email link, chat room, event calendar, functions that include search functions and surveys, rankings, and other formats that invite users to submit responses to hosted websites. Institutions that mediate such functions are the ones that facilitate the dialogue cycle. These institutions mobilize and thus interact with the visitors during their visit or return to the WEB. On the contrary, the situationality interaction is a process, in which the communication roles can be changed to fully interact, and which includes user, environment, and message. Situationality means that messages in an interactive communication process are linked to previous messages. The more the responses of the users to others are interdependent, numerous, and in an increasing nature, the more the communication becomes interactive (Zhang and Lin, 2015: 673–674; Kietzmann et al. 2011: 243–247). As a matter of fact, at the end of a study about the measurable effect of interactive communication on consumer attitudes, it was concluded that there were a number of relations between environmental stimuli and attitudes, and different environmental conditions had different effects on formation of attitudes (Nicovich, 1999).

2.3 Brand Equity

According to Aaker, brand equity is a combination of actives and passives related with the name and symbols of a brand. Aaker emphasized that the products and services that the brand provides for its customers are determinative in the increase or decrease of this equity (Aaker, 1992: 125). Koçak and Özer (2004: 192) stated that brand equity generally reflects the brand's strength in the marketplace, which provides competitive power, and that it is composed of assets and obligations that are related with symbols, brand name, or the benefit which an institution provides for its customers through goods and services. On the other hand, brand equity is a numerical figure which is based on the equity that consumers attribute to the brand and which shows the financial strength of the brand compared to other brands. As a result of this definition, brand equity is a consumer oriented concept (Fırat and Badem, 2008: 211). There is a correlation between the brand equity and the level of awareness of the brand, perceived quality, and total customer satisfaction (O'Neill and Mattila, 2004: 156).

2.4 Components of Brand Equity

Aaker (1992: 125) determined that, in the formation of a brand equity, there were five general categories belonging to the brand's assets. These are: (1) brand loyalty, (2) brand awareness, (3) perceived quality, (4) brand association in addition to perceived quality, and (5) registered brand assets such as patents, trademarks, and established channel relationships. At the end of their literature study, Zahoor and Qureshi (2017: 51) stated that brand equity should be assessed in six dimensions, taking into consideration all studies related to the subject. These are: brand loyalty, perceived quality, brand trust, brand image, brand awareness, and finally brand association.

Brand Loyalty: It is the positive attitude of the customer for a brand with regards to preference. A loyal customer group will ensure that the brand's profit and sales are predictable. In addition, the loyal customer group has a positive effect on the marketing costs of the brand. Because keeping the loyal customers at hand is much less costly than attracting new ones. In addition, the multitude of loyal customers in the brand's hand is a major obstacle for competitors for entry into the market (Çetinsöz and Artu, 2013: 203).

Perceived Quality is composed of feelings with regards to the brand, and customer perception pertaining to expectations, alternatives, and targets of the brand. Perceived quality, which represents the equity that customers define regarding the goods and services, is one of the most important reasons for purchasing as well as an important element of brand equity (Samsunlu and Baş, 2016: 344).

Brand Trust: It is conceptualized as the specific anticipations of the brand's credibility and intentions, in cases that pose risk to the consumer. Trust is a cornerstone in building a long-term business relationship and partnership.

Brand Image: It is briefly the impression, beliefs, and feelings of the individual about a company (del Bosque et al., 2006: 412). The brand image affects the consumer's decision-making process and ultimately contributes to the brand equity. A unique, strong, and positive brand image allows the brand to be strategically differentiated and positioned in the consumer's mind. And it contributes to an increase in brand equity.

Brand Awareness: It is defined as the ability of the consumer to identify a brand in different conditions. Brand awareness is related with how a brand name comes to mind and with the possibility of how simple it is. It is based on both brand recognition and recalling (Zahoor and Qureshi, 2017: 51).

Brand association: It is also very important what the brand first evokes in the consumer's mind. Its reason is that brand association is effective in creating brand loyalty for the customers, and it affects purchasing decisions positively. The sum of these brand association constitutes the brand equity (Samsunlu and Baş, 2016: 344). Many companies have not yet grasped the importance of the consumer association about the brands. However, perhaps the most important factor to reduce the effectiveness of product positioning should be sought in unsuccessful communication strategies. Brand associations are sometimes composed of a large spectrum that offers specific features of the product being advertised. A classification regarding the brand associations can be mentioned in three main categories of qualifications, benefits, and attitudes pertaining to the brand (Crayton, 2013: 27–28).

In a survey for measuring the brand equity of Antalya Province, "brand loyalty," "perceived quality," "brand image," and "brand awareness" were determined as brand equity dimensions. In the survey, it was determined that there was a positive moderate relationship among the brand equity dimensions. When Pearson correlation coefficients between dimensions are examined, it was determined that there was a moderate positive relation between "brand loyalty" and "perceived quality," a moderate positive relation between "brand loyalty"/"brand image" and "brand awareness," a moderate positive relation between "perceived quality"/"brand image" and "brand awareness," and finally a moderate positive relation between the dimensions of "brand image" and "brand awareness" (Çetinsöz and Artu, 2013: 208).

3 Research Hypotheses and Conceptual Model

Components of brand equity have been explained under different titles in different studies. In this study, components of brand equity were examined, in the light of scales used, under the titles brand loyalty, perceived quality, brand awareness, and general brand equity. Based on data obtained from literature, a theoretical model was developed in order to determine the role of social media communication on brand loyalty, perceived quality, brand awareness association, and general brand equity which are handled as the subdimensions of brand equity. Furthermore, the possible effects of social media communication on the latent variables of brand equity were also examined in the research. In this context, the conceptual model and hypotheses of the research are shown in Fig. 1.

3.1 Method

3.1.1 Population and Sample

This type of research is a cross-sectional study in context of handling the time. The universe of the research is composed of the Turkcell GSM brand users. Since Turkcell is the best brand to use social media among the GSM operators in Turkey according to social media brand index SocialBrands September 2017 data (www. boomsocial.com/social-brands, 2017), the universe of the research was limited to Turkcell GSM operator users. However, within the scope of the research, due to the limitation of time and cost, and difficulty of reaching to all of the Turkcell GSM operator users, the research was conducted with "Convenience Sampling Method" which is one of the "Non-Probability Sampling" methods, through the determined dates. In the scope of the research, 431 people were surveyed. Since 14 questionnaire forms contained incomplete and incorrect data, analyses were conducted on 417 questionnaire forms.

3.1.2 Data Collection Method and Tool

Questionnaire technique and face-to-face interview method, which are one of the most common data collection methods, were conducted to provide primary data of the research. In the first phase, a preliminary test, a pilot study on 53 participants was carried out with the first questionnaire, which included 26 attitude questions. As a result of the pilot study, determining that the indicator variables were grouped under the desired latent variables and that there was not any statement that was not understood, the survey continued with the questionnaire consisting of 30 questions including the demographic ones.

The questionnaire form used in the research consisted of two chapters. In the first chapter, "social media communication" scale that was adapted from studies of *Kim et al. (2010), Mangold and Faulds (2009), Laroche et al.* and "brand equity" scale adapted from the studies of *Yoo and Donthu (2001), Taşkın and Akat (2010)* were used. The second part of the questionnaire consisted of questions determining the demographic characteristics of the participants.

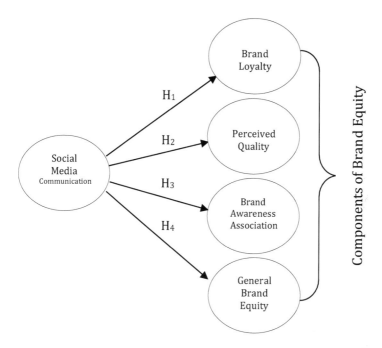

Fig. 1: Conceptual Model

H₁ *Social media communication has a positive significant effect on brand loyalty,*

H₂ *Social media communication has a positive significant effect on perceived quality,*

H₃ *Social media communication has a positive significant effect on brand awareness and association,*

H₄ *Social media communication has a positive significant effect on general brand equity.*

The questionnaire form of the research was prepared in Turkish language. The questionnaire form involved a total of 30 questions in two parts. The initial 26 questions were composed of statements prepared according to the Likert scale that were asked within the scope of the research model. During the preparation of the questionnaire questions, a detailed literature study was conducted, and scales that were published in international literature and used in the abovementioned studies were used regarding these questions. Additionally, scale expressions were created via Turkcell brand in this research.

All of the statements in the scales, that were formed to determine the effects of perceptions and opinions of Turkcell GSM operator users about social media communication on brand equity and subdimensions, were all scaled according to the 5-point Likert scale. Likert-scale questions in the questionnaire refer to: (1) Strongly Disagree, (2) Disagree, (3) Neutral, (4) Agree, and (5) Strongly Agree. SPSS 20.0 and AMOS 19.0 statistical programs were used in the analysis of the study. During the analysis, these two programs were used in coordination since they characteristically complemented each other.

3.2 Limitations of the Research

Due to time limitations and difficulty to reach all of the users, the data of the research was obtained from Konya-resided consumers using Turkcell GSM operator, with convenience sampling method. In this context, the generalizability and external validity of the research results are limited.

Another limitation of the research is that it only considered the social media communication, the subdimensions of brand equity components, and relational marketing elements, while not including in the scope of the research other variables that may be influential on brand equity.

The fact that this research was carried out through the Turkcell brand and that the scale expressions were adapted for the Turkcell brand constituted another limitation of this research.

Additionally, research results are limited to October 2017–November 2017, the dates during which research data was collected.

3.3 Findings and Comments

Demographic data of the participants regarding gender, age, educational status, and occupations are shown in Tab. 1.

Tab. 1 manifests that 69.5% of the participants were males and 30.5% were females. When age ranges of participants are examined, it is observed that the proportion of participants in the 22–26 age group is 34.8%, that of the participants in the 17–21 age group is 21.6%, and that of the participants in the 27–31 age group is 17.7%. On the other hand, when the educational status of the participants is examined, it is observed that the vast majority (58.8%) of the participants are university graduates. When the occupational knowledge of the participants is examined, it is observed that 41.0% are students, 20.6% are civil servants, and 17.7% are in the private sector category.

3.4 Social Media Communication Scale Exploratory Factor Analysis

An exploratory factor analysis was conducted to find out how many subdimensions the social media communication scale was perceived. Whether

Tab. 1: Sociodemographic Characteristics of the Participants (n = 417)

Demographic Variables	Value	Frequency	Percentage	Demographic Variables	Value	Frequency	Percentage
					Secondary School	38	9,1
	Male	290	69,5	Educational Status	High School	111	26,6
Gender					University	245	58,8
	Femal	127	30,5		Postgraduate	23	5,5
	Total	417	100,0		Total	417	100,0
	17–21	90	21,6		Self-Employment	35	8,4
	22–26	145	34,8	Occupation	Civil Servant	86	20,6
Age	27–31	74	17,7		Worker	29	7,0
	32–36	50	12,0		Private Sector	74	17,7
	37–41	28	6,7		Student	171	41,0
	42+	30	7,2		Others	22	5,3
	Total	417	100,0		Total	417	100,0

the data were consistent with explanatory factor analysis was tested with KMO and Barlett tests.

As a result of explanatory factor analysis, Kaiser-Meyer-Olkin (KMO = 0,924) and overall question group's consistency with factor analysis were measured. Moreover, each individual problem's compliance to factor analysis was measured. During this measurement, the anti-image correlation matrix of the variables was checked using the Measures of Sampling Adequacy (MSA) method. When the MSA values in the anti-image correlation matrix were examined, it was determined that all variables were above 0.50.

According to the explanatory factor analysis, the social media communication scale was perceived by the participants in a single dimension. The social media communication scale dimension accounted for 70,766% of the total variance of the scale.

The compliance of each factor in itself is measured by the Cronbach Alpha coefficient. This coefficient is the fit index depending on inter-question

Tab. 2: Social Media Communication Factor Structure

Factor	Variables	Factor Loads 1	Cronbach Alpha=,941
	S26	,870	,941
	S25	,864	
	S21	,862	
SMC	S20	,850	
	S24	,832	
	S22	,831	
	S23	,824	
	S19	,794	
Eigenvalue		5,661	
Explained Variance		70,766	
Total Explained Variance		70,766	
KMO		,924	
Barlett		2704,230 (sd.28; p=0,000)	

SMC (Social Media Communication)

correlation. As the Cronbach Alpha score of the social media communication was above 60%, it was concluded that the factor structure is very reliable (Tab. 2).

3.5 Brand Equity Scale Exploratory Factor Analysis

An exploratory factor analysis was conducted to find out how many subdimensions the brand equity scale was perceived. Whether the data were consistent with explanatory factor analysis was tested with KMO and Barlett tests (Tab. 3).

As a result of explanatory factor analysis, Kaiser-Meyer-Olkin (KMO = 0,928) and overall question group's consistency with factor analysis were measured. Moreover, each individual problem's compliance to factor analysis was measured. During this measurement, the anti-image correlation matrix of the variables was checked using the Measures of Sampling Adequacy (MSA) method. When the MSA values in the anti-image correlation matrix were examined, it was determined that all variables were above 0.50.

Additionally, the analysis was continued in this context since no variables with close factor weights were found under more than one factor at the end of exploratory factor analysis.

Tab. 3: Brand Equity Factor Structure

Factor	Variables	Factor Loads				Cronbach
		1	2	3	4	Alpha=,934
	S11	,789				
	S12	,785				
BAA	S13	,748				,909
	S9	,737				
	S10	,734				
	S16		,757			
	S15		,736			
GBE	S17		,721			,868
	S18		,715			
	S14		,661			
	S1			,858		
BL	S3			,797		,854
	S2			,733		
	S4			,582		
	S7				,786	
PQ	S6				,727	,804
	S8				,663	
	S5				,656	
Eigenvalue		8,500	1,507	1,335	1,152	
Explained Variance		20,359	19,136	15,363	14,554	
Total Explained Variance		69,412				
KMO		,928				
Barlett		4542,853 (sd.153;p=,000)				

BAA (Brand awareness/association), GBE (General Brand Equity), BL (Brand Loyalty), PQ (Perceived Quality)

According to the exploratory factor analysis, the brand equity scale was perceived by the participants in four subdimensions. Factors were named as Brand Awareness and Association (BAA), General Brand Equity (GBE), Brand Loyalty (BL), and Perceived Quality (PQ). BAA factor accounted for 20,359% of the scales, while GBE factor for 19,136%, BL factor for 15,363%, and PQ factor for 14,554%, all of the factors accounting for a total of 69,412% of the scales.

The compliance of each factor in itself is measured by the Cronbach Alpha coefficient. This coefficient is the fit index depending on inter-variable correlation.

Tab. 4: Confirmatory Factor Analysis

	χ^2	P	χ^2/df	CFI	NFI	IFI	GFI	AGFI	RMSEA	SRMR
Acceptable goodness of fit index	Lowest	>0,05 Insignificant	≤5	≥0,90	≥0,90	≥0,90	≥0,85	≥0,80	≤0,080	≤0,090
Model goodness of fit index	883,348	0,000	3,05	0,92	0,88	0,92	0,85	0,82	0,070	0,088

As the Cronbach Alpha score of the brand equity was above 60% in all of the subdimensions, it was concluded that the factor structure is very reliable.

3.6 Measurement Model (Confirmatory Factor Analysis) and Structural Equation Model (SEM)

"Goodness of fit index (gfi)" are used in defining how well conceptually gen-erated model explains the obtained data. Goodness of fit index (gfi) are tested via "Confirmatory Factor Analysis" (CFA), in other words via a measurement model. At the end of the Confirmatory Factor Analysis, model structure is accepted according to the goodness of fit index (gfi) as shown in Tab. 4.

Goodness of fit index (gfi) is the phase where the decision to accept or refuse the model is taken. In order for a model to have an acceptable goodness of fit index (gfi) structure, its RMSEA value must be 0,07; to have a perfect good-ness of fit index structure its RMSEA value must be 0,05 or lower (Jöreskog and Sörbom, 1993: 121; Arbuckle, 2013: 585). The RMSEA value of the research model is 0,070. χ^2/df=3,05 and p<0.000. When the other goodness of fit indexes are examined, it is observed that the acceptable values (CFI=0,92 - NFI=0,88 - IFI=0,92 - GFI=0,85 - AGFI=0,82 – SRMR=0,088) are provided by the model. The satisfactory result of the model compliance manifests that the predicted structural coefficients will be evaluated in terms of testing hypotheses (Ayyıldız and Cengiz, 2006: 77–80) (Fig. 2) (Tab. 5).

When the results are examined at the end of the analysis conducted, it was determined that the social media communication has above-medium and sig-nificant effects on brand equity subdimensions. Correspondingly, social media communication has a direct, positive, and significant effect (γ=0,634; p<0,001) on brand loyalty, which is one of the subdimensions of brand equity. Therefore, H_1 is supported. The (H_2) hypothesis defending that social media communica-tion has a positive and direct effect on quality variable, which is accepted among the brand equity subdimensions, is also verified.

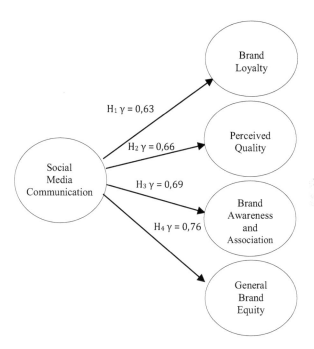

Fig. 2: Structural Equity Model

Tab. 5: Structural Model Results

Dependent Variables		Independent Variables	Total Effect (SRW)	S.E.	C.R.	P
Brand Loyalty	<---	Social Media Communication	,634	,039	11,733***	
Perceived Quality	<---	Social Media Communication	,663	,041	11,145***	
Brand Awareness and Association	<---	Social Media Communication	,689	,043	12,074***	
General Brand Equity	<---	Social Media Communication	,762	,043	13,648***	

***p<0,001, *p>0,05

Tab. 6: Results of Hypotheses Test

Hypotheses	Results
H_1 Social media communication has a positive significant effect on brand loyalty	Supported
H_2 Social media communication has a positive significant effect on perceived quality	Supported
H_3 Social media communication has a positive significant effect on brand awareness and association	Supported
H_4 Social media communication has a positive significant effect on general brand equity	Supported

Additionally, the hypothesis (H_3) defending that social media communication has direct, positive, and significant effect on brand awareness and association, which is among the brand equity subdimensions, is also supported. Furthermore, H_4 is supported by determining that social media communication has a statistically significant effect on general brand equity ($\beta=0{,}762$; $p<0{,}001$), which is the last one of the brand equity subdimensions.

In the light of these results, it was determined that social media communication of brands on online platforms has an above-medium, direct, positive, and significant effect on all of the subdimensions of the brand equity. In the light of all this information, the conceptual model was accepted, and all of the hypotheses tested were supported. The hypotheses results obtained with regards to the model are shown in Tab. 6.

4 Discussion and Conclusions

Social media platforms, which make the relational marketing communication process that compasses long-term customer-brand communication more effective, are not only increasing the awareness, recognition, and association of brands, but also make significant contributions to brand equity. Findings obtained in this research proved that brands, beyond creating instant impacts on customer relations, have to engage in social media communication in order to be effective with regards to awareness, association, and perceived quality. Findings also manifested that social media communication with an interactive structure is also driving brand loyalty to create long-term impact. In this context, one of the basic requirements for enhancing brand awareness, association, perceived quality, and brand loyalty is to develop an effective communication strategy on social media platforms where the target audience is also using it extensively.

In line with the findings of the research, if the brands or brand managers want to create a competitive advantage in favor of their brands, first of all, they have to implement strategic social media communication applications and correspondingly increase the brand association and awareness in the minds of the target audience. However, it is important to be able to drive the perception on the social media platforms by producing content that will attract interest and attention of the target audience. Additionally, the most popular social media platforms among online communication means are becoming an important component of increasing brand awareness and association, establishing long-term customer-relations and creating brand loyalty.

When the results of previous researches in the literature are examined, Nair and Subramaniam (2012: 8) mentioned that using social media platforms will provide a significant contribution to interactive communication, interactive product presentations, and creating a strong impact on customer; and social media networks can offer promising features by providing virtual shopping experience and interactive marketing opportunities. As a result of a study on how to control the interactive communication using social media (Zhang and Lin, 2015: 670), it was proved that while individual users attempt to provide increased protection for control, businesses try to engage in functional interaction.

According to researches on relationship between social media communication and brand equity, it was found that the relationship between social media marketing and brand equity is positive. In other words, social media marketing affects brand equity positively. Hanaysha (2016: 46) determined that social media ads had a significant positive effect on all dimensions of brand equity (brand image, brand loyalty, brand preference, and brand leadership). In the research conducted by Wright (2015: 97), it was concluded that (1) there was a positive relationship between social media communication, and reliability and equity dimensions of the brand equity; (2) there was a positive relationship between Facebook messages and brand equity in terms of image; (3) there was a positive relationship between reliability and equity dimensions of brand equity, and the intention to purchase; finally (4) it was concluded that communicating with potential fitness club customers via social media, customers could be indifferent to certain elements of the marketing mix (price, location, promotion, people, physical evidences and process, etc.).

Owing to social media, it is possible to communicate with a large number of followers regarding company products and services, which can contribute to an increase in brand equity of companies (Wright, 2015: 18). As a result of a research on luxury brands, examining social media marketing efforts on brand equity and consumer behavior (Godey et al., 2015: 1), it was concluded that there was a positive relation between social media marketing efforts and results (brand preference, price premium, and loyalty). As a result of a research (Callarisa et al., 2012: 77) on measuring customer-centered hotel brand equity via social media platforms, it was determined that brand awareness was at the center of all relations between the dimensions of brand equity.

Zauner et al. (2012: 689) emphasized that in marketing activities carried out via social media, sponsors have a positive effect on equity perceptions of customers. In a research on defining the effect of advertising awareness on brand equity in social media, it was concluded that advertising awareness had effect on both brand awareness and brand image. It was also observed that advertising awareness had an effect on brand equity (Alhaddad, 2015: 73).

Social media marketing has a significant effect on brand loyalty as well, which is one of the dimensions of brand equity. In a broader sense, brand awareness and equity awareness mediate the relation between social media marketing and brand loyalty (Ismail, 2017: 129). Can and Çetin (2016: 885) investigated the effects of social media marketing on brand loyalty, and they concluded that social media marketing influenced functional, social, and material benefits, while it had no effect on hedonic and psychological benefits. Moreover, it was observed that community involvement and brand trust had an effect on brand loyalty. Erdoğmuş and Çiçek (2012: 1353) concluded that brand loyalty of the customers was positively influenced when the brand offered (1) favorable campaigns, (2) affordable and (3) popular content, and when it was visible (4) on various platforms and when it carried out applications on social media. This is remarkable since it shows the effect of social media on formation of brand loyalty, which is one of the dimensions of brand equity.

Similar results were observed in studies pertaining to the effect of social media marketing on other dimensions of brand equity or on other elements with similar content. In an empirical study evaluating the importance of social media marketing on increasing the brand equity of e-commerce businesses, it was concluded that there was a significant relation between brand equity of online companies and social media marketing (Kavisekera and Abeysekera, 2016: 201). In the research about the influence of social media, brand credibility, and brand prestige on purchase tendency, Kazancı (2014) concluded that all three elements had a significant and positive effect on purchase tendency, and mentioned that brand credibility had a partial mediating role in the relationship between perceived social media and buying tendency. It was stated that the brand prestige had no mediating effect on this relation. Topal and Temizkan (2016: 1456) investigated the effect of consumers' use of mobile social media on brand awareness, and concluded that social motivation factor being in the first place, psychological and functional motivation factors, respectively, had a positive effect on explaining the use of "Mobile Social Media"; and the use of "Mobile Social Media" had a positive effect on explaining the brand awareness.

As a result of researches on the relation between brand equity and interactive communication on social media environment, it was observed that there was a positive relation between brand equity and interactive communication, in other words interactive communication had a positive effect on brand equity. Correspondingly, the results of a study evaluating the effect of brand communication on brand equity in Facebook context proved that the social media brand communication produced by both the company and the users affected brand awareness/association. Moreover, it was observed that user-generated social media brand communication had a positive effect on brand loyalty and perceived brand quality. On the other hand, significant differences were found (Schivinski and Dabrowski, 2015: 31) among the other industries (nonalcoholic beverages, clothing, and mobile network providers).

In a research on integrated marketing communication and brand identity, which are critical components of the brand identity strategy, the authors developed a schematic brand equity strategy. In this phase, the role of integrated marketing communication in creating and sustaining brand equity, and the role of brand identity in informing, guiding, supporting the development of these, and implementing the company's entire integrated marketing communications strategy were evaluated (Madhavaram et al., 2005: 69).

In the study that examined the effects of brand communities in social media on brand community indicators, value creation practices, brand credibility, and brand loyalty; the results of "Structural Equation Modeling" manifested that brand communities established in social media environment had a positive effect on value creation practices. Such communities can enhance brand loyalty through brand use and perception management practices. Brand trust plays a mediator role in transforming equity creation practices into brand loyalty (Laroche et al., 2012: 1755). In a study on the effects of online brand communities on brand equity in the luxury fashion sector (Brogi et al., 2013: 7), it was concluded that the dynamics of online brand communities (involvement of the brand community, brand content produced by the community, quality perceptions of members about the brand) had positive effects on brand equity.

Keller (2009: 139) introduced a customer-based brand equity model that highlighted the importance of understanding consumer-brand information structures to help the marketers build and manage their brands in a changing marketing communication environment. According to this model, which was called as the brand association pyramid, marketing communication integration involved blending and matching different communication options to create the desired awareness and image in the minds of the consumers. Additionally, online interactive marketing communication for marketers is also considered in the model as part of the versatility.

Even though it was concluded in the previous researches that interactive communication has a positive effect on the brand equity with regards to social media marketing, there are exceptional studies with negative consequences as well. For instance, in a study about fast moving consumer goods on Facebook, it was concluded that social media brand communication generated by the company had a direct effect on only four customer-based brand equity dimensions (brand awareness, brand-perceived quality, brand associations and brand reliability). Another consequence was that user-generated social media communication did not have a significant effect on brand-perceived quality, brand loyalty, and brand trust. An additional consequence was that the user-generated social media communication had a negative effect on brand awareness and brand association (Sadek et al., 2017: 237).

In the previous researches, the relations were examined between numerous variables and factors affecting brand equity. The findings of this study and conclusions of numerous similar researches are corresponding. Therefore, since the findings of this research support the results of the researches conducted to determine the effects of social media communication on brand equity, this research is remarkable with regards to its contribution to the literature.

Bibliography

Aaker, D. A. (1992). "Managing Brand Equity: Capitalizing on the Value of a Brand Name." *Journal of Marketing*, 56(2), pp. 125–128.

Alameddine, A. (2013). *Perceptions of Executives from Seven Selected Companies of the Use of Social Media in Marketing Practices*. Pepperdine University, Malibu, CA 90263 USA.

Alhaddad, A. A. (2015). "The Effect of Advertising Awareness on Brand Equity in Social Media." *International Journal of e-Education, e-Business, e-Management and e-Learning*, 5(2), pp. 73–84.

Arbuckle, J. L. (2013). *IBM SPSS Amos 22 User's Guide*. Florida: Amos Development Corporation.

Ayyıldız, H. and Cengiz, A. G. E. (2006). "Pazarlama Modellerinin Testinde Kullanılabilecek Yapısal Eşitlik Modeli (YEM) Üzerine Kavramsal Bir

İnceleme." *Süleyman Demirel Üniversitesi İktisadi ve İdari Bilimler Fakültesi Dergisi*, 11(2), pp. 63–84.

Bajpai, V., & Pandey, S. (2012). "Viral Marketing Through Social Networking Sites with Special Reference of Facebook." *International Journal of Marketing, Financial Services & Management Research*, 1(7), pp. 194–207.

Barefoot, D. and Szabo, J. (2010). *Friends with Benefits A Social Media Marketing Handbook*, No Starch Press, 555 De Haro Street, Suite 250, San Francisco, USA.

Bergh, J. V. and Behrer, M. (2013). *How Cool Brands Stay Hot. Branding to Generation Y.* (2. Baskı) United Kingdom, USA, India: Kogan Page Limited.

Brogi, S., Calabrese, A., Campisi, D., Capece, G., Costa, R., & Di Pillo, F. (2013). "The Effects of Online Brand Communities on Brand Equity in the Luxury Fashion Industry." *International Journal of Engineering Business Management*, 5(Godište 2013), pp. 5–32.

Callarisa, L. García, J. S. Cardiff, J. and Roshchina, A. (2012). "Harnessing Social Media Platforms to Measure Customer-Based Hotel Brand Equity." *Tourism Management Perspectives*, 4, pp. 73–79.

Can, P. and Çetin, İ. (2016). "Sosyal Medya Pazarlamasından Elde Edilen Faydaların Tüketici Marka Bağlılığına Etkisi Üzerine Bir Araştırma." *Atatürk Üniversitesi İktisadi ve İdari Bilimler Dergisi*, 30(4), pp. 885–906.

Crayton, M. K. (2013). *Examining the Relationship between the Usefulness of Multimedia Messaging Services and Brand Equity: A Conceptual Framework.* Minneapolis: Doctor of Philosophy, Capella University.

Çetinsöz, B. C. and Artuğer, S. (2013). "Antalya İli'nin Marka Değerinin Ölçülmesine Yönelik Bir Araştırma." *Anatolia: Turizm Araştırmaları Dergisi*, 24(2), pp. 200–210.

del Bosque, I. A. R. San Martín, H. and Collado, J. (2006). "The Role of Expectations in the Consumer Satisfaction Formation Process: Empirical Evidence in the Travel Agency Sector." *Tourism Management*, 27(3), pp. 410–419.

Eley, B. and Tilley, S. (2009). *Online Marketing Inside Out (First Edition).* Victoria: Sitepoint Pty. Ltd.

Erdoğmuş, İ. E. and Çiçek, M. (2012). "The Impact of Social Media Marketing on Brand Loyalty. SciVerse ScienceDirect." *Procedia – Social and Behavioral Sciences*, 58, pp. 1353–1360.

Fırat, D. and Badem, A. C. (2008). "Marka Değerleme Yöntemleri ve Marka Değerinin Mali Tablolara Yansıtılması." *Muhasebe ve Finansman Dergisi*, (38), 210–219.

Godey, B. Manthioua, A. Pederzoli, D. Rokka, J. Aiello, G. Donvito, R. and Singh, R. (2015). "Social Media Marketing Efforts of Luxury Brands: Influence on Brand Equity and Consumer Behavior." *Journal of Business Research*, 69(12), pp. 5833–5841.

Gunelius, S. (2011). 30 *Minute Social Media Marketing: Step-by-Step Techniques to Spread the Word about Your Business Fast and Free*. New York: Mcgraw Hill.

Hanaysha, J. (2016). "The Importance of Social Media Advertisements in Enhancing Brand Equity: A Study on Fast Food Restaurant Industry in Malaysia." *International Journal of Innovation, Management and Technology*, 7(2), p. 46.

Ismail, A. R. (2017). "The Influence of Perceived Social Media Marketing Activities on Brand Loyalty: The Mediation Effect of Brand and Value Consciousness." *Asia Pacific Journal of Marketing and Logistics*, 29(1), pp. 129–144.

Jin, X. L. Cheung, C. M. K. Lee, M. K.O. and Chen, H. P. (2009). "How to Keep Members Using the Information in a Computer-Supported Social Network." *Computers in Human Behavior*, 25(5), pp. 1172–1181.

Jöreskog, K. G., and Sörbom, D. (1993). *LISREL 8: Structural Equation Modeling with the SIMPLIS Command Language*. Scientific Software International, Microsoft Certified Partner, USA.

Kavisekera, S. and Abeysekera, N. (2016). "Effect of Social Media Marketing on Brand Equity of Online Companies." *Management & Marketing Journal*, 14(2), 201.

Kazancı, Ş. (2014). *Sosyal Medyanın, Marka Kredibilitesinin ve Marka Prestijinin Satın Alma Eğilimi Üzerine Etkileri*, Yüksek Lisans Tezi, Hacettepe Üniversitesi Sosyal Bilimler Enstitüsü, Ankara.

Keller, K. L. (2009). "Building Strong Brands in a Modern Marketing Communications Environment." *Journal of Marketing Communications*, 15(2–3), pp. 139–155.

Kelly, L. (2007). *Beyond Buzz: The Next Generation of Word-of-Mouth Marketing*. New York: Amacom.

Kietzmann, J. H., Hermkens, K., McCarthy, I. P., & Silvestre, B. S. (2011). "Social Media? Get Serious! Understanding the Functional Building Blocks of Social Media." *Business Horizons*, 54(3), pp. 241–251.

Kim, W., Jeong, O. R. and Lee, S. W. (2010). "On Social Web Sites." *Information Systems*, 35, pp. 215–236.

Koçak, A. and Özer, A. (2004). Marka Değeri Belirleyicileri: Bir Ölçek Değerlendirmesi, 9. Ulusal Pazarlama Kongresi, 6–8 Ekim 2004, PPAD, Gazi University, Ankara

Krajenke, B. (2014). *PETA's Use of Social Network Marketing* (Order No. 1525245). Available from ProQuest Dissertations & Theses Global. (1524993366).

Laccy, K. (2010). *Twitter Marketing for Dummies.* Indiana: Wiley Publishing Inc.

Laroche, M., Habibi, M. R., Richard, M. O. and Sankaranarayanan, R. (2012). "The Effects of Social Media Based Brand Communities on Brand Community Markers, Value Creation Practices, Brand Trust and Brand Loyalty." *Computers in Human Behavior*, 28, pp. 1755–1767.

Madhavaram, S. Badrinarayanan, V. and McDonald R. E. (2005). "Integrated Marketing Communication (Imc) and Brand Identity as Critical Components of Brand Equity Strategy." *Journal of Advertising*, 34(4), pp. 69–80.

Mangold, W. G. and Faulds, D. J. (2009). "Social Media: The New Hybrid Element of the Promotion Mix." *Business Horizons*, 52(4), pp. 357–365.

Nair, T. G. and Subramaniam, K. (2012). *Transformation of Traditional Marketing Communications in to Paradigms of Social Media Networking*, In Asia Pacific Business Research Conference.

Nicovich, S. G. (1999). *Interactive Communication: The Impact of Felt Presence on Consumer Attitudes* (Order No. 9949976). Available from ProQuest Dissertations & Theses Global.

O'Neill, J. W. and Mattıla, A. S. (2004). "Hotel Branding Strategy: Its Relationship to Guest Satisfaction and Room Revenue." *Journal of Hospitality & Tourism Research*, 28(2), pp. 156–165.

Ross, C. Orr, E. S. Sisic, M. Arseneault, J. M. Simmering, M. G. and Orr, R. R. (2009). "Personality and Motivations Associated with Facebook Use.", *Computers in Human Behavior*, 25(2), pp. 578–586.

Sadek, H. Elwy, S. and Eldallal, M. (2017). "The Impact of Social Media Brand Communication on Consumer-Based Brand Equity Dimensions Through Facebook in Fast Moving Consumer Goods: Egypt Case." *The Business and Management Review*, 8(5), pp. 237–251.

Samsunlu, G. and Baş, M. (2016). Marka Değerinin Tüketici Satın Alma Tutumları Üzerine Etkisi ve McDonald's ve Burger King Üzerine Bir Araştırma. 15. Ulusal İşletmecilik Kongresi, 26–28 Mayıs 2016, İstanbul.

Schivinski, B. and Dabrowski, D. (2015). "The Impact of Brand Communication on Brand Equity Through Facebook." *Journal of Research in Interactive Marketing*, 9(1, 9), pp. 31–53.

Taşkın, Ç. and Akat, Ö. (2010). "Tüketici Temelli Marka Değerinin Yapısal Eşitlik Modelleme ile Ölçümü ve Dayanıklı Tüketim Malları Sektöründe Bir Araştırma." *İşletme ve Ekonomi Araştırmaları Dergisi*, 1(2), pp. 1–16.

Topal, İ. and Temizkan, V. (2016). "Tüketicilerin Mobil Sosyal Medya Kullanımının Marka Farkındalığına Etkisi." *İnsan ve Toplum Bilimleri Araştırmaları Dergisi*, 5(5), pp. 1456–1473.

Tuten, T. L. (2008). *Advertising 2.0 Social Media Marketing in a Web 2.0 World*. Westport-London: Praeger Publishers.

Weinberg, T. (2009). *The New Community Rules: Marketing on the Social Web*. (First Edition). United States of America: O'Reilly Media.

Wright, B. K. (2015). *Brand Communication via Facebook: An Investigation of the Relationship Between the Marketing Mix, Brand Equity, and Purchase Intention in the Fitness Segment of the Sport Industry*. Indiana: Doctor of Philosophy in the School of Public Health, Indiana University.

Yoo, B. and Donthu, N. (2001). "Developing and Validating a Multidimensional Consumer-Based Brand Equity Scale." *Journal of Business Research*, 52, pp. 1–14.

Zahoor, S. Z. and Qureshi, I. H. (2017). "Social Media Marketing and Brand Equity: A Literature Review. IUP", *Journal of Marketing Management; Hyderabad*, 16(1), pp. 47–64.

Zauner, A. Koller, M. and Fink, M. (2012). "Sponsoring, Brand Value and Social Media." *RAE, São Paulo*, 52(6), pp. 681–691.

Zhang, C. B. and Lin, Y. H. (2015). "Exploring Interactive Communication Using Social Media." *The Service Industries Journal*, 35(11–12), pp. 670–693.

https://www.boomsocial.com/social-brands *(Turkey Social Media Brand Index (Accessed: 02/10/2017))*.

Fevziye Kalıpçı Çağıran and Alp Eren Kayasandık

Corporate Governance Rating and Profitability in Borsa İstanbul

1 Introduction

In general, all institutions, and in particular the businesses, are required to manage well in order to achieve their objectives with minimum cost and in the shortest time. In other words, good management is the process of achieving the objectives effectively and efficiently. This concept is much more important for businesses that want to survive profitably for generations. Especially for large-scale companies to live long term with sustainable profitability, they should consciously implement good managerial practices. In this respect, the concept of corporate governance is the implementation of the concept of good governance in companies.

As a result of the financial crises and bankruptcies in the world, corporate governance began to be used in business management. In order to ensure better performance of the companies and to put an end to mismanagement, various studies have been carried out in the field of corporate governance. As a result of these studies, Corporate Governance Principles were formed. The theoretical approaches that influence the development of corporate governance based on the different research fields such as economy, accounting, finance, psychology, sociology, law, management and organization (Özsoy, 2011: 17–18). The rapid development of corporate governance at the global concept has been echoed in Turkey and reproduced quickly in Turkey as a sense of management.

The Corporate Governance Practices Guide presented by the OECD in the international scope has been followed by Civil Society Organizations such as TÜSİAD, The Banks Association of Turkey (TBB) and Corporate Governance Association of Turkey (TKYD) and by market controllers such as Capital Market Board of Turkey (CMB) and Borsa İstanbul and corporate governance principles were formed in 2003. Within the framework of these principles, which have undergone some updates in the ongoing process, many studies have been conducted examining the relationship between the rating indicators of the listed companies and the ratings of financial indicators and board structures. In this study, firstly, after giving information about corporate governance and corporate governance rating, the application section was positioned. In the application part of the study, after determining the companies which have been in the index since the first calculation date of the BIST Corporate Governance Index (XKURY), tendencies of the corporate governance ratings and the different profitability ratios from years 2007 to 2017 were performed.

2 Corporate Governance

Corporate Governance is a concept that is frequently mentioned in both literature and applications. The concept of corporate governance which was first used in 1960 to point out the structure and functioning of company policy (Becht et al., 2002: 2). Corporate governance was initially perceived and defined as a system to regulate the relations between the owner or the owners and the managers.

The corporate governance should support managerial structure of the enterprise and efficient use of resources and at the same time it should ensure that the management is responsible for the loss arising from the misuse of these resources as required. The aim to be observed in management should be to ensure the balance between the interests of individuals, partnership and the society in general. One of the most important mechanisms that will ensure this is corporate governance (Çelik, 2007: 81).

The concept of corporate governance comes in many different forms according to its point of view and purpose. However, from the perspective of this study, it is possible to draw a background while explaining the corporate governance concept. In today's modern business structures, due to the transfer of management affairs to professionals, business founders may not be aware of the evolution of enterprises. This can lead to joint action problems. Due to the high number of partners and the information asymmetry, the management work becomes difficult. There may be conflict of interest between manager, investors and lenders. In addition, investor confidence is affected by the scandals that erupted by manipulating the financial statements in the interest of the entity. Such problems made the effective corporate governance practices inevitable (Doğan, 2018: 85; Dalğar & Çelik, 2011: 100).

The corporate governance approach is a concept that aims to protect the rights of all stakeholders, including shareholders, and to regulate the rules of the relations between the interest groups within this framework (Şehirli, 1999: 8).

It is possible to define corporate governance, the best management of a company, as well as a set of principles that enables to monitor and to control management process in a transparent manner. In other words, Denis & McConnell, (2003: 2) defines corporate governance as the set of mechanisms – both institutional and market-based – that induce the self-interested controllers of a company, to make decisions that maximize the value of the company to its owners.

Koçel (2014) defines corporate governance as an approach to be transparent and relaying information to both its internal and external stakeholders, while Gregory & Lillien (2000) have defined corporate governance as a set of regulations that protect the interests of shareholders and other stakeholders and increase the value of the company. Gill (2002) has associated corporate governance with discipline, independence, integrity and honesty, transparency, equality and accountability principles (Doğan, 2018: 86). TKYD (2013) defines corporate governance as legal, regulatory, and private sector practices for social expectations that help the business meet its legal obligations in achieving its objectives. Corporate governance is a variable that helps businesses attract capital and human resources and provides an efficient and high performance. Corporate governance is also a process related to the methods that provide financing to companies to make them feel safe in making a return on their investments (Shleifer & Vishny, 1997: 737).

In the broad sense, corporate governance is the formal and non-formal rules required for good company management via regulating the relations between the company and the society, and it regulates the relations between the company management and the shareholders and stakeholders. It also comprises all kinds of laws, regulations, codes and applications that allow value creation in long term by ensuring the recognition of the rights of the shareholders by the company and helps them to make effective use of these rights (Güler, 2017: 2; Kula & Baykut, 2013: 122).

Forming corporate governance basis was first studied by OECD in 1999. Corporate Governance Report at Banks are prepared by The Banks Association of Turkey, at the same year. Following this, TÜSİAD Corporate Governance Working Group presented the report "Corporate Governance-Best Practice Code: The Structure and Function of the Board of Directors" in 2002. Then in 2003, "Corporate Governance Principles" had been published by CMB. In 2005, it has been compulsory to include Corporate Governance Compliance Statements in the annual reports. In 2007, the Corporate Governance Index (XKURY) was added to the stock exchange in order to adapt capital markets to this change and to encourage companies and investors (TÜSİAD, 2002: 9; Kula & Baykut, 2013: 123).

Although there is no agreed "corporate governance" definition to cover each sector and practice, "equality", "transparency", "accountability" and "responsibility" are essential notions in all generally accepted corporate governance approaches. These notions are described as follows (Dalğar & Çelik, 2011: 101):

- *Equity*: The company management acts equally to shareholders and interest groups in all its activities and prevents any potential conflicts of interest between these groups.
- *Transparency*: It means that all financial and non-financial information related to the company, except for the information which is a trade secret and which has not been disclosed to the public, are shared with the public in a timely, accurate, complete, understandable manner, which can be interpreted by everyone and that all interest groups can reach at low cost. Moreover, according to Florini (1999), transparency can be defined as the release of relevant information for the evaluation of the companies by themselves.
- *Accountability*: Based on the fact that the members of the Board of Directors cannot manage the business in line with their own desires, managers have an obligation to account for the corporate legal entity and the shareholders.
- *Responsibility*: Inspection of compliance of all business activities carried out by the management on behalf of the incorporated company with the legislation, articles of association and internal regulations.

CMB carries out its activities to make capital markets more transparent and reliable. In addition to this, it also serves to increase the confidence in the market, by providing a more transparent structure of financial reports and thus to increase the demand for stocks and hence increase the transaction volume. Companies that are included in the Corporate Governance Index are encouraged to adopt corporate governance policies and to participate in the index by providing discount privileges on monthly quotation fees. The discount application for quotation fees has been abolished since February 2015. In order to support these objectives, four main headings as "Shareholders", "Public Disclosure and Transparency", "Stakeholders" and "Board of Management" and their subcriteria are formed by CMB (Karamustafa et al., 2009: 102–103).

- *Shareholders*: Shareholders' rights are to receive and review information about the company, to participate in and vote in the general assembly, to take part in the profit of the period, to participate in decisions related to the company. These rights mean protecting the shareholders through the corporate governance process.
- *Public Disclosure and Transparency*: To increase the visibility and corporate structure of the companies, it is the criterion that the correct and timely disclosure of information related to shareholders and preparation of annual reports on all financial and non-financial matters through Public Disclosure Platform (PDP) and company's websites.

- *Stakeholders*: The regulations contained in the third section are improving ability to communicate with the company management by groups of stakeholders who are directly or indirectly associated with the company. This criteria also suggests that there should be a standardized human resources policies and social responsibility activities.
- *Board of Directors*: In order for the company to have a corporate governance identity, an effective audit of the board of directors is required, and every individual involved in the management should be accountable to the company's legal entity and therefore to the shareholders. In this respect, this criteria emphasizes the duties and responsibilities that management has to fulfill in the interests of the shareholders.

Corporate governance provides benefits not only to companies that implement these management principles, but also to all stakeholders who are directly and/or indirectly associated with the entity. The benefits that the corporate governance practice can provide to businesses can be listed as follows (http://www.sobiadacademy.net/sobem/e-yonetim/kurumsal-yonetim/amaclar.htm):

- The most important benefit that corporate governance provides to the business is to reduce the cost of capital.
- Corporate governance provides cash inflow to the company with liquidity shortage.
- It also enhances confidence of domestic and foreign investors and thus the long-term capital inflow is accelerated.
- It allows financial crises to be overcome more easily.
- The better the business is managed, the higher the returns on assets. Therefore, corporate governance increases the value of the company.
- Corruption is reduced due to transparency and accountability in business management. Eliminates arbitrary management.
- It contributes to increase the relations between the company and stakeholders as it will serve the interests of all stakeholders.
- It increases the competitiveness and profitability of the company.
- The benefits of corporate governance to the country and society can be listed as follows (http://www.sobiadacademy.net/sobem/e-yonetim/kurumsal-yonetim/amaclar.htm):
- It helps to overcome economic crises more easily.
- It facilitates financial deepening by protecting rights of shareholders. In this respect, corporate governance has positive contributions to the development of banking and financial sector.

- It allows the development of capital markets. There is a linear relationship between good protection of shareholder rights and stock market capitalization.
- It contributes to increase macroeconomic performance. Ease of access to financing opportunities increases the total investments of companies by reducing their capital costs. The increase in investments creates new job opportunities and broadens the employment capacity in the economy.

3 Corporate Governance Rating

The competition that emerged as a natural result of globalization has made the corporate governance rating a new tool that determines the conditions for entering the corporate governance index for economies that want to attract more investors to the financial system (Toraman and Abdioğlu, 2008: 108). The corporate governance rating is an independent, objective and fair evaluation of the companies' compliance with the Corporate Governance Principles published by CMB (www.spk.gov.tr).

Corporate Governance Index was established within Borsa İstanbul in order to contribute to the establishment of the best corporate governance practices in Turkey, to encourage companies that are sensitive about the corporate governance, to create references to others and especially to attract foreign investors (Cebeci ve Özbilgin, 2015: 53).

The weights of the four main sections of the Corporate Governance Principles in the corporate governance rating were determined by the CMB. The weighting of the principles under the main sections is made by rating institutions. It is seen that the explanatory information made by the rating companies about the importance of corporate governance principles in the mentioned weighting is quite low (Güçlü, 2010: 4).

Corporate governance rating of the companies are maintained by SAHA Corporate Governance and Credit Rating Services Inc., Kobirate International Credit Rating and Corporate Governance Services Inc., JCR Eurasia Rating, DRC Rating Services Inc. in Turkey (www.spk.gov.tr).

The corporate governance rating is determined by the rating institutions incorporated by CMB in its list of rating agencies as a result of their assessment of the company's compliance with the corporate governance principles. The rating must be issued and renewed annually due to the request of the company that wants to make a rating. The companies that meet the minimum rating requirement shall be included in the BIST Corporate Governance Index on the working day following the date on which the rating is published at PDP.

Tab. 1: Companies in BIST Corporate Governance Index (2013–2017). Source: Borsa İstanbul, Corporate Governance Association of Turkey

Years	2013	2014	2015	2016	2017
Number of Companies in XKURY	47	53	54	51	51
BIST Companies	424	425	416	405	481
%	11,08	12,47	12,98	12,59	10,06

The corporate governance rating is based on the Corporate Governance Principles published in 2003 and revised later by CMB.

In corporate governance, rating of the companies is calculated by weighting 25 % of the Shareholders' criteria, 25 % of the Public Disclosure and Transparency criteria, 15 % of the Stakeholders' criteria and 35 % of the Board of Directors' criteria. Independent rating institutions give a rating of between 1 and 10 for each of the main sections mentioned according to the degree of compliance with these criteria. Companies that can get 7 or more in total from 10 are eligible to be traded in the Corporate Governance Index (XKURY). The Corporate Governance Index, which is an important step to support the corporate governance perception in Borsa İstanbul, is one of Borsa İstanbul's share indices and is an index that includes companies with minimum corporate governance rating requirement. BIST Corporate Governance Index aims to measure the price and return performances of companies traded on Borsa İstanbul Markets with a corporate governance rating of minimum 7 over 10 as a whole and minimum of 6.5 for each main section (www.borsaistanbul.com).

Vestel Elektronik Sanayi ve Ticaret A.Ş. met the criteria for inclusion in the Corporate Governance Index on 07.03.2007. Respectively, Y&Y Gayrimenkul Yatırım Ortaklığı A.Ş. on 20.04.2007, Tofaş Türk Otomobil Fabrikası A.Ş. on 28.05.2007, Doğan Yayın Holding A.Ş. on 02.08.2007. BIST Corporate Governance Index has been calculated on 31.08.2007 since Türk Traktör ve Ziraat Makinaları A.Ş. met the criteria for being included in the Corporate Governance Index on 23.08.2007 with the number of companies that met these criteria reached to 5 (www.hakanguclu.com/kurumsal-yonetim/soru-cevap/imkb-kurumsal-yonetim-endeksi/). End of year 2017, the number of companies in the index increased from 5 to 51 (www.kap.org.tr).

The number of companies in BIST Corporate Governance Index and the number of companies traded in the stock exchange in the last five-year period are given in Tab. 1.

Tab. 2: Corporate Governance Ratings by Years. Source: Borsa İstanbul, Corporate Governance Association of Turkey

Years	Vestel Elektronik Sanayi ve Ticaret A.Ş.	Tofaş Türk Otomobil Fabrikası A.Ş.	Türk Traktör ve Ziraat Makineleri A.Ş.
2007	7.59	7.74	7.52
2008	8.26	8.16	7.83
2009	8.34	8.24	8.12
2010	8.40	8.42	8.30
2011	8.59	8.58	8.50
2012	8.83	9.02	8.90
2013	9.09	9.14	9.10
2014	9.04	9.01	9.05
2015	9.12	9.06	9.08
2016	9.36	9.14	9.15
2017	9.49	9.15	9.21

Tab. 1 shows that there has been a decrease in the companies included in BIST Corporate Governance Index after the abolition of discounts in the quotation fee applied by Borsa İstanbul, and there is no increase in the companies in the Corporate Governance Index despite the increase in the number of companies traded in Borsa İstanbul.

Tab. 2 shows corporate governance ratings by years of the companies mentioned in this study.

4 The Application

In this section, after companies that have been in BIST Corporate Governance Index (XKURY) since the first calculation of index are identified, the trend of different profitability ratios and corporate governance ratings given by rating institutions to these companies between 2007 and 2017 will be analyzed. For this purpose, the change in the different profitability ratios (ROA, ROE, ROS, ROCE) and corporate governance ratings of the three companies which firstly were included in the index and which are still in the index are examined both in terms of each company and by comparison between companies. In the scope of the study, it has been tried to determine whether the corporate governance ratings and the profitability ratios show a certain tendency.

In the study, Vestel Elektronik Sanayi ve Ticaret A.Ş. (VESTL), Tofaş Türk Otomobil Fabrikası A.Ş. (TOASO) and Türk Traktör ve Ziraat Makineleri A.Ş.

Tab. 3: Profitability Ratios

ROA	Return on Assets	Net Profit/Total Assets
ROE	Return on Equity	Net Profit/Total Owners' Equity
ROS	Return on Sales	Net Profit/Net Sales
ROCE	Return on Capital Employed	EBIT/(Total Assets – Short Term Liabilities)

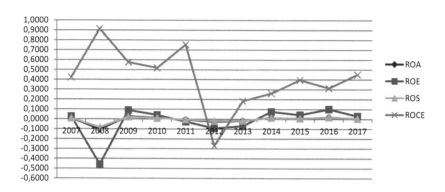

Fig. 1: Changes in the Profitability Ratios of Vestel Elektronik San. ve Tic. A.Ş.

(TTRAK), which are the three companies in the index since the first calculation of BIST Corporate Governance Index, have been included in the study. These companies were selected because they have been in index.

Within the scope of this study, the data on the required different profitability ratios of the three companies currently operating in the BIST Corporate Governance Index are obtained from the financial statements of the years 2007–2017, which are included in the Public Disclosure Platform (www.kap.gov.tr). The companies of corporate governance ratings have been reached via Corporate Governance Association of Turkey website (www.tkyd.org).

In the study, as profitability ratios ROA, ROE, ROS and ROCE were included. The selected ratios of profitability are frequently used in the literature. The ratios used in the analysis to be performed are given in Tab. 3.

Fig. 1, Fig. 2 and Fig. 3 show the change in four different profitability ratios in terms of all three companies from 2007 to 2017. Each of the following graphs include changes in the profitability ratios of each company.

According to Fig. 1, return on assets and return on sales of Vestel Elektronik Sanayi ve Ticaret A.Ş. show a very similar tendency to be called the same over the years.

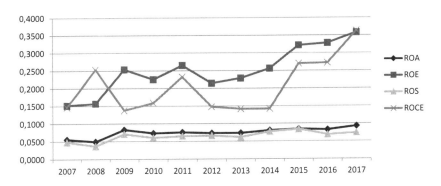

Fig. 2: Changes in the Profitability Ratios of Tofaş Türk A.Ş.

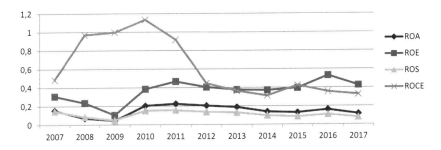

Fig. 3: Changes in the Profitability Ratios of Türk Traktör ve Ziraat Mak. A.Ş.

Fig. 2 shows that return on assets and return on sales of Tofaş Türk Otomobil Fabrikası A.Ş. have parallel trend.

According to Fig. 3, it is seen that ROA and ROS of Türk Traktör ve Ziraat Makineleri A.Ş. show a similar tendency over the years.

As can be seen in Fig. 4, the corporate governance rating of the companies between 2007 and 2017 is an upward trend. Only in 2014, the corporate governance ratings of all three companies decreased. The increasing in ratings continued in other years.

In 2007 when the index was first calculated, the corporate governance ratings of the companies were about 7, and after 10 years, the rating of the companies increased to 9 as a result of the importance given to corporate governance.

Ratings between 9 and 10 are an indication that the companies are in compliance with the CMB Corporate Governance Principles. At the same time, the rights of the shareholders and stakeholders are best respected; public

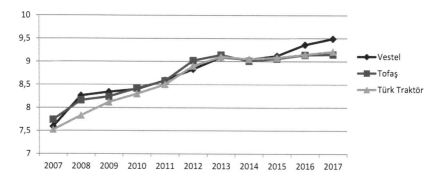

Fig. 4: Change in the Corporate Governance Ratings of the Companies

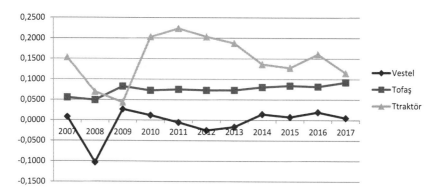

Fig. 5: Change in Return on Assets of Companies by Years

disclosure and transparency activities are at the highest level; the structure and operation of the board of directors is in the best practice category   (www.saharating.com/~saharati/kurumsal-yonetim-derecelendirmesi/kurumsal-yonetim-derecelendirme-notlarinin-anlami/).

In Fig. 5, Fig. 6, Fig. 7 and Fig. 8 below, the changes in each profitability ratio over the years are given comparatively among companies.

As can be seen in the graphs in Fig. 5, Fig. 6, Fig. 7 and Fig. 8, profitability ratios do not show a regular uptrend between 2007 and 2017 as in corporate governance ratings. There is no doubt that it is not surprising that such a trend is encountered because of sectoral and economic fluctuations that affect profitability. Nevertheless, it can be concluded that profitability ratios of Tofaş Türk

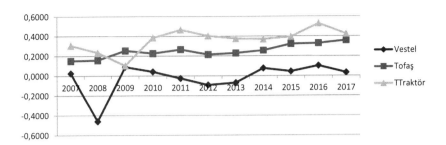

Fig. 6: Change in Return on Equity of Companies by Years

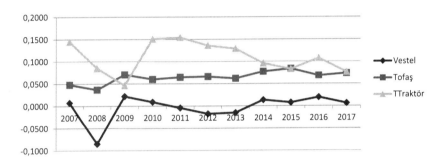

Fig. 7: Change in Return on Sales of Companies by Years

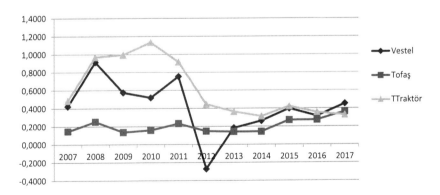

Fig. 8: Change in Return on Capital Employed of Companies by Years

Otomobil Fabrikası A.Ş. shows no more fluctuations between 2007–2017 and has a more regular trend compared to others.

Conclusion

Corporate governance and corporate governance rating has gained importance in companies with global financial crises and business insolvencies.

Corporate governance refers to a management approach in which the relations between business management and all interest groups are adhered to principles in order to provide a sustainable value for the company and to ensure the continuity of the company in the long term.

Corporate governance practices are an important fact that increase the accountability and transparency of companies. The companies that comply with the corporate governance principles and have had the appropriate corporate governance rating are included in the corporate governance index.

In this study, which examines the tendency in corporate governance ratings and profitability ratios by years, three companies which are listed in BIST Corporate Governance Index and which continue to be included in the index since 31.08.2007, the first calculation date of the index has been selected. In the study, return on assets, return on equity, return on sales and return on capital employed were determined as profitability ratios.

It has been concluded that the corporate governance ratings of the identified companies between years 2007 and 2017 are upward trend except for one year (2014). This result can be interpreted as an indication that the value of corporate and financially high standard companies increased importance given to corporate governance.

According to the results, it is seen that these companies have very high ratings (at least 9), especially in the last five years. In addition, it can be said that Tofaş Türk Otomobil Fabrikası A.Ş. does not have much fluctuations in profitability ratios and it has shown a more regular trend compared to the other two companies. Furthermore, a similar tendency has been determined between the return on assets and return on sales of the companies over the years.

Bibliography

Becht, M., Bolton, P., Röell, A. (2002). "Corporate Governance and Control", Working Paper. http://ssrn.com/abstract_id=343461 (Accessed on: 05.01.2019)

Cebeci, G. and Özbilgin, İ. G. (2015), "Borsa İstanbul Bilişim Endeksinde Yer Alan Şirketlerin Kurumsal Yönetim ve Finansal Performans Açısından Değerlendirilmesi", Gazi Üniversitesi Sosyal Bilimler Dergisi, 2(4), 47–64.

Çelik, O. (2007), İşletmelerde Muhasebe Bilgisi ve Şirket Demokrasisi, Ankara: Siyasal Kitabevi.

Dalğar, H. and Çelik, İ. (2011), "Kurumsal Yönetimin İşletmelerin Finansal Yapısına Etkileri: İMKB Kurumsal Yönetim Endeksi (XKURY) Üzerine Bir İnceleme", Finans Politik & Ekonomik Yorumlar Dergisi, 48(557), 99–110.

Denis, D. K. & McConnell, J. J. (2003), "International Corporate Governance", Journal of Financial and Quantitative Analysis, 38(1), 1–36.

Doğan, M. (2018), "Kurumsal Yönetimin Teorik Temelleri", Uluslararası Yönetim Akademisi Dergisi, 1(1), 84–96.

Florini, A. (1999), "Does the Invisible Hand Need a Transparent Glove? The Politics of Transparency", Annual World Bank Conference on Development Economics, Washington, http://www.worldbank.org/research/abcde/washington_11/pdfs/florini.pdf(Accessed on: 10.02.2019).

Gill, A. (2002). Corporate Governance in Emerging Markets- Saints and Sinners: Who's Got Religion?, Symposium on Corporate Governance and Disclosure: The Impact of Globalization, The School of Accountancy, The Chinese University of Hong Kong.

Gregory, H. J. and Lilien, J. R. (2000), Corporate Governance and the Role of the Board of Directors, Great Britian, Egon Zehnder International.

Güçlü, H. (2010), Kurumsal Yönetim Uyum Derecelendirmesi, İstanbul: İMKB Yayını.

Güler, E. (2017), "The Relationship of Corporate Governance and Financial Performance an Application on Manufacturing Enterprises Covered By ISE Corporate Governance Index", Journal of Applied Research in Finance and Economics, 3(2), 1–12.

Karamustafa, O., Varıcı, İ. and Er, B. (2009), "Kurumsal Yönetim ve Firma Performansı: İMKB Kurumsal Yönetim Endeksi Kapsamındaki Firmalar Üzerinde Bir Uygulama", Kocaeli Üniversitesi Sosyal Bilimler Enstitüsü Dergisi, 17, 100–119.

Koçel, T. (2014), İşletme Yöneticiliği (15. Baskı), İstanbul: Beta.

Kula, V. and Baykut, E. (2013), "Kurumsal Yönetim Endeksinde Yer Almanın Mevduat Bankalarının Performansına Etkisi: BIST Örneği", Afyon Kocatepe Üniversitesi Sosyal Bilimler Dergisi, 15(2), 121–136.

Özsoy, Z. (2011), Kurumsal Yönetim ve Yönetim Kurulları, Ankara: İmge Kitabevi.

Shleifer, R. and Vishny, W. (1997), "A Survey of Corporate Governance", The Journal of Finance, 52(2), pp. 737–783.

SPK, (2005), "Kurumsal Yönetim İlkeleri", http://www.spk.gov.tr/Sayfa/Dosya/845.

Şehirli, K. (1999), "Kurumsal Yönetim", SPK Yeterlilik Etütleri, S.P.K. Denetleme Dairesi.

TKYD, (2013), "Kurumsal Yönetim İlkeleri Işığında Aile Şirketleri Yönetim Rehberi", İstanbul, http://www.tkyd.org/files/downloads/faaliyet_alanlari/yayinlarimiz/tkyd_yayinlari/aile_sirketleri_yonetim_rehberi_2013_2.pdf. (Accessed on 05.03.2019)..

Toraman, C. V. and Abdioğlu, H. (2008), "İMKB Kurumsal Yönetim Endeksinde Yer Alan Şirketlerin Kurumsal Yönetim Uygulamalarında Zayıf ve Güçlü Yanları: Derecelendirme Raporlarının İncelenmesi", MUFAD Muhasebe ve Finansman Dergisi, 40, pp. 96–109.

TÜSİAD, (2002). "Kurumsal Yönetim En İyi Uygulama Kodu: Yönetim Kurulunun Yapısı ve İşleyişi", https://tusiad.org/tr/tum/item/1877-kurumsal-yonetim-en-iyi-uygulama-kodu--yonetim-kurulunun-yapisi-ve-isleyisi, Yayın No. TÜSİAD-T/2002-12/336

https://cgf.ku.edu.tr/tr/content/kurumsal-yonetim-nedir

http://www.saharating.com/~saharati/kurumsal-yonetim-derecelendirmesi/kurumsal-yonetim-derecelendirme-notlarinin-anlami/

http://www.spk.gov.tr/sayfa/index/6/10/1

http://www.spk.gov.tr/Sayfa/Index/6/10/2

http://www.sobiadacademy.net/sobem/e-yonetim/kurumsal-yonetim/amaclar.htm

www.borsaistanbul.com/endeksler/bist-pay-endeksleri/kurumsal-yonetim-endeksi

www.kap.gov.tr

www.tkyd.org.tr

www.hakanguclu.com/kurumsal-yonetim/soru-cevap/kurumsal-yonetim/

List of Figures

List of Tables

List of Tables

List of Tables